From Woodstock to the Moon

the Moon

The Cultural Evolution of Rock Music

Second Edition

Chas Smith
Cleveland State University

KENDALL/HUNT PUBLISHING COMPANY
4050 Westmark Drive   Dubuque, Iowa 52002

Contents

1 The Roots of the Roots

In the beginning . . . there was nothing. No sound . . . no anything. Then out of an infinitely dense point exploded the "Big Bang," as this essential moment of creation is called by physicists, and our universe was born. Even our name for that moment suggests an essentially musical moment. I've heard it redefined as the "Big Ring," which strongly appeals to any musician.

To answer the question of why is music we must root out the essence of music. From our present form as Homo sapiens—dominant life form on this planet—right on back to the "Big Ring." What is this baggage we carry called music? Where is it written in our being that music is important to us as a species? Is it in our DNA? Our minds? Our souls? (What is soul?) Is it learned, or does it travel with us from generation to generation? Either we learn music, or it's embedded in our very being. Maybe a combination of both.

The effort of this book is to explore these questions as viewed through the grass-roots music of the American working class of the 20th-century . . . country, hillbilly, blues, and gospel music. Or, if you will, Rock and Roll.

✫✫✫✫✫✫✫✫✫✫✫✫✫✫✫✫✫

Of all the peoples of the planet, there has never been documentation of even one tribe or civilization that did not, or does not, have music. Yet music is not something of vital importance. Or is it? As an organism, we would not die without music. Unlike air to breathe, water to drink, food to eat, or shelter to protect us, music is not one of the things that prevent us from perishing. Yet not one culture exists without it.

Maybe music is more akin to our dreams. Not something for our bodies, but for our mind, our heart, our soul. It speaks to something inside of us that is not definable. Music, as a language, exists more in our creative right side of the brain than the logical left. A language without words, speaking to that side of us that interprets the world creatively and spiritually. Music bypasses our mind's internal dialogue, the place of language, and speaks to something in us beyond word-based language and thought.

Now, much music has words, and does indeed speak to our logical left brain. But again . . . why the music? Why not just speak the words? What is it about setting words to music that lets those words settle deeper into our consciousness? There have been so many instances of a song—ONE song—that inspired whole populations to rally a cause. Or, how many times has a person begun to cry upon hearing certain songs? (I know some-one who can't listen to *Puff the Magic Dragon* without welling up in tears.) These are precisely the effects of music and songwriting we will be discussing throughout this book. Our primary concern will be an understanding of the relationship between authentic grass-roots music and human culture as seen through the prism of 20th-century America.

Voyager and Our Worlds of Music.

As the song says, "let's go back . . . way back . . ." Let's take a walk back down the cosmic calendar, an idea of Carl Sagan's to plot out all of time from today back to the "Big Bang." Today we are human. As stated, dominant species on the planet Earth. But this was not always the case. We evolved from other species through large amounts of time. We, as Homo sapiens, are the only human species walking around the planet, but not long ago we shared the available resources with other human species. There were still Neanderthal humans walking around northern Europe just 15,000 years ago. Hardly a blink on the cosmic calendar. A completely different line of Man existing right along side of us, the Neanderthal competed for the same resources. Did they completely disappear, or did they merge with us? That question is still a hot topic of debate. Other human species as well shared the planet with us as we evolved beyond them. Where are they? They are all gone. Every single one of them . . . extinct. We won. Did they have music too? We can never know. We do know that they did have art from their cave drawings. We also know that they had buried their dead ceremoniously. Both indicate a strong sense of culture and community.

But before we were Homo sapien, we were Home habillis, before that, Homo erectus. Cave men—cave women. Were we there? Yes, in some way we were. Before we were biped humanoid, we were primates—monkeys living in the trees. Again, were we there? Again, yes . . . in some way we were. Before that, when mammals made their entry onto this earthly stage—timid little creatures scratching out an existence under the feet of the dinosaurs. In some way, we were there too. Before that, we were reptilian creatures first crawling out of the waters . . . before that we swam in the oceans and warm pools around the planet . . . before that we attached ourselves to the ocean floors . . . before that we were free floating cells. At every stage, and even there at the dawn of life on Earth, when the first cells began the biological race of natural selection . . . were we there? Yes . . . in some way far beyond anything our brains can remember . . . our DNA does.

When the earth was forming out of what was left of our sun's formation—that violent, molten era of our now fair planet. Were we there? Yes again, in some way you were. Every atom that makes up your physical body was already in existence. Our sun and the whole solar system itself is a second generation star formed from the exploded remnants of some older ancient star. In some way we were there too. Every atom in your body was once inside of that ancient star. As the late cosmologist Carl Sagan said, "We are the ash of stellar alchemy that has achieved awareness. We are a way for the universe to know itself."

So what's the connection to music? In 1977, NASA launched the Voyager I and II spacecrafts. On board those crafts, traveling throughout the solar system and now voyaging into the deep void beyond, among all the instruments, meters, experiments, and cameras was a microphone that could "hear" space. Not like a regular microphone which, like our ears, needs the movement of air to "hear," but microphones that can "hear" the solar wind, charged particles, electromagnetic waves, and ionized fields that permeate space. The sound of space.

When you listen to these recordings, you cannot help but feel an organic nature to these sounds. They sound very similar to the sound of the ocean surf or distant howling winds. There's something very familiar . . . yet slightly foreign about these recordings. Soothing yet engaging. When you listen to this, make sure you do so in a non-distracting environment. Allow yourself to *really* listen to it. In music, we call this "active listening" . . . when you shut out the world and focus entirely on what you are hearing.

> 🎼 **Listen:**   *NASA Voyager recording Symphony of the Planets*

This is our starting point. The sound of space. Where we come from and live. Listening to the organic nature of the NASA Voyager deep space recordings inspires a sense of intrigue in view of our long path of evolution out of that space.

Now let us jump back up on the cosmic calendar to today. Humans living in many different ways. Living vastly differing lives based on differences in environment, spirituality, history, culture, arts, and music, yet we are bonded by the fact that regardless of how different we may seem, we are, every one of us, members of the same race . . . the human race . . . floating on our little spaceship in the vastness of the universe. So many different tribes, and if you listen, so many different musical styles. Almost all of which comes together to some degree in America, forming wholly new forms of music: jazz, country, western, bluegrass, gospel, rhythm and blues, and rock and roll. All of it should be counted as the folk music of America. And in the discussion of world folk music, these are the contributions of the various people of America. However they may have arrived or emigrated to America, whether fleeing noble tyrants, enslaved in bondage, or pursuing the land of milk and honey; the working classes of America have developed a variety of folk music styles all their own.

The variety of these musical styles can be traced to two primary factors: upbringing and regionality are strong factors in discussing the variety of musical forms coming out of America.

For instance, a freed slave blues singer living in New Orleans at the turn of the 20th-century has many influences going into his or her musical style: griot-style storytelling, gospel, blues, and worksongs (styles the musician learned growing up in the close knit family environment), as well as early jazz and hillbilly boogie (styles the musician may have picked up in the cities or on other adventures of adulthood in the open environment of public society). Now let's say that blues singer heads out west and spends some time herding cattle. Cowboy ballad songs are added into the mix. As well, every other musician that any other musician might encounter will foster an exchange of musical ideas. Now our blues singer, after tiring of breaking cattle, settles in a central city like Memphis, TN. A crossroads city where lots of people and their many varied ideas and musical styles pass through on their way from east to west or south to north in the early 20th-century. Now we might add country swing, bluegrass, other jazz, and gospel styles. All of which our blues singer absorbs and synthesizes into his or her own style.

And it goes on and on just like that. Dick Dale introduces surf rock, but uses Middle-Eastern modes and rhythms to do so. Jim Morrison and the Doors have one of the most distinctive and original sounds in all of rock and roll, but use heavy amounts of Native American influences to do so. The many bands associated with the psychedelic era used so many East Indian influences that the stock price for sitar makers must have topped out with IBM. World music is such a large part of the American rock and roll story. It is, in fact, the primary basis of all things rock. Even early blues and gospel, which we will spend much time on, roots back to storytelling griots, the historians and living encyclopedias of African tribal society. Early gospel recordings are nearly indistinguishable from modern recordings of authentic African music. Regardless of how the rest of America was functioning throughout the 20th-century, one thing is certain: America truly was in the strongest sense, and still is, a melting pot of musical ideas. If there was any part of American society that embraced the melting pot idea, it was certainly the musicians. To this day, the thing Little Richard is proudest of is that his music helped to bring the races together. No small feat in the deep south of the 1950s. But his music *did* bring the races together like no other music did . . . or like *any* aspect of society did. As did the music of Elvis, Chuck Berry, and all the other great songwriters, performers and musicians who changed the face of America simply by singing a song.

The Elements of Music.

Music, very much like biology or chemistry, can be broken down to fundamental primary elements. In your physics classes, you may talk about the nucleus of the atom being composed of quarks, strangeness and charm, and those possibly composed of little vibrating strings. The atom itself being composed of neutrons, protons, and electrons as primary elements. Music can be viewed in the same way. There are three primary elements that we can use to describe music: **rhythm**, **melody**, and **harmony**, with many secondary elements like **dynamics**, **timbre**, and **texture** in supporting roles.

Primary Elements of Music

Rhythm

In its strictest sense, **rhythm** can be thought of as the controlled movement of music in time. As time moves along never slowing or stopping—so does music. It is the aspect of rhythm that animates music, that makes it go from point A to point B.

You can compare the idea of rhythm to the difference between a still photograph and a movie. The still photograph just sits there in a persistent state of stasis. But take a large amount of still photographs one after another, say of a person running, then look at those pictures in sequence at a fast rate and all of a sudden the pictures create the illusion of action. The brain does not interpret what you see at the movie theater as a large amount of individual photographs. However, you watch what is in reality a large sequence of photographs shown to you at a rate of 24 pictures per second and your brain creates the impression of animation. The pictures now come alive, so to speak. One picture merges into the next as the brain creates fluidity.

Without rhythm there is no movement through time. However, it is impossible to imagine a state of no rhythm. Take any individual musical event, say a cosmic violinist playing one single note. The cosmic violinist began playing that single note at the beginning of the universe and will keep playing it for another four billion years. That's a pretty long note. In that time, wars are fought and dreams are followed. Empires rise up, conquer, and are conquered. Species on earth evolve into being and are long gone by the time our violinist stops playing. Even stars and planets are created and destroyed, the star running out of fuel and blowing off its spent self into the void of space before our violinist stops playing. Yet even a note played that long has a rhythm. It may be a very long rhythmic music event, but it is a rhythm.

So many aspects of our lives and the universe we live in are rhythmic. On a macro scale . . . The moon revolves around the earth to a rhythm. Did you know the earth is never truly round? It always bulges just a bit in the direction of the moon, creating the rhythmic high and low tides. The earth revolves around the sun to a rhythm, creating our varied seasons. Our sun even revolves around the Milky Way galaxy every 400,000 years or so. That's a pretty long tempo marking—but is still a rhythm. Earth revolves to a 24 hour rhythm—creating the day and night cycles we wake and sleep to. When we disturb this cycle, we experience what is known as jet lag. Our hearts beat to a rhythm, pulsing blood through our bodies to a rhythm. Rhythm is life.

So that we can talk about the musical ideas in this book, first let's gain an understanding of common traditional music terms related to rhythm.

The Beat, Measure, and Meter

The beat is the essential unit of musical time. Just like the seconds of the clock are the essential counting units of real time. Beats move right along with time, only we decide how fast or slow the beats occur. The speed of the beat repetition is called **tempo (time)**. The tempo can be slow, or fast, or anywhere in between. Generally in music we think of the quarter note as the beat.

As beats go by at a specific and steady tempo, we organize the beats into groups. We measure those groups in what's called, simply enough, a **measure**. There can be any number of beats in a measure, but the most common numbers of beats per measure are 3 or 4. Measures with 3 beats, or multiples of 3, are known as triple meter, and measures with 2 beats, or multiple of 2, like 4 and 8, are known as duple meter. Measures are what we call the cyclical repetition of beat. **Meter** is the name for the cyclical repetition of the measure. In standard notation, measures look like this, with meter indicated by the **time signature**:

4 beats per measure   *3 beats per measure*   *5 beats per measure*
(simple blues & rock meter)   *(simple waltz meter)*   *(Irregular meter that would*
                                                                  be felt as a combination
                                                                  of 2+3 or 3+2)

The top number of the metrical time signature indicates how many beats there are per measure. The bottom number indicates what those beats are. In this case 4 indicates quarter notes. If the bottom number was 8, they would be eighth notes, 2 and they would be half notes:

The beat can be subdivided or compounded:

Much of the music we will be looking at and listening to will be in standard 4/4 or 3/4 meter. But on occasion we will see some very creative manipulation and subdivision of meter, especially when we get to the music of the middle to mid to late 1960s.

Syncopation

Not all music happens *on* the beat. There is an *off* beat as well. In music, we call the offbeat *and*, as in a - 1 - **and** - 2 - **and** - 3 - **and** - 4 - **and** - 1 - **and** - 2 - **and** - 3 - **and** - 4 - **and** - etc . . . If all music happened only on the beat, music would get quite boring quite fast. So composers and songwriters utilize the offbeat to create variety in the rhythms of their music. As listeners, it keeps us interested in the music. Repetitive use of the offbeat is called *syncopation*. There are some forms of music that rely quite strongly, or even entirely, on syncopation. Caribbean music, ska, and its first cousin, reggae, all make heavy use of syncopation. The accent is almost always on the offbeat in these styles. Pick any reggae song . . . the bass plays on 1, but everyone else plays on the *and* of each beat, or . . . on the offbeat. It's an uplifting feel. It makes people dance.

Melody

Melody, in a very strict academic sense, is defined as a succession of pitches perceived as a whole unit. "Perceived" is the key word there, as a melody is made up of notes just like a sentence is made up of words (remember . . . music *is* a language). Melody fills linear space and fills the role of the dominant single line in the music. It's the tune you whistle . . . or the tune you can't get out of your head. In rock and roll, if it's a catchy and inspired melody, it's called a **hook**. And in the big money world of pop music, one really good hook can make you rich.

If we dissect it, a melody is made up phrases, and the phrases are made up of notes (or pitches). As previously stated, just like a sentence is made up of phrases which are made up of words. Here is where the word "perceived" is of vital importance. Each note of a melody is heard in relation to the notes that came before and the ones that come after. Again, just like the words of a sentence. Any single word in a sentence, taken out of its context, is just that word. But start stringing words together to illustrate an idea, and you have a sentence. In music, any single note is usually just that note, but start stringing differing notes together and our brains start to hear them in relation to each other.

An interval is the distance between any two notes. Some intervals sound good to us. Some don't. There are solid acoustical reasons why an octave or an open fifth sounds stable and "right" to us, and a tritone (the devil's interval—halfway between an octave) sounds unresolved and disturbing. But melodies made up of just octaves and fifths would also get quite boring quite fast. And that is the true art of the composer; to figure out just the right combinations of notes and intervals, and string them together into a melody that will hopefully, for the composer, elicit emotional response from the listener, and thus have that hook.

There are three main characteristics of any melody. **Range** is the high and the low; the distance between the highest pitch and the lowest pitch. **Shape** is the ups and downs as the melody moves linearly through time. **Type of Movement** is the differences between leaping and stepping. To figure out type of movement, you have to ask: do the intervals in the melody leap and jump large distances? This is known as **disjunct** movement. Or does the melody move in small steps, from one note to the next available notes? This is known as **conjunct** movement. The same primary rule of composition applies here as before. A melody that is all conjunct or all disjunct gets quite boring quite fast too, so most good composers and songwriters utilize a combination of the two. Combinations of all of the musical parameters is the key to good composition and songwriting, regardless of the context. Classical composers of three hundred years ago used the same parameters as the songwriter of today.

Major and Minor Scales

The scale, a.k.a. mode, is the available notes and intervals that we choose from to create melody. Most of us in America are very familiar with the major scale. We all learn it in grade school. In solfege syllables we sing it:

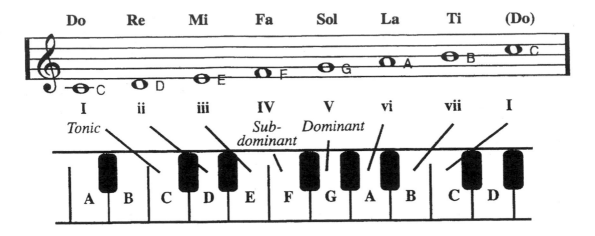

Notice that there are seven available notes to choose from in this scale, and that each note is also numbered with roman numerals, some upper case, some lower. In this example I have listed all the notes of the major scale from C to C (you can play this at the piano by playing all the white notes between Cs), and assigned C as I (tonic), but any note can be I (tonic). This system in completely transposable, so that we can play a major scale in any key. It's the half step and whole step relationships between notes that must remain the same in order to maintain the major (or minor) tonality.

Because this book is meant for use by non-musicians, and because the topic of key transposition is a deep one, we will not delve further here. If you are interested in learning the theory involved, sign up for a general music theory course offered by your music department. If you are an aspiring songwriter, completing a general theory course is mandatory in order to understand these fundamentals.

To play a minor scale, simply play all the white notes between A and A. Notice the difference in quality between the major and the minor scale. While the major scale has a feeling of stability and lightness, the minor scale has a restless and darker feel. This difference is utilized to great effect by composers to manipulate our emotions. The most classic example, and the most potent use of the difference between major and minor, is that whenever a composer wants to depict a movement from night into day, there is usually always an accompanying shift from minor to major mode.

Other Modes

While many of us in the west grew up firmly entrenched in major/minor tonality, they are not the only musical modes in use around the world. When we look at rock music in the 1950s, we will find the great preponderance of it written in major keys, but as the music evolves we will find that musicians of the 1960s were fond of exploring other options. During the psychedelic era of the late 1960s, many bands found that they could improvise for extended periods (sometimes all night) using combinations of all the known modes, especially Middle Eastern and Native American modes, mixed in with the standard major and minor blues scales. These other modes are a fresh sound to your ears, unless you grew up in the cultures from where they came, and even then, their infusion into western music would be a new experience. Experimentation was a hallmark of music in the 1960s, whether we're talking about rock music or classical based art-music.

East Indian and Middle Eastern modes are deeply interesting simply because we are not used to them. They have an exotic feel to our ears. Notice the half step relationships.

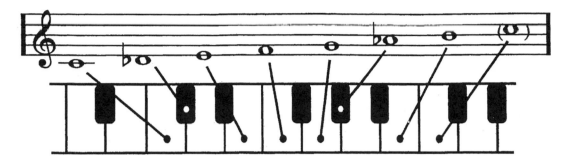

Pentatonic Scale

As the name implies, a pentatonic scale has five notes to the scale (the tonic repeated as six in this example).

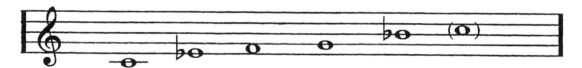

Pentatonic scales are one of the most common scales found in Native American, Asian, and African music and can be found in great abundance in the music of certain bands of the 1960s, particularly that of The Doors.

Harmony

Very similar to melody, **harmony** can be defined as a succession of chords perceived in relation to one another, and to the melody. The primary difference between melody and harmony is that while melody fills linear space, harmony fills vertical space. Both, however, move together in time.

It is also important to note that melody can imply harmony, and harmony can imply melody. This means that you can take a melody and derive an accompanying harmony from the notes used in the melody. Likewise you can derive a melody from a harmonic progression by utilizing the notes used in the chords of the harmony.

Chords

Chords are more than two notes or pitches played at the same time. The standard chords that follow are based on what is called **tercel harmony**—chords built on intervals of a third.

Chords can be built out of other intervals besides our traditional tercel system. Chords built on intervals of fourths (*quartal harmony*) and fifths (*quintal harmony*) are common throughout music of the world, and, again, we will see musicians experimenting with these ideas in the 1960s.

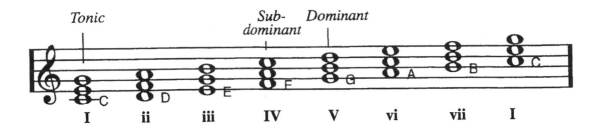

Tonal Relationships

When someone sets out to write a piece of music, the main goal of the composer is to take the listener somewhere and return them *home*. The idea of *home* is very important. You wouldn't want to take someone for a ride in your car and then drop them off a few miles away from where you started. You'd want to take them *home*. In music, *home* is called **tonic**. Home = tonic = **I**. The most stable interval relative to tonic, besides an octave, is a perfect fifth . . . the **V** note or chord above tonic . . . also known as **dominant**. The second most stable interval relative to tonic is the perfect fourth . . . the **IV** note or chord above tonic . . . also known as **subdominant**.

These close relatives to tonic are of vital importance to us in our study of rock music. Though it is certainly an over generalization, it has been said—even by very successful rock musicians—that "There are three chords in rock and roll. The trick is to learn to play them just the right way." These are the three chords they are talking about. The **I-IV-V** progression, and its variations, are the primary formal ingredient of popular, gospel, blues, folk, and rock music, but to say that rock music is all made up of three chords is simply not a true statement in any era of the music or its development. Though it can be argued that some of the most powerful, popular, and best selling songs in the history of rock were, in fact, three-chord songs, or on some occasions, even less, there is a deeper history of versatile and creative manipulation of harmony, especially in the experimental environment of the 1960s.

The next most important interval relationships to tonic are the major third . . . the **iii** chord—which is a minor chord naturally, and the major sixth . . . the **vi** chord—also a minor chord. These chords work in very well into the **I-IV-V** format. There are more than a few romantic ballad and doo-wop songs based on a **I-vi-IV-V** progression. The **ii** and the **vii** chords have special use with songwriters, as they can function as a substitute for V, adding color by deepening the chord. Remember, chords are made up of *more than two* notes played simultaneously. However, they don't have to be *just* three note chords. Four and five note chords are quite common, and six notes and more chords are not uncommon.

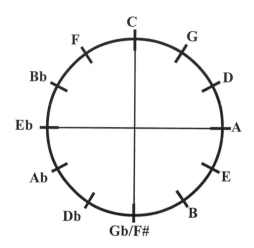

The **circle of fifths**, illustrated here, is the acoustical basis of Western tonal relationships. If C is our tonic, then the note directly clockwise is the dominant (G), and the note directly counterclockwise is the subdominant (F). Any note can be tonic. The relationships stay the same regardless of what note is picked as tonic. If D is tonic, then A is dominant, and G is subdominant. The closer a note is in the circle to any given tonic, or home key, the closer the tonal relationship is acoustically.

A Note About Popular Music Notation

Many books of popular music are printed in a different format than standard notation classical scores. Usually there is a single line melody written in standard notation with the words, if any, printed below the notes, and the chord name with a graphic guitar chord notation printed above. These are commonly known as **fake books**. They give you limited information, just the melody and its rhythm, and what chords (harmony) go with that melody. Fake books leave much room for interpretation and improvisation on the part of the performer.

Secondary Elements

Texture

Think of musical **texture** in terms of thickness and density on one end of the scale, and thinness and transparency on the other. Ask yourself, how many people are playing and what are they doing? An example of thick texture could be any heavy rock song, but even then there are moments where the texture becomes thin and more transparent, providing contrast for when the wall of sound kicks back in. That is the role of texture: to provide contrast. We hear good examples of texture variation every day on the radio. A song starts soft, maybe just an acoustic guitar and vocals, then—wham! The whole band kicks in and there goes the eardrums.

But texture is not dynamics. You can have very thick texture at very low volume and very thin texture with very high volume, but generally the two do go hand-in-hand. When a composer utilizes thick texture, there is usually an accompanying rise in volume. Likewise, thin textures are usually played at softer volumes.

Dynamics

Dynamics are the loudness and softness, or the volume. Here also, variations in dynamics are a vital tool of the composer/songwriter. If everything is always loud, or always soft, things can get quite boring quite fast. (Do you see a pattern emerging? Over and over we see that variation in all the aspects of music is the key to good composition and songwriting.)

Mostly in popular and rock music we just speak in terms of "this is a loud section— this is a soft section." But in traditional notation you will see the dynamics indicated in the Italian markings as follows:

ppp —	*pianissimo* —	**very soft (a whisper)**
p —	*piano* —	**soft**
mp —	*mezzopiano* —	**somewhat soft**
mf —	*mezzoforte* —	**somewhat loud**
f —	*forte* —	**loud**
fff —	*fortissimo* —	**very loud**

A Note about Piano:

Notice that the term **piano** is used for playing soft, and is also the name of a keyboard instrument in great popularity today. Commonly called a piano, the instrument's real name is the **piano forte**, for the ability to play soft or loud. Before the piano was invented, keyboard instruments like the harpsichord had only one volume. With these keyboards, dynamics had to be achieved in other ways besides just playing the keys harder or softer. A popular dynamics tool for harpsichord composers was to achieve a sense of more volume by simply playing more notes at the same time. When the piano-forte became popular in the 18th-century, the palette of available dynamics increased dramatically. The early pianos were not the sturdy instruments we see today. At first they would last only a year or two before the tension of the strings would warp the instrument (remember, you've got a lot of steel cable in there pulled very tight). But as time went on the instrument was reinforced and refined.

During the late 19th-century, the now fully developed piano became a household item for many people in Europe and America. A century ago, before radio . . . before television . . . before computers and home entertainment centers, almost everyone had some ability on the piano. It *was* the home entertainment system for a lot of people before the advent of electronic media.

Timbre

Also known as tone-color, **timbre** (pronounced tamber) is the specific sound and quality of sound that individual instruments make, or can make. For instance, a violin sounds very different from a trombone. It's the tone color, or timbre, of those instruments that differentiate them to our ears. That's the big view of timbre, but any individual instrument has a variety of tone colors available depending on how the instrument is played. A violin can sound strong, full, and forceful, or can be played in ways to make it sound very soft, glassy, and haunting. A trombone can blow your ears out in piercing brassy force or can be muted to sound like far off boats in the harbor. Those differences, not to be confused with dynamics, are tone color, or timbre differences.

Form—Macro Structure

Everything discussed until now has been micro-structural ideas. They are the little things that go into making up the bigger picture. Form is the big picture—the macro structure. We've been looking at the stars . . . the planets . . . the clouds of gas, but now we want to look at the whole galaxy—the song structure.

Just like in math and algebra, in music we use variables to talk about differing sections of a musical work, only in music we start at the beginning of the alphabet.

Intro = Introductory material: not necessarily thematically important to the body of the work.
A = First section
Bridge = Material that bridges the A and B sections together. A modulation bar(s) between A and B
B = Second contrasting section
A' = Called A-prime, similar to A section but with variation
C = Yet more new material, usually with bridge between A' or B and C

A simple song form then might look like this:

Intro - A - A - Bridge - B - A' - A - B

Many times we will talk about song form as verse and chorus (refrain). In this case A or B might be either verse or chorus, depending on its assignment. If in the previous example A represents the verses and B the chorus, then we could write it:

Intro - Verse 1 - Verse 2 - Bridge - Chorus - Verse 3' - Verse 4 - Chorus

The 12-Bar Blues Form

Without a doubt, the most important formal structure we will be dealing with in our discussions of soul and rock music is the **12-bar blues form**. As indicated by the name, there are 12 bars (measures) to the form in 4/4 meter. The first four bars are in tonic **(I)**. Bars 5 and 6 are in subdominant **(IV)** then shift back to tonic (I) for bars 7 and 8. Bar 9 shifts to the dominant **(V)**. Bar 10 drops to the subdominant **(IV)**. Bar 11 goes back to tonic **(I)**, and bar 12 makes the turn around back to the beginning using the dominant **(V)** with a seventh added. Below is a graphic example of the 12-bar blues form.

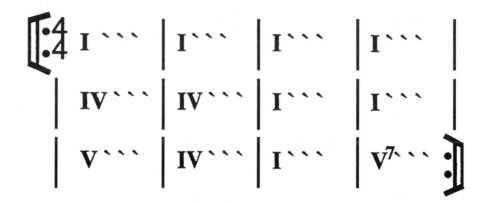

No one knows for certain when the 12-bar blues form developed, but we do know that it came from the Mississippi delta region. And we do know that it was developed by the African slaves in America. By the time recording technology finally got around to documenting the sounds of the southern black population, freed slaves and their children, the blues and gospel music is heard in its 12-bar form. But just when did it solidify into this form? And who helped develop it? Those questions will forever remain a mystery, as our "fossil record" (recorded material) of black music in America only goes back to the 1920s. Whatever happened before that is woefully lost to the ages and can only be speculated.

The music comes from a people with a long oral tradition, meaning that the blues and gospel were handed down, generation to generation, via oral transmission, sitting around the fire on cold winter nights or on the porch steps on hot summer days. But none of it was notated or written down in any way; unlike European classical music, it was simply learned from the elders as the new generations grew up listening and watching.

There is no rule stating that if you play the blues, you *must* use this form to the letter. In fact, there are so many deviations from this strict 12-bar form to be found in early blues recordings that it seems obvious that musicians made strong intention to deviate the form whenever inspired. Bars may be added, different chords substituted, and even just adding a couple of extra beats to the last bar as a turnaround to tonic is common.

As much deviation as can be found in the blues, deviation can only come from a full understanding of the original form. As a musician, if you went into a studio to record for someone, or to an audition for a band, and you *couldn't* play the 12-bar blues, you would find that not a lot of people would be hiring you. In the world of rock music, 12-bar blues is where we all come from. It is the original tree to which we all, as musicians and songwriters, graft a little bit of ourselves.

Notice that the form contains three chords: tonic, dominant, and subdominant. There they are folks, the three chords of rock and roll. The mighty I—IV—V progression that has propelled American music for over 100 years. The importance and impact of the American 12-bar blues form on music of the 20th-century cannot be overstated.

Words / Lyrics

"They put down our music, but do they ever listen to the words?" This statement, a common mantra of youth in the 1960s, expresses the strong emotional and social connection that rock music has always had within its relative generation. As we explore the social context of soul and rock music in America, we will find an increasing urgency in the lyrics of the songs from the dance music of the 1950s to the civil rights explosion of the late 1960s. Rock lyrics gave voice to a generation that was part of an explosion of new ideas in all sectors of American society.

One of the most interesting aspects of rock music of the 1960s is the musical shift of focus from vocals to instrumental virtuosity and improvisation, yet at precisely the same time that rock music shifted its focus to instrumental exploration, the words of the songs became even more vital to the cultural changes. Vocals may not have been as important as they were in the 1950s to the emerging and constantly evolving musical landscape, but the lyrics that were there carried much stronger and socially conscious messages than ever before.

This is not to say that no real social change resulted from the rock music of the 1950s. Quite the contrary, as we shall see. The music of Little Richard and his contemporaries helped bring the races together in America more than *any* other force, and they did it at a time when segregation was the law of the land. If it hadn't been for the shift in social attitudes that saw white teens on the same dance floor as black teens in the 1950s, American society simply would not have been primed and open to the deep civil rights changes of the 1960s.

We will examine song lyrics from all of the various developments and styles of American rock music, as the words in the music provide an important insight for our examination into the symbiotic relationship between music and culture. To even understand the question of "Why is music?", much less attempt an answer, we will need all the insight we can muster. As we examine the music, from the delta blues men to the Haight-Ashbury hippie and all points in between; the story of life in America emerges. The great experiment called freedom found so many different voices who sang of the pain and hardships, the good times and Saturday nights, the triumphs and glory, the every day struggles of the common man and woman, and the working class Joe who built the American dream. By understanding their words, we gain a deeper insight into who *we* are.

Worksheet Assignment: Chapter 1
The Roots of the Roots

1. Rhythm is a primary element of music, as well as the guiding force in the Universe. Name five non-musical aspects of life and/or cosmology that are guided by rhythm.

   _____

   _____

   _____

   _____

   _____

2. In music, the essential unit of time is called the

   _____

3. The cyclical clumping of beats is how we humans organize musical time. These rhythmic cycles are called the

   _____

4. The number of beats assigned to a cycle is called the

   _____

5. Playing, or emphasizing, the offbeat (a.k.a. backbeat) in known as

   _____

6. Melody is defined as a succession of _____ perceived as a whole unit.

7. The available notes or pitches in any melody scale are called

   _____

8. The common major and minor modes have how many notes in them?

   _____

9. A pentatonic mode has how many notes or pitches in it?

   _____

10. Playing three or more notes at the same time is called a

    _____

11. The home note of any key or mode is called

———————————————————————————————————————

12. An interval of a fifth above the home note is the most stable interval besides an octave and is known as

———————————————————————————————————————

13. An interval of a fourth above the home note is the second most stable interval and is known as

———————————————————————————————————————

14. Density or transparency, two ends of the musical spectrum, of sound within music is called

———————————————————————————————————————

15. The variations between loudness and softness in music are known as

———————————————————————————————————————

16. In regard to musical formula, musicians use the same system as mathematicians do by replacing chord progressions with

———————————————————————————————————————

17. Using the Roman numerical system, write out a standard 12-bar blues form.

$$\begin{array}{l}\|\begin{smallmatrix}4\\4\end{smallmatrix}\end{array}$$

2 20th-Century America
The Landscape of Possibilities

The Many Voices of the New World

As the people of America merged together, regardless of the circumstances that brought them there, it was inevitable that their cultures, art, music, and beliefs would merge together to form a wholly new culture. The results of this mass merging, sometimes referred to as the melting pot, climaxed in the late 1960s as America exploded with new ideas about civil rights (free speech, black rights, and women's liberation), technology (space, communications, and computers), politics and international policy (Vietnam), and renewed spirituality (neo-paganism, Eastern mysticism). Rock music united all of these ideas into a new view of the world and the possibilities of the human race and gave voice to the concerns of a generation that was prepared to question all authority.

But taken a step or two back, the ideas of rebelling against dominating authority seem part of the American landscape. The underdogs and their struggles and concerns are exactly what makes rock music so endearing. It is the music of the lower and middle classes of America—the underdogs. And when we root out the evolution of the music, we find countless stories in every era of its development of the music giving voice to their concerns.

The Story of the Delta

The story of the Africans brought to America as slaves is indeed a sad chapter in U.S. history. It is the story of a collective people who endured hundreds of years of denial of property, family, mind, and self. They could own no property. Their families were torn apart, with children torn from mothers' arms and sold off. The slaves were severely whipped, beaten and murdered on a daily basis. They were kept uneducated and ignorant of the world they came from. Most horrific of all, their sense of community and self, of who they were as a people and individually, that they even were human, was systematically removed from their awareness. Or so the slave masters thought.

The Oral Tradition

The American bound slaves from Africa, like native America and all tribal cultures, came from what is known as an oral tradition. Meaning that the history and varied stories and beliefs of the tribes were handed down orally. One generation to the next, the collective memory of tribal culture is passed down via storytelling and song. Nothing is written down, as western and Asian civilizations had been doing for hundreds, even thousands, of years. Every bit of information in the collective knowledge of a tribe must be protected and transmitted around fires at night and in the fields at day. There were no books, no magazines, no encyclopedias, no documents, not even glyphs chiselled into stone. There are transitional tribes, who painted picture stories on cave walls or created visual earthworks indicating some sense of mythos and spirituality (a good example is the earthwork of the Adena Serpent Mound in Ohio, which is the image of a snake with mouth open and either swallowing or producing from its mouth a large egg), but by and large the tribes passed the detailed majority of their history through oral transmission. When coming into contact with a culture with a written tradition this puts the oral based tribal culture at a grave disadvantage.

One of the most striking examples of the awareness of this disadvantage and the clash of culture can be heard in the song *The Talking Leaves* by Johnny Cash, off of his *Bitter Tears* album *(Columbia Rec. 66507)*. It is the true story of Saquoia of the Cherokee nation.

🎼 **Listen:**   *The Talking Leaves*   **Johnny Cash**

This song illustrates the strong conflict of culture between societies based on oral tradition versus those based on written tradition. The written tradition culture stands at a strong advantage over the oral tradition culture, and this advantage was exploited to great affect by American slave masters and the Indian killers alike. The oral tradition, however, facilitates a storytelling, song singing culture that actually was the only means by which the African slaves in America had to hang on to their sense of self, culture, and society.

Griots

The most important people to a tribe are the ones that keep that tradition alive. **Griots** are just that to Africans' tribal culture. The griot of any tribe is usually also the shaman (or medicine man) of the tribe. Griots are the living journals and encyclopedias of tribal culture. They are the keepers and transmitters of the tribe's history, beliefs, customs, mythology, and folklore; and they ply their craft, for the most part, through storytelling in song form. The topics of the griots songs may be anything having to do with that tribe, but usually with a focus on important events like hunting, planting, harvesting, births, deaths, and celebrations. The griot is important to the tribe not only sitting around the fires at night, but also in their day-to-day struggles to feed and care for themselves. Thus the griot might preside over celebrations and rituals, but also keep the field workers happy as they toiled the land during the day with rhythmically upbeat worksongs.

The one thing that the griot is not is a scribe. Griots must, before they die, pass their knowledge and craft to the next generation. The songs are not written down, and remain alive only as long as they remain in the tribal memory. If there is only one griot in a tribe, and he or she dies before passing on the comprehensive body of information they hold, then the tribal continuity is in trouble. They immediately lose the vast majority of their history. Fortunately, tribal culture is aware of this danger, and there is usually a small school of apprentices whom the griot teaches over very extended periods of time. In fact, once taken as an apprentice, the future griot will spend their life in the trade.

In addition to their voices, the primary tool of the griot, and shamans in general, regardless of tribal geography on this planet, is the drum. The drum, and thus rhythm, is utilized by shamans on all occasions, but most particularly when they are involved in spiritual quests and healing.

As America was being built on the backs of the slaves, the slave masters found that the griots could keep the slaves working through those rhythmically upbeat work songs. Thus griots and their work songs became quite important to the goals of the slave masters in keeping the slaves working. The slave masters, at first, were not even concerned with what words were being used in the work songs. Frequently the griot was allowed to sing in their own language, or it was the case that, to the slave masters, the English spoken by the slaves was so bastardized and mixed with their own languages, and in many cases, Native American languages as well, that the slave masters permitted whatever words the singers wanted to use, as long as the slaves kept working. This labor management technique would conspire against the slave masters.

Brush Arbor

In order to hold on to their traditions and culture, the American slaves would frequently hold secret night time meetings in the deep forests surrounding the plantations. **Brush Arbor**, as these gatherings were called, was a time (the only time) for the slaves to get together, share news and each others company, sing songs and dance together around the fires, and sometimes, to plot rebellion against their slave masters. The slaves were simply trying to hold on and maintain continuity to their collective sense of self, community, and culture through these meetings. Brush Arbor usually went late into the night, and it was the only time they had to catch up on news from neighboring plantations. But Brush Arbor was anything but a party in the woods. The slaves held a strong sense of anger against their slave masters and unjust bondage. Rebellions and escapes were plotted at Brush Arbors as well, and the details of these plots were spread from plantation to plantation, right under the noses of the slave masters, via work songs. To the slave master, the slaves were simply working and singing songs to keep their work rhythm going. But to the slaves, the words of the work songs held the information—the where, when, how, and other details they needed for rebellion.

One such rebellion, plotted at a Brush Arbor, was the Nat Turner Rebellion of 1831 in Virginia. Seventy-three people died in the rebellion, creating a desperate sense of fear of blacks by their white slave masters. When it was found out that the rebellion was planned at a Brush Arbor, the meetings were outlawed and the slave masters' oppression increased.

The Sacred versus Secular Conflict

Sacred music, like spirituals and gospel songs, are songs with religious and spiritual topics, while **secular** music, like the blues, is any music not about religious topics. By the mid-1800s the blues and spirituals coexisted and emanated from the same people. The primary difference between the two is that the blues burns deep with straight truth, with lyrical topics of everyday struggles and the burden and repression of life in a slave society, while gospel and spirituals focused on the promised land, heaven, and the non-earthly rewards awaiting the faithful.

Although in most cases it was sung and played by the same people who sang and played sacred gospel music, blues musicians were frequently derided in their own communities for singing secular music. Most blues singers grew up learning music in the church. When they shifted to the secular blues forms, they found that even in their own families they were derided for singing "the devil's music." The conflict arises from the idea that God gave you this gift to sing and play and how dare you *not* use your talents for that sacred purpose. This sacred versus secular conflict has been a concern in American culture, for both black and white musicians, especially those from southern states and the Mississippi delta region into the 1950s and 1960s. Little Richard and Aretha Franklin had to deal with this conflict just as much as Bessie Smith and Son House did.

Early Gospel

Black gospel music was strongly associated with certain musical techniques. Though gospel did not originate these ideas, it was strongly responsible for its popularization in American music. **Call and response** refers to the technique of one person "calling" alone, then having the rest of the people in the congregation respond to that call. The call and response technique comes right from the pulpit, where a preacher might call for the congregation to witness to something just said. Almost every church service has moments where the preacher says a prayer, then the people say "amen" (meaning I agree).

We can find examples of call and response in every style of music on this planet. Literally, everyone does it, whether gospel, blues, hillbilly, cowboy, jazz, classical, Native American, or Indian. All forms of music created by humans have some elements of call and response. No matter what music you listen to, no matter what culture you come from, call and response is woven into the music of all cultures. Call and response is certainly woven into the fabric of our being far beyond a human level. We hear it being used in the majority of species of the animal world, from monkeys, to wolves, to whales, to frogs, to crickets.

Another aspect of early gospel forms that plays a large role in the emergence of rock and roll is the use of strong vocal harmony. So much vocal music from the 20th-century, including the complete genre of doo wop, is heavily influenced by the vocal harmony styles set down by early gospel harmony. Another very important aspect of gospel vocal music is that it was the first music from black America to cross over to white American audiences. Traveling shows featuring gospel singers and choirs, known as **Jubilees**, were the first popular exposure that most of America had to black music and culture. The Jubilee shows also provided black musicians with a respectable means of support, as opposed to the hard road life of the blues singer. Jubilees performed in large theaters in big cities for white audiences; a far cry from the crossroad honky tonks and chitlin houses of the south.

Listen:	*My Soul Is A Witness*	Austin Coleman—circa 1925
	I Got A Hiding Place	The Church of God in Christ—circa 1930

Work Songs and Gandy Dancers

Gandies and **gandy dancers** were, and actually still are, railroad track laborers whose work songs were once heard along the railroad tracks that crisscross the South. The gandy dancer's job is to straighten the miles of railroad tracks after heavy use by heavy trains shift and warp the path of the track. The gandy is the caller, while the gandy dancers answer his call (sound familiar?). A very rhythmic vocal line, much like a military cadence, is sung by the gandy, while the gandy dancers, armed with long steel crow bars, grunt, groan, and wedge their bars under the track, slowly loosening the track with small but forceful shimmies of the bar. Then when the call cycles to the next 8, 12, or 16 bars, the dancers reel back and give one combined strong lift on their bars and the train track moves. All of this work is done to the rhythm of the gandy, and when the moment comes for the heavy move of the track, the dancers all grunt in unison to the downbeat. The gandy technique of using strongly rhythmic music was utilized in other aspects of building the nation's railroad system as well. Driving the steel spikes that secures the track to the thick wooden ties, and carving tunnels out of mountains using pickaxes and shovels were all done to the rhythm of the gandy's song.

The vital aspect of this technique of straightening railroad track is that all of the workers need to be in perfect rhythm with each other in order to shift the heavy track. The constant, repetitive vocal songs of the gandy, and the downbeat grunts of the gandy dancers supplies that rhythm. Their songs traveled with them throughout the south, heard by anyone who wished to watch this seeming miracle of a handful of men moving what seems to be the immovable. Today, gandy dancing is a performed art at folk festivals. At these festivals the music must be placed in context in order to authentically perform it. Fifty to 100 feet of real railroad track (with ties) are set down at the festival, and a handful of men, frequently retired railroad workers, actually perform the art of moving that track using nothing more than their muscles, a six-foot steel-bar, and a song. The fact that gandy dancing is still done today, transformed from a hard, thankless job into a highly respected performed art, is a tribute to the rhythmic vitality of the work song form and its role in transforming the American landscape of possibilities.

Gandy dancers doing their dance. © Jim Sugar Photography/CORBIS

Delta Blues

A primary difference in the previously mentioned sacred versus secular conflict is that sacred music was sung in community, meaning that it was performed with, and including, other people of the congregation. It is a music for the people to share in to create a sense of fellowship. Blues music, on the other hand, was performed mostly by one man and his guitar, roaming the country and living a more solitary, transient lifestyle. Blues musicians traveled the south and performed and stayed wherever they could, from chitlin houses to backwoods honky tonks, all the while laboring in the day. They worked wherever someone would hire them, frequently working for a few weeks on a farm, plantation, or herding cattle, then moving on to the next adventure. Many times the pay for this work was simply a place to stay and meals to eat. Many times they were locked up in jails or imprisoned on chain gangs on trumped-up charges by a white sheriff who feared this roaming freed slave. And in some cases the blues singer just got tired of the delta region and traveled to western states to herd cattle and work as a cowboy. (This mix of culture— the black and white cowboys working together and sharing musical styles—creates its own style of music that we will discuss later.)

But for all the drawbacks to this lifestyle, this adventurous calling and the experiences they had traveling the land and constantly meeting new people provided the blues singer with a vast variety of stories and song topics, as well as expanded the scope of their musical influences. The classic picture of the traveling blues singer is a young black man with absolutely no alternative than to travel the land and sing about the good times and the bad. As Leadbelly said, "When you got the blues, you wear out your shoes." That says it all.

Early blues music from the south, also called **Delta Blues** or **Country Blues**, has a vital ingredient that gives the music a gritty edge . . . *truth*. The blues singer sang mostly about the truth of an all too prevalent racist society that was at the core of American culture. This truth was frequently not welcome. Blues music, and even its primary instrument, the guitar, were, in some circles, considered decadent and unsavory, sometimes even among the black community from which it came.

But in order to understand where the blues comes from, we must understand that blues music tells a story: the story of Africans in America. Blues music and spirituals project the collective voice of the people who endured the horrors of slavery: of being forcibly removed from their homeland, shipped across the Atlantic Ocean like packed cargo, and placed into a completely unfamiliar environment thousands of miles and an ocean away from everything they knew. The family separations, the hard labor, the whippings, the beatings, and the unjust murder of so many. In order to keep the slaves ignorant and docile, the slave masters were quite successful at removing from the slaves a sense of self. They could own no property, their family structures were torn apart, and their minds were kept in the darkness of ignorance. For what, you may ask?! To pick cotton and tobacco. It is certain that if they could have enslaved the Native American into forced labor, we would be studying the roots of rock music through very different musical channels. But America was the natives' home turf. In the eyes of the people in charge of the new American agricultural system, the Native American was too savage and independent to enslave in cotton fields. The only choice seemed to be to wipe them out of the picture completely, which came pretty close to happening.

But the slave masters' strategy never worked. As seen in Brush Arbor, the slaves did retain, frequently at great personal risk, a sense of community and self; of themselves as a people. And they did it through their music. Given this historic scenario, and the fact that the most popular forms of music around the planet today, namely rock and roll and its musical descendants, evolved primarily from the blues, it seems the question of "Who really won the battle for self?" can still be hotly debated. Now we find ourselves in the 21st-century, and the game, as it were, is still being played out.

As the 20th-century bore on, emancipated slaves and their children spread

A passive image of slavery. © CORBIS

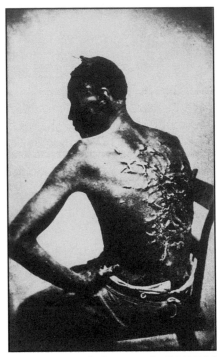

The reality of slavery. © CORBIS

the sound of the blues throughout the country. From its home in New Orleans and the Mississippi delta region, the blues spread around the southern states first, then slowly moved west into Arkansas and Texas, and up into St. Louis and Memphis. But soon the call of the industrial northern states led black Americans and their families to more lucrative jobs in cities like Chicago, New York, Detroit, Cleveland, and Pittsburgh.

A new version of the blues started to evolve out of these urban environments, primarily centered in Chicago, called **electric blues**. Electric guitars and amplifiers replaced the acoustic guitar, but the emotion, 12-bar form, and lyric content remained. The essence of the blues singer, one person with a guitar standing up against the world, also remained. It is really this essence that drives the spirit of true rock and roll. The underdogs, with no other options than to stand up and let their voices be heard, is a hallmark of the American experiment. Whether that experience comes from emancipated black America or immigrant white America, the very essence of what it is to be American is defined by this music. The hard-working family struggling to create a life for themselves is, in fact, what is sometimes called the American way. It's even on the Statue of Liberty: "Give me your tired, your hungry, your huddled masses yearning to be free . . ." Blues music resonates that yearning like no other, as so many 20th-century Americans were legally free, but institutionally bound in cultural slavery, racial stereotypes, and discrimination.

In this way, the blues, and rock and roll, are the logical musical results of the toil, the hardships, the insecurities, and uncertainties of the future; the personal tragedies and triumphs, and the melting pot of cultures found in the history of this young nation. Sadly, the only voice that seems to be missing from this cultural fugue, with few exceptions, is the voice of the people who settled America long before the Europeans. The Native American is, by and large, left out of this picture. Their voice, all too often, stands alone, removed from the cultural fugue called America.

Early Pioneers of the Blues

There were few opportunities for early blues men to record their music. The music of black America was woefully neglected until the 1920s when Mamie Smith recorded *Crazy Blues*. However, the first blues recordings were more on the jazz side of the blues. The real grit and dirt of authentic delta blues took some getting used to. The blues men wandered throughout the delta regions, working, performing, and just trying to get by. For

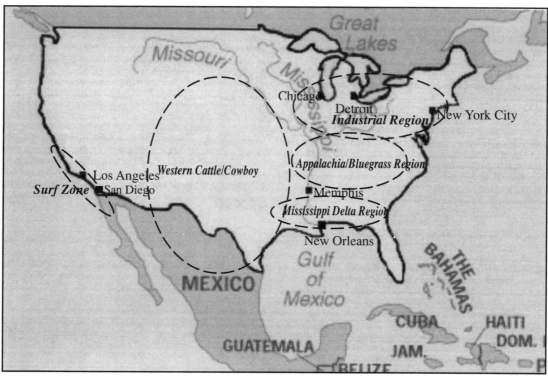

Dominant regional influences in 20th-century American music.

most blues singers, only on rare occasion would there be an opportunity to travel to the big cities where the recording studios were. Even then, there was no profit or fame in it for the musician. Many of the names we now associate with early blues masters were virtually unknown in their time, and only in the blues revivals of the 1960s did some of them find a more appreciative audience in mainstream American culture.

Charley Patton (1887–1934)

Charley Patton broke ground for all country blues musicians by being one of the first to record authentic delta blues. Patton was the mold into which so many blues musicians poured themselves. He richly embodied the lifestyle previously described of the traveling blues man, constantly on the road, performing in crossroad shacks and chitlin houses, and only on a few occasions traveling to the big cities to record. His musical style had a strong feel of grassroots authenticity. His worn, raspy voice, heavy southern black dialect, and heavy-handed guitar playing style became the standard for authentic blues. His recording of his song, *High Sheriff Blues*, illustrates the gruff, authentic qualities and spirit of the blues, and is truly our point of embarkment into the evolution of rock and roll. His soulful interpretation of the blues heavily influenced later blues men that came along. One of his students in the blues was Robert Johnson, the King of the Blues Guitar.

Robert Johnson (1911–1938)

Known as the "King of the Blues Guitar," Robert Johnson cut a name for himself as the best and most controversial blues guitarist of all time, and he did it in just 27 years of life. His influence on the musical and mythopoeic essence of the blues is prodigious, and still growing. He may, in fact, have perpetrated one of the first sensational publicity stunts in the history of rock music, convincing the public that he had sold his soul to the devil in exchange for his talent and seven years with which to take his place in history. His song, *Crossroad Blues*, recorded in 1936 in a Texas hotel room, details how you go about selling your soul to the devil. This song certainly did not hinder the Johnson mythos. In fact, Robert Johnson, aside from the sensationalism, possessed extraordinary natural talent and the good fortune to have been taught the blues by some heavy names in the genre, like Charlie Patton and Son House. However, Johnson loved the attention and fed into the myth, which seems to grow stronger as the years pass. Even though he recorded a total of only 29 songs, the CD boxed set of those songs is one of the top selling box sets today in any genre. Through those few recordings, he is still teaching those who want to play the blues. Johnson also lived the life of the classic blues man, constantly traveling and performing the juke-joint and chitlin house circuit throughout the delta region. Like a self-fulfilling prophesy, Johnson died at the age of twenty-seven after he drank whiskey poisoned by the jealous husband of a woman he had an affair with. In that short twenty-seven years, Johnson created a name for himself that still holds true as one of the best blues men to ever live.

Huddie Ledbetter aka. Leadbelly (1888–1949)

Huddie Ledbetter, better known as Leadbelly, didn't fit into any of the blues men molds. Though he did travel extensively in his youth, he truly was his own person, and is heralded in blues and folk music circles alike. He is, in fact, the most griot-like personality of all the blues men in his early years. After traveling and performing all over the southern United States gaining great popularity in grassroots circles, he then spent the last fifteen years of his life in New York City recording all of the rich music of the land he had learned for the Smithsonian archives. His voice was clear, his diction meticulously precise, and his 12-string guitar playing created a rich bodied fullness of sound to accompany that voice, creating a style all his own. He

Leadbelly. © Bettmann/CORBIS

sang the blues, folk legend songs, gospel songs, and worksongs. He even sang cowboy songs, and was one of the first blues men to use the walking bass type accompaniment known as boogie woogie. Because he sang all genres of folk music, his voice resonates from the people of the land stronger than any other, and his passion was for the people as a whole, not black, not white, but for the common folk and folk heroes of America.

Eddie James "Son" House Jr. (1902–1988)

Eddie James House Jr., better known as Son House, is certainly one of the most intense musical figures to come out of the blues. In his guitar playing style he utilized the power chord long before Link Wray's *Rumble* or Dick Dale's *Miselou*. He played a strong, hard-hitting attack at the instrument, combined with jabbing bottleneck slides, and his voice was extremely powerful, raspy, gruff, and soaked in deep southern black dialect. Along with Willie Brown and his mentor, Charlie Patton, Son House is one of the major figures in the development of the delta blues style and maintained a lifelong commitment to preserving the authenticity of that style. In the music of Son House, you can almost taste the mud of the Mississippi delta.

Son House actually came to the blues in his 20s, after he had already begun a life as a preacher. If there was ever a good example of the sacred versus secular conflict of the blues singer, this is it. He even chronicles the tempestuous nature of this conflict in his song *Preachin' Blues*.

Son House moved to Rochester, New York in the early 1940s and disappeared from the blues scene until the blues revival of the mid-1960s, when his music was rediscovered by the blues revivalists. He returned to the recording studio and left us a legacy of what it means to play authentic blues.

Big Bill Broonzy (1893–1958)

William Lee Conley Jr., better known as Big Bill Broonzy, represents *THE* classic example of the transplantation and transformation of southern country blues to big-city Chicago electric blues. His musical stylings on the guitar helped to steer blues music into new directions in the 1930s as electric blues gradually replaced the country blues style. He moved from Arkansas to Chicago in the 1920s and eventually became one of the biggest names in the emerging Chicago blues scene of the 1930s and 1940s. Broonzy's work on the guitar and the blues form represents a bridge between country blues and electric blues. He would end up being shadowed in the electric blues realm by names like Muddy Waters and T. Bone Walker, but his impact on the transformation from one style to another is still highly regarded among blues fans.

Early Country and Rockabilly Roots

The picture of the American folk landscape that rock and roll emerges from is certainly not a study of black America alone. The rich musical traditions of poor and working class white America also played heavily into the mixture, and most particularly, the folk music from Appalachia, commonly called country or hillbilly music. Not to be confused with the polished stylings of what is today called country music, the most direct descendent of hillbilly music today is bluegrass. Again, just like the blues, this is the music of the poor and working class of America that spent most of their lives toiling in farm fields, mines, shipyards, railroads, and factories that helped build the nation, celebrated from their own heritage and traditions. Ethnically, hillbilly music descends predominantly from English, Irish, Scottish, and western and some central European 19th and early 20th-century immigrants to America, bringing with them Celtic and European instruments and song styles.

Just as the southern blues men had good reason to sing the blues, hillbilly and bluegrass music stems from the lifestyle of the people who created it. It also expresses the concerns, trials and tribulations, failures and triumphs, loves gained and lost, the happiness and sorrows, the love of the land, and everyday existence of the people whose sweat and labor built America. Centered in the Appalachian mountain mid-regions of America east of the Mississippi, country and hillbilly music is the voice of a people who have

Pickin' and grinnin' with First Lady Roosevelt. © Bettmann/CORBIS

endured the hard work of eking out an existence in the rugged, isolated, and frequently hostile mountain life.

The spirit of grassroots America is not easily foiled by ruggedness of life. Frequently, that rugged life became the inspiration for art. One way for the mountain folk to bear the hard work and uncertainty of mountain life was to celebrate it. The Saturday night **Barn Dance** was nearly as sacred to the hillbillies as was Sunday morning church service. There are many slow and sad country songs, but there is no slow mournful crooning at the barn dance. Tempos in barn dance music are lightning fast, songs are upbeat and danceable, and the whole point is to have fun in a community social setting after laboring so hard all week long. Another reason for partying so hard on Saturday might also be to get the week's sins out of the way before Sunday morning service.

Bluegrass music today maintains the up tempo spirit of authentic hillbilly music. The instruments used by bluegrass musicians today are the same as the hillbilly musician of years past, though authentic hillbilly music is frequently performed on homemade instruments. The washtub bass (eventually replaced by the stand-up bass in western and rockabilly music), washboard percussion, along with fiddles, guitars, harmonicas (aka. mouth organ) and banjos were common tools for these musicians. How the banjo ended up in hillbilly music is a unique story all its own, considering that the instrument has African origins and was introduced to America by the slaves.

Another aspect of hillbilly music, bluegrass culture, and mountain life in general, is that in any household everyone works and everyone plays. Ability on some instrument or another was common for all family members, and in fact, many bands were made up of complete families. The extended family structure of mountain culture facilitates the passing of musical ability, traditions, beliefs, culture, and folklore from one generation to the next. Mountain communities are close knit social structures where everyone knows each other and are strongly tied together by a shared sense of attachment to the land and each other as a people of that land.

Calling

Calling is a specific vocal style used on fast songs at the barn dances, commonly called contra dances today. The person who sings the lyrics is known as the **caller**. Extremely fast and rhythmically precise song lyrics contain the instructions for the dance. In this traditional *"swing your partner"* call, every one of the lines below are delivered in a single breath. Breaths are indicated by ^.

^All join your hands and circle to the south and little bit o' moonshine in your mouth.
^Lose your hold with a grand lean back and the lady in the lead.
^All men turn left turn right your partner go right and left and hurry up boys and don't
    be slow and shift your heel 'n meet your doe 'n meet your partner walk slow.
^ Take her home.
^First couple out to the right and around that couple go through and swing.
^Back through that couple go 'round and swing and lead 'em up to circle a ring.

^Change a right hand lady with a left hand 'round and point her to the right as she
    comes 'round through your hole and take a little natural and swing your honey
    and watch her plant.

All of these lyrics are delivered within 50 seconds of the song *Round that Couple Go Through and Swing* on a recording by Roy Rogers in 1940. The song then continues on for another two minutes of nonstop lyric delivery. Today the tradition is kept alive at contra dance halls, where the advertised main attraction of the night isn't the bands or who may be playing, but the caller. Barn dances go late into the night, and the dancers are just as fanatical about learning their steps for the dance as the musicians are about virtuosity on their instruments. It's not just a group of couples dancing together, but an entire group of people interwoven together into the dance, which makes for a wonderful analogy to their way of life.

Hillbilly Boogie and Western Swing

Arising out of Tennessee, Oklahoma, Texas, and the southwest, hillbilly boogie, and western swing came about in the 1930s and flowered in the 1940s as musicians merged heavy doses of boogie woogie and rhythm and blues with the country feel and instruments of bluegrass—fiddles, mandolins, banjos, guitars, accordions, and steel slide guitars (an offshoot of the Hawaiian slide guitar), mixed also with the popular stylings of swing jazz and the romantic image of the singing cowboy.

Bands like Spade Cooley and His Orchestra, Leon McAuliffe and His Western Swing Band, Bob Wills and His Texas Playboys, and Tex Williams and His Western Caravan thrilled radio audiences throughout the 1940s and into the 1950s with their lively, foot stomping songs; breakneck speed slide guitar; fiddle, mandolin, and accordion solos; and precise vocal harmony. This is music that you literally can *not* sit still through. It is made for cheerful times and dancing through and through and is performed with big smiles, wide brim cowboy hats, polished boots, white shirts, and an enthusiasm for virtuosity and speed that has no equal in western music. Western swing and hillbilly boogie and the musicians who played it were, in fact, some of the most popular styles of music and well known band names in mainstream America before the explosion of rock and roll in the early to mid-1950s.

Listen:	*Smoke, Smoke, Smoke That Cigarette*	Tex Williams and His Western Caravan
	Take It Away, Leon	Leon McAuliffe and His Western Swing Band
	Oklahoma Stomp	Spade Cooley and His Orchestra
	Cowboy Stomp	Bob Wills and His Texas Playboys

To the cowboy swingsters, virtuosity and speed were everything. Extraordinary ability at extraordinary tempos is the hallmark of the guitar and slide guitar legends of country music and is certainly the element that still attracts so many to the rockabilly and bluegrass sound. The heavy emphasis on the back beat—the two guitars, one electric and one steel slide—dueling it out, first one solos while the other plays rhythm, then reversing roles, and the **breakdown** tempos conspire against the listener to bring them to their feet. If you ever meet anyone who says, "Oh . . . I don't dance," then you've certainly met someone who has never heard this music.

Like the blues, the impact and influence of cowboy swing and hillbilly boogie on the emergence of rock and roll cannot be overstated. In fact, Elvis Presley introduced America to rock and roll using what is now seen as a standard rockabilly band and sound. But once Elvis opened the door to mainstream America, everybody else came through as well, whether from the country-rockabilly realm, the New Orleans rhythm and blues realm, the Chicago electric blues realm, or the gospel and doo wop realm. Every one of these genres are like the separate cars of a train, a little different but linked together. As the rock and roll train gained momentum, regardless of whether it was rhythm and blues, blues, doo wop, or country rooted, more and more people fell in line to the diversity of sounds and the infectious dance rhythms and tempos. At the front of the rock and roll train was a locomotive engine called rockabilly.

 Listen: *Hurricane* **Larry Collins and Joe Maphis (Rhino, Legends of Guitar Vol. 1 Country)**

Would rock and roll have emerged without this impetus? Yes, it certainly would have. The times were changing, and whether his name was Elvis or not, whether he came from Memphis, New Orleans, or Chicago, sooner or later someone would have come along to blow the doors open for all of the rich regional flavors of music evolving in America. Rock and roll was already firmly in place and growing before Elvis ever met Sam Phillips. The advent of electric instruments and amplification and the fact that there was room for all (*except the Native American*) of the many and varied voices and music found in America insured that the rock and roll train could not be derailed.

The Singing Cowboy and the American Balladeer

The romantic image of the American cowboy played heavily into the image of America itself in the first half of the 20th-century. The cowboy was independent, brave, bold, daring, rustic, and strong, and shared a binding sense of camaraderie honed through many years and many hard miles of driving cattle over vast territories of the country. Though this romantic image captured the public's fancy around the turn of the 20th-century through traveling cowboy shows and silent film and was used as costume for the western swing bands later on, it was in the new age of *talky* movies and radio theatre that the cowboy would rise to mythological grandeur. In the movies and on radio the singing cowboy was born and soon dominated American culture.

The singing cowboy was not, however, something made up by Hollywood directors. The technology simply caught up with what the cowboy was good at besides herding and driving cattle. Then that image was fed to the public, who loved it and elevated the singing cowboy to star status. Once the formula was proven to work with the public, cowboy stars were cultivated by Hollywood and radio, and soon everyone was wearing a Stetson and cowboy boots and having portraits taken of their children sitting on ponies and dressed in leather chaps and cowboy hats, but the essence of where the singing cowboy came from was real.

Cowboys were truly on their own out in the wilderness of western America. If they wanted a meal, they had to cook it. If something broke, they had to fix it. If they wanted to be entertained at night, they had to do the entertaining. Singing songs and storytelling around the campfire and under the stars was a staple of cowboy night life on the prairies. But the functionality of the cowboy being able to sing soothing ballads and strum a guitar went beyond their own entertainment and chronicling their exploits. The phrase "music calms the savage beast" was not just a phrase to the cowboy.

Circle herding is a technique used by the cowboys to bed the cattle down for the night. After a long day of driving them non-stop through the great plains of the West, the cattle were often reluctant to lie down and sleep. The cowboys would herd them into a circle until there was no front of the line, and slowed their pace until the cattle stopped their march. Once the cowboys achieved this, the next step was getting a few of them to lie down. Once one laid down, the rest would follow suit and the cowboy could finally set up camp, eat, and relax for the night. But getting them to bed down was not easy, as the cattle were always restless from the day's drive and the sounds of the wilderness around them. Until the cattle were down, there was the danger of stampede; the cowboy's worst

© CORBIS

fear. The cowboys found that if they sang to the cattle, it calmed them. They would slowly ride around the circled herd strumming and singing soft and low ballads. This verse of the traditional *Circle Herding Song* perfectly captures the cowboys sentiment. *"Oh slow up doggies, quit roaming around. And stop this forever a shifting around. Lie still, little doggies and drown the wild sound—that'll leave when the day rolls around. Lie still, little doggies, lie still."*

Cowboy songs give us a tremendously clear picture of early 20th-century life in America west of the Mississippi. The repertoire of cowboy songs provide very colorful interpretations of how those people viewed themselves, their lives, and the land they worked. Cowboy song forms are also the mold into which so many American ballads were poured. Songs like *Tumbling Tumbleweeds, Red River Valley, The Streets of Laredo, Back In the Saddle, High Noon, Riders in the Sky*, and the many odes to Texas, Arizona, and Montana are detailed storytelling songs reflecting the lives of the American cowboy.

The one song most associated with cowboys, *Home On the Range*, wasn't a cowboy song at first at all, but the cowboys knew a good ballad when they heard it and changed a few key words to fit their need, a very common practice among the cowboys. Songs would change in time as cowboys added their

Actor and singer Gene Autry with Champion. © Bettmann/CORBIS

own lyrics to already established songs. *Home On the Range* was originally composed by a homesteader in Kansas, and the change in one word transformed the song. The line "I would not exchange my home on the range," was originally penned "I would not exchange my home *here* to range". The old English implication of the original is that the singer would not exchange his freedom to roam the land and to keep moving from valley to valley. The cowboys changed the lyric to "home on the range" to reflect their feeling that the range itself was home to them.

The American cowboys captured the imagination of the country, and the spirit of freedom that they represented gave many of the people of America a sense of identity and independence. Their music is associated with everything from western swing to rockabilly to American ballads. Their crooning style was emulated by many musicians, and their image, like the blues men of the south, of a lone man and his guitar exploring and traveling the land, plays into the sense of liberty, freedom, and hope for the common man that became the hallmark image for rock and roll.

| Listen: | *Back In the Saddle Again* | Gene Autry |

Roots Americana

Uncle Dave Macon

Uncle Dave Macon, beginning his professional musical career after the age of fifty, brought musical and performance traditions of the 19th-century South to the radio shows and the recording catalogues of the early country music industry. In 1925, he became one of two charter members of the Grand Ole Opry, then called the WSM Barn Dance. A consummate showman on the banjo and a one-man repository of countless old songs and comic routines, Macon remained a well-loved icon of country music until and beyond his death in 1952.

Born David Harrison Macon in Smartt Station in middle Tennessee's Warren County, he was the son of a Confederate officer who owned a large farm. Macon heard the folk music of the area when he was young, but he was also a product of the urban South: after the family moved to Nashville and began operating a hotel, Macon hobnobbed with traveling vaudeville musicians who performed there. After his father was stabbed near the hotel, Macon left Nashville with the rest of his family. He worked on a farm and later operated a wagon freight line, performing music only at local parties and dances. Macon's return to music was due partly to the advent of motorized trucks, for his wagon line fell on hard times in the early 1920s after a competitor invested in the horseless novelties. In 1923, he struck up a few tunes in a Nashville barbershop with fiddler Sid Harkreader, and an agent from the Loew's theater chain happened to stop in. Soon Macon and Harkreader were touring as far afield as New England, and when George D. Hay began bringing together performers two years later for what would become the Opry, Macon was a natural choice. The tour also brought Macon the first of his many recording dates, held in New York for the Vocalion label in 1924. Macon would record prolifically through the 1930s (and occasionally up to 1950) for various labels, accompanied at different times by Harkreader, the brother duo of Sam and Kirk McGee, the Delmore Brothers, the young Roy Acuff, and other string players including a then-unknown Bill Monroe.

Macon's recordings are richly enjoyable in themselves and are priceless historical documents, both for the large variety of banjo styles they preserve and for the window they afford on American song of the late 19th century. Macon performed musical-comic routines such as the *Uncle Dave's Travels* series, topical songs, often of his own composition (*Governor Al Smith*), playful folk songs (*I'll Tickle Nancy*), gospel with his Dixie Sacred Singers, blackface minstrel songs, unique proto-blues pieces that Macon learned from African-American freight workers (*Keep My Skillet Good and Greasy*), and songs of many other types. Yet "the Dixie Dewdrop" was loved most of all for his presence as a live musician, captured not only on the weekly Opry broadcasts (which were broadcast nationally for a time in the 1930s) but also in the 1940 film *Grand Ole Opry*.

Macon delivered what an 1880s southern vaudeville audience would have demanded for its hard-earned dollar: showmanship (he handled the banjo with Harlem Globetrotters-like trick dexterity), humor, political commentary (often of the incorrect variety by modern standards), and unflagging energy. Macon continued to appear on the Opry almost until his death, gradually taking on the status of a great-hearted living link to country music's origins. He became the tenth member of the Country Music Hall of Fame in 1966, and the revival of old-time music that flourished as part of the folk movement focused the attention of younger listeners on his music. Yet Macon remains less well understood, and less present in the musical minds of country listeners, than Jimmie Rodgers or the Carter Family, even though he was nearly as well known in his own day. Perhaps that's because he represents an older layer of American music-making than almost any other performer known to country audiences. Modern hearers can easily connect with Rodgers' blues or the Carters' homespun sentiment, but Macon may require greater effort. Such effort, in any case, is well repaid by an acquaintance with his musical legacy. Probably the most significant aspect of Uncle Dave Macon is that he opened the gates for all performers and musicians to be characters.

Deford Bailey

Deford Bailey was another early Opry regular. Known as "The Harmonica Wizard," Bailey played what he liked to call "black hillbilly music." His solo performance of *Pan American Blues*, named after a train that passed near his house, soon became an Opry favorite, garnering Bailey more Opry appearances than any other performer in 1928. Bailey was for a time a familiar act at the Grand Ole Opry. That is, until a tiff with Opry founder George Hay led to his dismissal.

Bailey was a professional musician from the age of fourteen, by which time he was already supporting himself around Smith County, Tenn., by playing the harmonica. He had also picked up a few other instruments that were required items in country music from his dad and uncle. The music that was being passed around was something Bailey described as black hillbilly, half country and half blues. And nobody listening cared if a particular song had a bit more country than blues and vice versa. Bailey was given a chance and went on to become the Opry's first solo star as well as its first black artist. Historians lobbying for Bailey's importance go on to point out that in 1928, the Opry's first year, the harmonica player did his thing on 49 of the 52 programs. No other artist even came close to that record of appearances. A symbolically more important event was the fact that immediately after the audience heard the phrase Grand Ole Opry announced for the very first time, on came Bailey blowing his train imitation on the harp.

He remained secure in this contract with the Opry for about fifteen years. He recorded in the late 1920s on labels such as Columbia, Brunswick, and Victor. His sessions were the first decently recorded examples of harmonica playing and were incredibly influential. His effect on the history of the instrument itself is measurable, because his success led to opportunities for many other harmonica players to record and perform.

Bailey also helped establish several performers by appearing as a solo artist in front of their bands, including Roy Acuff. Venues at this time included tent shows and county fairs as well as theatres. Wherever the tour might lead, Bailey always had to be back in Nashville for the Saturday night Opry show.

Even after his death, the fight between Bailey and the Nashville establishment continues, with Roy Acuff bristling at the idea of honoring the man with a membership in the Country Music Hall of Fame, although many other old-time performers of Bailey's generation have already been inducted. After all, it was these original old-time performers who, with their personality and unique music, had managed to launch what would become an unstoppable institution in country music.

Jimmie Rodgers

His brass plaque in the Country Music Hall of Fame reads, "Jimmie Rodgers' name stands foremost in the country music field as *the man who started it all*." This is a fair assessment. The "Singing Brakeman" and the "Mississippi Blue Yodeler," whose six-year career was cut short by tuberculosis, became the first nationally known star of country music and the direct influence of many later performers—from Hank Snow, Ernest Tubb, and Hank Williams to Lefty Frizzell and Merle Haggard. Rodgers sang about rounders and gamblers, bounders and ramblers—and he knew what he sang about. At age fourteen he went to work as a railroad brakeman, and on the rails he stayed until a pulmonary hemorrhage sidetracked him to the medicine show circuit in 1925. The years with the trains harmed his health but helped his music.

In an era when Rodgers' contemporaries were singing only mountain and mountain/folk music, he fused hillbilly country, gospel, jazz, blues, pop, cowboy, and folk; and many of his best songs were his compositions, including *TB Blues*, *Waiting for a Train*, *Travelin' Blues*, *Train Whistle Blues*, and his thirteen blue yodels. Although Rodgers wasn't the first to yodel on records, his style was distinct from all the others. His yodel wasn't merely sugar-coating on the song, it was as important as the lyric, mournful and plaintive or happy and carefree, depending on a song's emotional content. His instrumental accompaniment consisted sometimes of his guitar only, while at other times a full jazz band (horns and all) backed him up.

Country fans could have asked for no better hero/star—someone who thought what they thought, felt what they felt, and sang about the common person honestly and beautifully. In his last recording session, Rodgers was so racked and ravaged by tuberculosis that a cot had to be set up in the studio, so he could rest before attempting that one song more. No wonder Rodgers is to this day loved by country music fans.

The youngest son of a railroad man, Rodgers was born and raised in Meridian, Miss. Following his mother's death in 1904, he and his older brother went to live with their mother's sister, where he first became interested in music. Rodgers' aunt was a former teacher who held degrees in music and English, and she exposed him to a number of different styles of music, including vaudeville, pop, and dancehall. Though he was attracted to music, he was a mischievous boy and often got into trouble. When he returned to his father's care in 1911, Rodgers ran wild, hanging out in pool halls and dives, yet he never got into any serious trouble. When he was twelve, he experienced his first taste of fame when he sang *Steamboat Bill* at a local talent contest. Rodgers won the concert and, inspired by his success, decided to head out on the road in his own traveling tent show.

His father immediately tracked him down and brought him back home, yet he ran away again, this time joining a medicine show. The romance of performing with the show wore off by the time his father hunted him down. Given the choice of school or the railroad, Rodgers chose to join his father on the tracks.

For the next ten years, Rodgers worked on the railroad, performing a variety of jobs along the South and West Coasts. In May of 1917, he married Sandra Kelly after knowing her for only a handful of weeks; by the fall, they had separated, even though she was pregnant (their daughter died in 1938). Two years later, they officially divorced, and around the same time, he met Carrie Williamson, a preacher's daughter. Rodgers married Carrie in April of 1920 while she was still in high school. Shortly after their marriage, Rodgers was laid off by the New Orleans and Northeastern Railroad, and he began performing various blue-collar jobs, looking for opportunities to sing. Over the next three years, the couple was plagued with problems, ranging from financial to health—the second of their two daughters died of diphtheria six months after her birth in 1923. By that time, Rodgers had begun to regularly play in traveling shows, and he was on the road at the time of her death. Though these years were difficult, they were important in the development of Rodgers' musical style as he began to develop his distinctive blue yodel and worked on his guitar skills.

In 1924, Rodgers was diagnosed with tuberculosis (TB), but instead of heeding the doctor's warning about the seriousness of the disease, he discharged himself from the hospital to form a trio with fiddler Slim Rozell and his sister-in-law Elsie McWilliams. Rodgers continued to work on the railroad and perform blackface comedy with medicine shows while he sang. Two years after being diagnosed with TB, he moved his family out to Tucson, Ariz., believing the change in location would improve his health. In Tucson, he continued to sing at local clubs and events. The railroad believed these extracurricular activities interfered with his work and fired him. Moving back to Meridian, Rodgers and Carrie lived with her parents before he moved away to Asheville, N.C., in 1927. Rodgers was going to work on the railroad, but his health was so poor he couldn't handle the labor; he would never work the rails again. Instead, he began working as a janitor and a cab driver, singing on a local radio station and events as well. Soon, he moved to Johnson City, Tenn., where he began singing with the string band the Tenneva Ramblers. Prior to Rodgers, the group had existed as a trio, but he persuaded the members to become his backing band because he had a regular show in Asheville. The Ramblers relented, and the group's name took second billing to Rodgers, and the group began playing various concerts in addition to the radio show. Eventually, Rodgers heard that Ralph Peer, an RCA talent scout, was recording hillbilly and string bands in Bristol, Tenn. Rodgers convinced the band to travel to Bristol, but on the eve of the audition, they had a huge argument about the proper way they should be billed, resulting in the Tenneva Ramblers breaking away from Rodgers. He went to the audition as a solo artist, and Peer recorded two songs—the old standards *The Soldier's Sweetheart* and *Sleep, Baby, Sleep*—after rejecting Rodgers' signature song, *T for Texas*.

Released in October of 1927, the record was not a hit, but Victor Records did agree to record Rodgers again, this time as a solo artist. In November of 1927, he cut four songs, including *T for Texas*. Retitled *Blue Yodel* upon its release, the song became a huge hit and one of only a handful of early country records to sell a million copies. Shortly after its release, Rodgers and Carrie moved to Washington, where he began appearing on a weekly local radio show billed as the Singing Brakeman.

Though *Blue Yodel* was a success, its sales grew steadily throughout early 1928, which meant that the couple wasn't able to reap the financial benefits until the end of the year. By that time, Rodgers had recorded several more singles, including the hits *Way Out on the Mountain*, *Blue Yodel No. 4*, *Waiting for a Train*, and *In the Jailhouse Now*. On various sessions, Peer experimented with Rodgers' backing band, occasionally recording him with two other string instrumentalists and recording his solo as well. Over the next two years, Peer and Rodgers tried out a number of different backing bands, including a jazz group featuring Louis Armstrong, orchestras, and a Hawaiian combo.

By 1929, Rodgers had become an official star, as his concerts became major attractions and his records consistently sold well. During 1929, he made a small film called *The Singing Brakeman*, recorded many songs, and toured throughout the country. Though his activity kept his star shining and the money rolling in, his health began to decline under all the stress. Nevertheless, he continued to plow forward, recording numerous songs and building a large home in Kerrville, Tex., as well as working with Will Rogers on several fundraising tours for the Red Cross that were designed to help those suffering from the Depression. By the middle of 1931, the Depression was beginning to affect Rodgers as well, as his concert bookings decreased dramatically and his records stopped selling. Despite the financial hardships, Rodgers continued to record.

Not only did the Great Depression cut into Rodgers' career, but so did his poor health. He had to decrease the number of concerts he performed in both 1931 and 1932, and by 1933, his health affected his recording and forced him to cancel plans for several films. Despite his condition, he refused to stop performing, telling his wife that "I want to die with my shoes on." By early 1933, the family was running short on money, and he had to perform anywhere he could—including vaudeville shows and nickelodeons—to make ends meet. For a while, he performed on a radio show in San Antonio, but in February he collapsed and was sent to the hospital. Realizing that he was close to death, he convinced Peer to schedule a recording session in May. Rodgers used that session to provide needed financial support for his family. At that session, Rodgers was accompanied by a nurse and rested on a cot in between songs. Two days after the sessions were completed, he died of a lung hemorrhage on May 26, 1933. Following his death, his body was taken to Meridian by train, riding in a converted baggage car. Hundreds of country fans awaited the body's arrival in Meridian, and the train blew its whistle consistently throughout its journey. For several days after the body arrived in Rodgers' hometown, it lay in state as hundreds, if not thousands, of people paid tribute to the departed musician.

The massive display of affection at Rodgers' funeral services indicated what a popular and beloved star he was during his time. His influence wasn't limited to the 1930s, however. Throughout country music's history, echoes of Rodgers can be heard, from Hank Williams to Merle Haggard. In 1961, Rodgers became the first artist inducted into the Country Music Hall of Fame; 25 years later, he was inducted as a founding father at the Rock and Roll Hall of Fame. Though both honors are impressive, they only give a small indication of what Rodgers accomplished—and how he affected the history of country music by making it a viable, commercially popular medium—during his lifetime.

The Carter Family

The most influential group in country music history, the Carter Family, switched the emphasis from hillbilly instrumentals to vocals, made scores of their songs part of the standard country music canon, and made a style of guitar playing, "Carter picking," the dominant technique for decades. Along with Jimmie Rodgers, the Carter Family were among the first country music stars. Comprised of a gaunt, shy gospel quartet member named Alvin P. Carter and two reserved country girls—his wife, Sara, and their sister-in-law, Maybelle—the Carter Family sang a pure, simple harmony that influenced not only the numerous other family groups of the 1930s and the 1940s, but folk, bluegrass, and rock musicians like Woody Guthrie, Bill Monroe, the Kingston Trio, Doc Watson, Bob Dylan, and Emmylou Harris, to mention just a few.

It's unlikely that bluegrass music would have existed without the Carter Family. A.P., the family patriarch, collected hundreds of British/Appalachian folk songs and, in arranging these for recording, enhanced the pure beauty of these "facts-of-life tunes" and at the same time saved them for future generations. Those hundreds of songs the trio members found around their Virginia and Tennessee homes, after being sung by A.P., Sara, and Maybelle, became *Carter* songs, even though these were folk songs and in the public domain. Among the more than 300 sides they recorded are *Worried Man Blues*, *Wabash Cannonball*, *Will the Circle Be Unbroken*, *Wildwood Flower*, and *Keep on the Sunny Side*.

The Carter Family's instrumental backup, like their vocals, was unique. On her Gibson L-5 guitar, Maybelle played a bass-strings lead (the guitar being tuned down from the standard pitch) that is the mainstay of bluegrass guitarists to the present. Sara accompanied her on the autoharp or on a second guitar, while A.P. devoted his talent to singing in a haunting though idiosyncratic bass or baritone. Although the original Carter Family disbanded in 1943, enough of their recordings remained in the vaults to keep the group current through the '40s. Furthermore, their influence was evident through further generations of musicians, in all forms of popular music, through the end of the century.

Initially, the Carter Family consisted of just A.P. and Sara. Born and raised in the Clinch Mountains of Virginia, A.P. (b. Alvin Pleasant Delaney Carter, April 15, 1891; d. November 7, 1960) learned to play fiddle as a child, with his mother teaching him several traditional and old-time songs; his father had played violin as a young man but abandoned the instrument once he married. Once he became an adult, he began singing with two uncles and his older sister in a gospel quartet, but he became restless and soon moved to Indiana where he worked on the railroad. By 1911, he had returned to Virginia, where he sold fruit trees and wrote songs in his spare time.

While he was traveling and selling trees, he met Sara (b. Sara Dougherty, July 21, 1898; d. January 8, 1979). According to legend, she was on her porch playing the autoharp and singing *Engine 143* when he met her. Like A.P., Sara learned how to sing and play through her family. As a child, she learned a variety of instruments, including autoharp, guitar, and banjo, and she played with her friends and cousins.

A.P. and Sara fell in love and married on June 18, 1915, settling in Maces Springs, where he worked various jobs while the two of them sang at local parties, socials, and gatherings. For the next eleven years, they played locally. During that time, the duo auditioned for Brunswick Records, but the label was only willing to sign A.P., and only if he recorded fiddle dance songs under the name Fiddlin' Doc; he rejected their offer, believing that it was against his parents' religious beliefs.

Eventually, Maybelle Carter (b. Maybelle Addington, May 10, 1909; d. October 23, 1978)—who had married A.P.'s brother Ezra—began singing and playing guitar with Sara and A.P. Following Maybelle's addition to the Carter Family in 1926, the group began auditioning at labels in earnest. In 1927, the group auditioned for Ralph Peer, a New York-based A&R man for Victor Records who was scouting for local talent in Bristol, Tenn. The Carters recorded six tracks, including *The Wandering Boy* and *Single Girl, Married Girl*. Victor released several of the songs as singles, and when the records sold well, the label offered the group a long-range contract.

The Carter Family signed with Victor in 1928, and over the next seven years the group recorded most of its most famous songs, including *Wabash Cannonball*, *I'm Thinking Tonight of My Blue Eyes*, *John Hardy Was a Desperate Little Man*, *Wildwood Flower*, and *Keep on the Sunny Side*, which became the Carters' signature song. By the end of the '20s, the group had become a well-known national act, but its income was hurt considerably by the Great Depression. Because of the financial crisis, the Carters were unable to play concerts in cities across the United States and were stuck playing schoolhouses in Virginia. Eventually, all of the members became so strapped for cash they had to move away from home to find work. In 1929, A.P. moved to Detroit temporarily while Maybelle and her husband relocated to Washington, D.C.

In addition to the stress of the Great Depression, A.P. and Sara's marriage began to fray, and the couple separated in 1932. For the next few years, the Carters only saw each other at recording sessions, partially because the Depression had cut into the country audience and partially because the women were raising their families. In 1935, the Carters left Victor for ARC, where they re-recorded their most famous songs. The following year, they signed to Decca.

Eventually, the group signed a lucrative radio contract with XERF in Del Rio, Texas, which led to contracts at a few other stations along the Mexican and Texas border. Because of their locations, these stations could broadcast at levels that were far stronger than other American radio stations, so the Carters' radio performances could be heard throughout the nation, either in their live form or as radio transcriptions. As a result, the band's popularity increased dramatically, and their Decca records became extremely popular.

Just as their career was back in full swing, Sara and A.P.'s marriage fell apart, with the couple divorcing in 1939. Nevertheless, the Carter Family continued to perform, remaining in Texas until 1941, when they moved to a radio station in Charlotte, N.C. During the early 1940s, the band briefly recorded for Columbia before re-signing with Victor in 1941. Two years later, Sara decided to retire and move out to California with her new husband, Coy Bayes (who was A.P.'s cousin), while A.P. moved back to Virginia, where he ran a country store. Maybelle Carter began recording and touring with her daughters, Helen, June, and Anita.

A.P. and Sara re-formed the Carter Family with their grown children in 1952, performing a concert in Maces Spring. Following the successful concert, the Kentucky-based Acme signed A.P., Sara, and their daughter Janette to a contract, and over the next four years they recorded nearly 100 songs that didn't gain much attention at the time. In 1956, the Carter Family disbanded for the second time. Four years later, A.P. died at his Maces Spring home. Following his death, the Carter Family's original recordings began to be reissued. In 1966, Maybelle persuaded Sara to reunite to play a number of folk festivals and record an album for Columbia. In 1970, the Carter Family became the first group to be elected into the Country Music Hall of Fame, which is a fitting tribute to their immense influence and legacy.

Grand Ole Opry

Perhaps no other institution is more synonymous with country music than WSM Radio's Grand Ole Opry in Nashville, Tenn. Since 1925, it has featured country music acts on its stage for live Saturday night broadcasts. This program has introduced the nation to most, if not all, of the greats of country music. To this day, membership on the Opry remains one of the greatest ambitions of a country music artist.

The Opry began as a show with primarily part-time artists who used the show to promote their live appearances throughout the South and Midwest, but with the help of Roy Acuff, the professionalism of country music became established at the Opry.

The King of Country Music could well have become another Lou Gehrig or Babe Ruth. Born in Maynardville, Tenn., Roy Claxton Acuff seemed destined to become an athlete. Following a move to Fountain City (near Knoxville), Acuff gained thirteen varsity letters in high school, eventually playing minor league ball and being considered for the New York Yankees. Severe sunstroke in 1929 put an end to that career.

By 1933, Acuff formed a group, the Tennessee Crackerjacks, in which Clell Summey played dobro, thus providing the distinctive sound that came to be associated with Acuff (and later provided by Pete 'Bashful Brother Oswald' Kirby). Acuff married Mildred Douglas in 1936, that same year recording two sessions for ARC (a company controlling a host of labels that later merged with Columbia). Tracks from these sessions included two of his greatest hits: *Wabash Cannonball* (featuring vocals by Dynamite Hatcher) and *The Great Speckle Bird*.

Making his first appearance on the Grand Ole Opry in 1938, Acuff soon became a regular on the show, changing the name of the band once more to the Smoky Mountain

Boys. He won many friends with his sincere, mountain-boy vocal style and his dobro-flavored band sound, and eventually became as popular as Uncle Dave Macon, who was the Opry's main attraction at the time.

During the 1940s, Acuff's recordings became so popular that he headed Frank Sinatra in some major music polls and reportedly caused Japanese troops to yell 'To hell with Roosevelt, to hell with Babe Ruth, to hell with Roy Acuff' as they banzai-charged at Okinawa. These years also saw some of his biggest hits, including *Wreck on the Highway* (1942), *Fireball Mail* (1942), *Night Train to Memphis* (1943), *Tied Down, That's What Makes the Jukebox Play,* and his classic *The Precious Jewel.*

Acuff's tremendous contribution to country music was recognized in November 1962, when he became the first living musician to be honored as a member of the Country Music Hall of Fame. He guested on the Nitty Gritty Dirt Band's triple album set *Will The Circle Be Unbroken?* in 1972, lending credence to contemporary and country-rock music. He continued to appear regularly on the Grand Ole Opry throughout the '70s and '80s, but cut down on his previously extensive touring schedule, until by the early '90s his only appearances were infrequent guest spots at Opryland. He died on November 23, 1992, following a short illness.

Bob Wills & His Texas Playboys

Bob Wills' name will forever be associated with Western swing. Although he did not invent the genre single-handedly, he did popularize the genre and changed its rules. In the process, he reinvented the rules of popular music. Bob Wills & His Texas Playboys were a dance band with a country string section that played pop songs as if they were jazz numbers. Their music expanded and erased boundaries between genres. It was also some of the most popular music of its era. Throughout the 1940s, the band was one of the most popular groups in the country and the musicians in the Playboys were among the finest of their era. As the popularity of Western swing declined, so did Wills' popularity, but his influence is immeasurable. From the first honky tonkers to Western swing revivalists, generations of country artists owe him a significant debt, as do certain rock and jazz musicians. Bob Wills was a maverick and his spirit infused American popular music of the 20th-century with a renegade, virtuosic flair.

Bob Wills was born outside of Kosse, Tex., in 1905. From his father and grandfather, Wills learned how to play mandolin, guitar, and eventually fiddle, and he regularly played local dances in his teens. In 1929, he joined a medicine show in Fort Worth, where he played fiddle and did blackface comedy. At one performance, he met guitarist Herman Arnspiger and the duo formed the Wills Fiddle Band. Within a year, they were playing dances and radio stations around Fort Worth. During one of the performances, the pair met a vocalist called Milton Brown who joined the band. Soon, Brown's guitarist brother Durwood joined the group, as did Clifton "Sleepy" Johnson, a tenor banjo player.

In early 1931, the band landed their own radio show, which was sponsored by the Burris Mill and Elevator company, the manufacturers of Light Crust Flour. The group re-christened themselves the Light Crust Doughboys and their show was being broadcast throughout Texas, hosted and organized by W. Lee O'Daniel, the manager of Burris Mill. By 1932, the band was famous in Texas but there was some trouble behind the scenes; O'Daniel wasn't allowing the band to play anything but the radio show. This situation led to the departure of Milton Brown; Wills eventually replaced Brown with Tommy Duncan, who he would work with for the next sixteen years. By late summer 1933, Wills, aggravated by a series of fights with O'Daniel, left the Light Crust Doughboys and Duncan left with him.

Wills and Duncan relocated to Waco, Texas, and formed the Playboys, which featured Wills on fiddle, Duncan on piano and vocals, rhythm guitarist June Whalin, tenor banjoist Johnnie Lee Wills, and Kermit Whalin, who played steel guitar and bass. For the next year, the Playboys moved through a number of radio stations, as O'Daniel tried to force them off the air. Finally, the group settled in Tulsa, where they had a job at KVOO.

Tulsa is where Bob Wills & His Texas Playboys began to refine their sound. Wills added an eighteen-year-old electric steel guitarist called Leon McAuliffe, pianist Al Stricklin, drummer Smokey Dacus, and a horn section to the band's lineup. Soon, the Texas Playboys were the most popular band in Oklahoma and Texas. The band made their first record in 1935 for the American Recording Company, which would later become part of Columbia Records. At ARC, they were produced by Uncle Art Satherley, who would wind up as Wills' producer for the next twelve years.

The bandleader had his way and they cut a number of tracks that were released on a series of 78s. The singles were successful enough that Wills could demand that steel guitarist Leon McAuliffe—who wasn't on the first sessions due to ARC's abundance of steel players under contract—was featured on the Playboys' next record, 1936's *Steel Guitar Rag*. The song became a standard for steel guitar. Also released from that session was *Right or Wrong*, which featured Tommy Duncan on lead vocals.

Toward the end of the decade, big bands were dominating popular music and Wills wanted a band capable of playing complex, jazz-inspired arrangements. To help him achieve his sound, he hired arranger and guitarist Eldon Shamblin, who wrote charts that fused country with big band music for the Texas Playboys. By 1940, he had replaced some of the weaker musicians in the lineup, winding up with a full eighteen-piece band. The Texas Playboys were breaking concert attendance records across the country, filling out venues from Tulsa to California; and they also had their first genuine national hit with *New San Antonio Rose*, which climbed to number eleven in 1940.

Throughout 1941 and 1942, Bob Wills & His Texas Playboys continued to record and perform, and they were one of the most popular bands in the country. However, their popularity was quickly derailed by the arrival of World War II. Tommy Duncan enlisted in the Army after Pearl Harbor and Al Stricklin became a defense plant worker. Late in 1942, Leon McAuliffe and Eldon Shamblin both left the group. Bob Wills enlisted in the Army late in 1942, but he was discharged as being unfit for service in the summer of 1943, primarily because he was out of shape and disagreeable. Duncan was discharged around the same time and the pair moved to California by the end of 1943. Wills revamped the sound of the Texas Playboys after World War II, cutting out the horn section and relying on amplified string instruments.

During the 1940s, Art Satherley had moved from ARC to OKeh Records and Wills followed him to the new label. His first single for OKeh was a new version of *New San Antonio Rose* and it became a Top Ten hit early in 1944, crossing over into the Top Twenty on the pop charts. Wills stayed with OKeh for about a year, having several Top Ten hits, as well as the number ones, *Smoke on the Water* and *Stars and Stripes on Iwo Jima*. After he left OKeh, he signed with Columbia Records, releasing his first single for the label, *Texas Playboy Rag*, toward the end of 1945.

In 1946, the Texas Playboys began recording a series of transcriptions for Oakland, Calif.'s Tiffany Music Corporation. Tiffany's plan was to syndicate the transcriptions throughout the Southwest, but their goal was never fulfilled. Nevertheless, the Texas Playboys made a number of transcriptions in 1946 and 1947, and these are the only recordings of the band playing extended jams. Consequently, they are close approximations of the group's live sound. Though the Tiffany transcriptions would turn out to be important historical items, the recordings that kept Wills & The Texas Playboys in the charts were their singles for Columbia, which were consistently reaching the Top Five between 1945 and 1948; in the summer of 1946, they had their biggest hit, *New Spanish Two Step*, which spent sixteen weeks at number one.

Guitarist Eldon Shamblin returned to the Playboys in 1947, the final year Wills recorded for Columbia Records. Beginning in late 1947, Wills was signed to MGM. His first single for the label, *Bubbles in My Beer*, was a Top Ten hit early in 1948, as was its follow-up, *Keeper of My Heart*. Though the Texas Playboys were one of the most popular bands in the nation, they were beginning to fight internally, mainly because Wills had developed a drinking problem that caused him to behave erratically. Furthermore, Wills came to believe Tommy Duncan was demanding too much attention and asking for too much money. By the end of 1948, he had fired the singer.

Duncan's departure couldn't have come at a worse time. Western swing was beginning to fall out of public favor, and Wills' recordings weren't as consistently successful as they had been before; he had no hits at all in 1949. That year, he relocated to Oklahoma, beginning a fifteen-year stretch of frequent moves, all designed to find a thriving market for the band. In 1950, he had two Top Ten hits: *Ida Red Likes the Boogie* and *Faded Love*, which would become a country standard; they would be his last hits for a decade. Throughout the 1950s, he struggled with poor health and poor finances, but he continued to perform frequently. However, his audience continued to shrink, despite his attempts to hold on to it. Wills moved throughout the Southwest during the decade, without ever finding a new home base. Audiences at dance halls plummeted with the advent of television and rock and roll. The Texas Playboys made some records for Decca that went unnoticed in the mid-1950s. In 1959, Wills signed with Liberty Records, where he was produced by Tommy Allsup, a former Playboy. Before recording his first sessions with Liberty, Wills expanded the lineup of the band again and reunited with Tommy Duncan. The results were a success, with *Heart to Heart Talk* climbing into the Top Ten during the summer of 1960. Again, the Texas Playboys were drawing sizable crowds and selling a respectable amount of records.

In 1962, Wills had a heart attack that temporarily debilitated him, but by 1963, he was making an album for Kapp Records. The following year, he had a second heart attack that forced him to disband the Playboys. After the second heart attack, he performed and recorded as a solo performer. His solo recordings for Kapp were made in Nashville with studio musicians and were generally ignored, though he continued to be successful in concert.

In 1968, the Country Music Hall of Fame inducted Bob Wills, and the following year the Texas State Legislature honored him for his contribution to American music. The day after he appeared in both houses of the Texas state government, Wills suffered a massive stroke, which paralyzed his right side. During his recovery, Merle Haggard—the most popular country singer of the late '60s—recorded an album dedicated to Bob Wills, *A Tribute to the Best Damn Fiddle Player*, which helped return Wills to public consciousness and spark a wide-spread Western swing revival. In 1972, Wills was well enough to accept a citation from ASCAP in Nashville, as well as appear at several Texas Playboy reunions, which were all very popular. In the fall of 1973, Wills and Haggard began planning a Texas Playboys reunion album, featuring Leon McAuliffe, Al Stricklin, Eldon Shamblin, and Smokey Dacus, among others. The first session was held on December 3, 1973, with Wills leading the band from his wheelchair. That night, he suffered another massive stroke in his sleep; the stroke left him comatose. The Texas Playboys finished the album without him. Bob Wills never regained consciousness and he died on May 15, 1975, in a nursing home. Wills was buried in Tulsa, the place where his legend began.

Hank Williams

Hank Williams is the father of contemporary country music. Williams was a superstar by the age of twenty-five; he was dead at the age of twenty-nine. In those four short years, he established the rules for all the country performers that followed him and, in the process, much of popular music. Williams wrote a body of songs that became popular classics, and his direct, emotional lyrics and vocals became the standard for most popular performers. Williams lived a life as troubled and reckless as that depicted in his songs.

Hank Williams was born in Mount Olive, Al., on September 17, 1923. When he was eight years old, Williams was given a guitar by his mother. His musical education was provided by a local blues street singer, Rufus Payne, who was called Tee Tot. From Tee Tot, Williams learned how to play the guitar and sing the blues, which would come to provide a strong undercurrent in his songwriting. Williams began performing around the Georgiana and Greenville areas of Alabama in his early teens. His mother moved the family to Montgomery, Al., in 1937, where she opened a boarding house. In Montgomery, he formed a band called the Drifting Cowboys and landed a regular spot on a local radio station, WSFA, in 1941. During his shows, Williams would sing songs from his idol, Roy Acuff, as well as several other country hits of the day. WSFA dubbed him "the Singing Kid" and Williams stayed with the station for the rest of the decade.

Williams met Audrey Mae Sheppard, a farm girl from Banks, Ala., in 1943, while he was playing a medicine show. The following year, the couple married and moved into

Lilly's boarding house. Audrey became Williams' manager just before the marriage. By 1946, he was a local celebrity, but he was unable to make much headway nationally. That year, Hank Williams and Audrey visited Nashville with the intent of meeting songwriter/music publisher Fred Rose, one of the heads of Acuff-Rose Publishing. Rose liked Williams' songs and asked him to record two sessions for Sterling Records, which resulted in two singles. Both of the singles—*Never Again* in December 1946 and *Honky Tonkin'* in February 1947—were successful and Williams signed a contract with MGM Records early in 1947. Rose became the singer's manager and record producer.

Move It On Over, released later in 1947, became Hank Williams' first single for MGM. It was an immediate hit, climbing into the country Top Five. By the summer of 1948, he had joined the Louisiana Hayride, appearing both on its tours and radio programs. *Honky Tonkin'* was released in 1948, followed by *I'm a Long Gone Daddy*. While neither song was as successful as *Move It On Over*, they were popular, with the latter peaking in the Top Ten. Early in 1949, he recorded *Lovesick Blues*, a Tin Pan Alley song initially recorded by Emmett Miller and made popular by Rex Griffin. The single became a huge hit upon its release in the spring of 1949, staying at number one for sixteen weeks and crossing over into the pop Top Twenty-five. Williams sang the song at the Grand Ole Opry, where he performed an unprecedented six encores. He had become a star.

Hank and Audrey Williams had their first child, Randall Hank, in the spring of 1949. Also in the spring, Hank Williams assembled the most famous edition of the Drifting Cowboys, featuring guitarist Bob McNett, bassist Hillous Butrum, fiddler Jerry Rivers, and steel guitarist Don Helms. Soon, he and the band were earning $1,000 per concert and were selling out shows across the country. Williams had no fewer than seven hits in 1949 after *Lovesick Blues*, including the Top Fives *Wedding Bells*, *Mind Your Own Business*, *You're Gonna Change (Or I'm Gonna Leave)*, and *My Bucket's Got a Hole in It*; in addition to having a string of hit singles in 1950 including the number ones *Long Gone Lonesome Blues*, *Why Don't You Love Me*, and *Moanin' the Blues*; as well as the Top Tens *I Just Don't Like This Kind of Livin'*, *My Son Calls Another Man Daddy*, *They'll Never Take Her Love From Me*, *Why Should We Try*, and *Nobody's Lonesome for Me*. That same year, Williams began recording a series of spiritual records under the name Luke the Drifter.

Williams continued to rack up hits in 1951, beginning with the Top Ten hit *Dear John* and its number one flip-side *Cold, Cold Heart*. That same year, pop vocalist Tony Bennett recorded *Cold, Cold Heart* and had a hit, leading to a stream of covers from such mainstream artists as Jo Stafford, Guy Mitchell, Frankie Laine, Teresa Brewer, and several others. Williams had also begun to experience the fruits of crossover success, appearing on the Perry Como television show and being part of a package tour that also featured Bob Hope, Jack Benny, and Minnie Pearl. In addition to *Dear John* and *Cold, Cold Heart*, Williams had several other hits in 1951, including the number one *Hey, Good Lookin'* and *Howlin' at the Moon*, *I Can't Help It (If I'm Still in Love With You)*, *Crazy Heart*, *Lonesome Whistle*, and *Baby, We're Really in Love*, which all charted in the Top Ten.

Though his professional career was soaring, Hank Williams' personal life was beginning to spin out of control. Before he became a star, he had a mild drinking problem, but it had been more or less controlled during his first few years of fame. However, as he began to earn large amounts of money and spend long times away from home, he began to drink frequently. Furthermore, Hank's marriage to Audrey was deteriorating. Not only were they fighting, resulting in occasional separations, but Audrey was trying to create her own recording career without any success. In the fall of 1951, Hank was on a hunting trip on his Tennessee farm when he tripped and fell, re-activating a dormant back injury. Williams began taking morphine and other pain killers for his back and quickly became addicted.

In January of 1952, Hank and Audrey separated for a final time and he headed back to Montgomery to live with his mother. The hits were still coming fast for Williams, with *Honky Tonk Blues* hitting number two in the spring. In fact, he released five more singles in 1952—*Half As Much, Jambalaya, Settin' the Woods on Fire, You Win Again,* and *I'll Never Get Out of This World Alive*—which all went Top Ten. In spite of all of his success, Hank turned completely reckless in 1952, spending nearly all of his waking hours drunk and taking drugs, while he was frequently destroying property and playing with guns.

Williams left his mother in early spring, moving in with Ray Price in Nashville. In May, Audrey and Hank were officially divorced. She was awarded the house and their child, as well as half of his future royalties. Williams continued to play a large number of concerts, but he was always drunk during the show, or he missed the gig altogether. In August, the Grand Ole Opry fired Williams for that very reason. He was told that he could return once he was sober. Instead of heeding the Opry's warning, he just sank deeper into his self-destructive behavior. Soon, his friends were leaving him, as the Drifting Cowboys began working with Ray Price and Fred Rose no longer supported him. Williams was still playing the Louisiana Hayride, but he was performing with local pickup bands and was earning reduced wages. That fall, he met Billie Jean Jones Eshlimar, the nineteen-year-old daughter of a Louisiana policeman. By October, they were married. Hank also signed an agreement to support the baby—who had yet to be delivered—of one of his other girlfriends, Bobbie Jett, in October. By the end of the year, Williams was having heart problems, and Toby Marshall, a con-man doctor, was giving him various prescription drugs to help soothe the pain.

Hank Williams was scheduled to play a concert in Canton, Ohio, on January 1, 1953. He was scheduled to fly out of Knoxville, Tenn., on New Year's Eve, but the weather was so bad he had to hire a chauffeur to drive him to Ohio in his new Cadillac. Before they left for Ohio, Williams was injected with two shots of the vitamin B-12 and morphine by a doctor. Williams got into the backseat of the Cadillac with a bottle of whiskey and the teenage chauffeur headed out for Canton. The driver was stopped for speeding when the policeman noticed that Williams looked like a dead man. Williams was taken to a West Virginia hospital and he was officially declared dead at 7:00 A.M. on January 1, 1953. Hank Williams had died in the back of the Cadillac, on his way to a concert. The last single released in his lifetime was *I'll Never Get Out of This World Alive.*

Hank Williams was buried in Montgomery, Al., three days later. His funeral drew a record crowd, larger than any crowd since Jefferson Davis was inaugurated as the President of the Confederacy in 1861. Dozens of country music stars attended, as did Audrey Williams, Billie Jean Jones, and Bobbie Jett, who happened to give birth to a daughter three days later. *I'll Never Get Out of This World Alive* reached number one immediately after his death and it was followed by a number of hit records throughout 1953, including the number ones *Your Cheatin' Heart*, *Kaw-Liga*, and *Take These Chains From My Heart*.

After his death, MGM wanted to keep issuing Hank Williams records, so they took some of his original demos and overdubbed bands onto the original recording. The first of these, *Weary Blues from Waitin'*, was a hit but the others weren't quite as successful. In 1961, Hank Williams was one of the first inductees to the Country Music Hall of Fame. Throughout the 1960s, Williams' records were released in overdubbed versions featuring heavy strings, as well as reprocessed stereo. For years, these bastardized versions were the only records in print and only in the 1980s, when his music was released on compact disc, was his catalog restored to its original form. Even during those years when only overdubbed versions of his hits existed, Hank Williams' impact never diminished. His songs have become classics, his recordings have stood the test of time, and his life story is legendary. It's easy to see why Hank Williams is considered by many as the defining figure of country music.

Johnny Cash: The Man in Black

Johnny Cash was one of the most imposing and influential figures in post-World War II country music. He is one of those few people whose tremendous impact on American music grows deeper as the years progress. With his deep, resonant baritone and spare, percussive guitar, he had a basic, distinctive sound. Cash didn't sound like Nashville, nor did he sound like honky tonk or rock and roll. He created his own sub-genre, falling halfway between the blunt emotional honesty of folk, the rebelliousness of rock and roll, and the world weariness of country. Cash's career coincided with the birth of rock and roll, and his rebellious attitude and simple, direct musical attack shared a lot of similarities with rock. However, there was a deep sense of history—as he would later illustrate with his series of historical albums, particularly on the album *Bitter Tears*—that kept him forever tied with country. And he was one of country music's biggest stars of the 1950s and 1960s, scoring well over 100 hit singles.

Johnny Cash was born and raised in Arkansas, moving to Dyess when he was three. By the time he was twelve years old, Cash had begun writing his own songs. Johnny was inspired by the country songs he had heard on the radio. While he was in high school, he sang on the Arkansas radio station KLCN. Johnny Cash graduated from college in 1950, moving to Detroit to work in an auto factory for a brief while. With the outbreak of the Korean War, he enlisted in the Air Force. While he was in the Air Force, Cash bought his first guitar and taught himself to play. He began writing songs in earnest, including *Folsom Prison Blues*. Cash left the Air Force in 1954, married a Texas woman named Vivian Leberto, and moved to Memphis, where he took a radio announcing course at a broadcasting school on the GI Bill. During the evenings, he played country music in a trio that also consisted of guitarist Luther Perkins and bassist Marshall Grant. The trio occasionally played for free on a local radio station, KWEM, and tried to secure gigs and an audition at Sun Records.

Cash finally landed an audition with Sun Records and its founder, Sam Phillips, in 1955. Initially, Cash presented himself as a gospel singer, but Phillips turned him down. Phillips asked him to come back with something more commercial. Cash returned with *Hey Porter*, which immediately caught Phillips' ear. Soon, Cash released *Cry Cry Cry/ Hey Porter* as his debut single for Sun. On the single, Phillips billed Cash as "Johnny," which upset the singer, because he felt it sounded too young; the record producer also dubbed Perkins and Grant the Tennessee Two. *Cry Cry Cry* became a success upon its release in 1955, entering the country charts at number fourteen and leading to a spot on the Louisiana Hayride, where he stayed for nearly a year. A second single, *Folsom Prison Blues*, reached the country Top Five in early 1956 and its follow-up, *I Walk the Line*, was number one for six weeks and crossed over into the pop Top Twenty.

Johnny Cash had an equally successful year in 1957, scoring several Top Ten country hits including the Top Fifteen *Give My Love to Rose*. Cash also made his Grand Ole Opry debut that year, appearing all in black where the other performers were decked out in flamboyant, rhinestone-studded outfits. Eventually, he earned the nickname of *The Man in Black*. Cash became the first Sun artist to release a long-playing album in November of 1957, when *Johnny Cash With His Hot and Blue Guitar* hit the stores. Cash's success continued to roll throughout 1958, as he earned his biggest hit, *Ballad of a Teenage Queen* (number one for ten weeks), as well as another number one single, *Guess Things Happen That Way*. For most of 1958, Cash attempted to record a gospel album, but Sun refused to allow him to record one. Sun also was unwilling to increase Cash's record royalties. Both of these were deciding factors in the vocalist's decision to sign with Columbia Records in 1958. By the end of the year, he had released his first single for the label, *All Over Again*, which became another Top Five success. Sun continued to release singles and albums of unissued Cash material into the 1960s.

Don't Take Your Guns to Town, Cash's second single for Columbia, was one of his biggest hits, reaching the top of the country charts and crossing over into the pop charts in the beginning of 1959. Throughout that year, Columbia and Sun singles vied for the top of the charts. Generally, the Columbia releases—*Frankie's Man Johnny*, *I Got Stripes*, and *Five Feet High and Rising*—fared better than the Sun singles, but *Luther Played the Boogie* did climb into the Top Ten. That same year, Cash had the chance to make his gospel record—*Hymns by Johnny Cash*—which kicked off a series of thematic albums that ran into the 1970s.

The Tennessee Two became the Tennessee Three in 1960 with the addition of drummer W.S. Holland. Though he was continuing to have hits, the relentless pace of his career was beginning to take a toll on Cash. In 1959, he had begun taking amphetamines to help him get through his schedule of nearly 300 shows a year. By 1961, his drug intake had increased dramatically and his work was affected, which was reflected by a declining number of hit singles and albums. By 1963, he had moved to New York, leaving his family behind. He was running into trouble with the law, most notably for starting a forest fire out West.

June Carter—who was the wife of one of Cash's drinking buddies, Carl Smith—would provide Cash with his return to the top of the charts with *Ring of Fire*, which she co-wrote with Merle Kilgore. *Ring of Fire* spent seven weeks on the top of the charts and was a Top Twenty pop hit. Cash continued his success in 1964, as *Understand Your Man* became a number one hit. However, Cash's comeback was short-lived, as he sank further into addiction and his hit singles arrived sporadically. Cash was arrested in El Paso for attempting to smuggle amphetamines into the country through his guitar case in 1965. That same year, the Grand Ole Opry refused to have him perform and he wrecked the establishment's footlights. In 1966, his wife Vivian filed for divorce. After the divorce, Cash moved to Nashville. At first, he was as destructive as he ever had been, but he became close friends with June Carter, who had divorced Carl Smith. With Carter's help, he was able to shake his addictions; she also converted Cash to fundamentalist Christianity. His career began to bounce back as *Jackson* and *Rosanna's Going Wild* became Top Ten hits. Early in 1968, Cash proposed marriage to Carter during a concert; the pair were married in the spring of 1968.

In 1968, Johnny Cash recorded and released his most popular album, *Johnny Cash at Folsom Prison*. Recorded during a prison concert, the album spawned the number one country hit *Folsom Prison Blues*, which also crossed over into the pop charts. By the end of the year, the record had gone gold. The following year, he released a sequel, *Johnny Cash at San Quentin*, which had his only Top Ten pop single, *A Boy Named Sue*, which peaked at number three; it also hit number one on the country charts. Johnny Cash guested on Bob Dylan's 1969 country-rock album, *Nashville Skyline*. Dylan returned the favor by appearing on the first episode of *The Johnny Cash Show*, the singer's television program for ABC. *The Johnny Cash Show* ran for two years, between 1969 and 1971.

Johnny Cash was reaching a second peak of popularity in 1970. In addition to his television show, he performed for President Richard Nixon at the White House, acted with Kirk Douglas in *The Gunfight*, sang with John Williams and the Boston Pops Orchestra, and he was the subject of a documentary film. His record sales were equally healthy, as *Sunday Morning Coming Down* and *Flesh and Blood* were number one hits. Throughout 1971, Cash continued to have hits, including the Top Three *Man in Black*. Both Cash and Carter became more socially active in the early 1970s, campaigning for the civil rights of Native-Americans and prisoners, as well as frequently working with Billy Graham.

In the mid-1970s, Cash's presence on the country charts began to decline, but he continued to have a series of minor hits and the occasional chart topper like 1976's *One Piece at a Time*, or Top Ten hits like the Waylon Jennings duet *There Ain't No Good Chain Gang* and *(Ghost) Riders in the Sky*. *Man in Black*, Johnny Cash's autobiography, was published in 1975. In 1980, Johnny Cash became the youngest inductee to the Country Music Hall of Fame. However, the 1980s were a rough time for Cash, as his record sales continued to decline and he ran into trouble with Columbia. Cash, Carl Perkins, and Jerry Lee Lewis teamed up to record *The Survivors* in 1982, which was a mild success. The Highwaymen—a band featuring Cash, Waylon Jennings, Willie Nelson, and Kris Kristofferson—released their first album in 1985, which was also moderately successful. The following year, Cash and Columbia Records ended their relationship and he signed with Mercury Nashville. The new label didn't prove to be a success, as the company and the singer fought over stylistic direction. Furthermore, country radio had begun to favor more contemporary artists and pop formulaic formats for their musical direction, and Cash soon found himself shut out of the charts.

Johnny Cash is the embodiment of the life he sang about. A true American icon right on up to today. His legacy will undoubtedly carry on for many years as an American musical institution. He has never been afraid to evolve musically, constantly reinvented himself while maintaining that unique sound that is Cash.

Bill Monroe: the Birth of Breakdown Bluegrass

The person responsible for popularizing the bluegrass sound and regarded as a heavy influence on rockabilly styles is singer, band leader, and mandolinist *Bill Monroe*. Monroe grew up on a family farm in Kentucky where he learned the styles and forms of fast hillbilly (breakdowns), country blues (soulful ballad), and church music (spirituals). Monroe formed his band, Bill Monroe and his Blue Grass Boys, in 1939 and was invited to join the Grand Ole Opry radio show. With faster tempos and thin, high vocals in the music, The Blue Grass Boys redefined the spirit of how country music should be played. Monroe was a master of reshaping older styles like country blues to fit his new, spirited model of bluegrass. In his book, *Bluegrass: A History*, Neil Rosenburg illustrates a curious irony. *"Monroe had done to 'Mule Skinner Blues' what Elvis Presley would later do to his 'Blue Moon Of Kentucky' in 1954."* An even bigger irony is that Presley completely transforms *Blue Moon Of Kentucky* on his very first record for Sun Records using his own style of rockabilly, the direct rock descendent of hillbilly and bluegrass music.

Listen:	*Blue Moon of Kentucky*	**Bill Monroe and His Blue Grass Boys**
	Blue Moon Of Kentucky	**Elvis Presley**
	Katy Hill	**Bill Monroe and His Blue Grass Boys**
	Goin' To the Barn Dance Tonight	**Carson Robinson and His Pioneers**

Bill Monroe is the father of bluegrass. He invented the style, invented the name, and for the great majority of the twentieth-century, embodied the art form. Beginning with his Blue Grass Boys in the 1940s, Monroe defined a hard-edged style of country that emphasized instrumental virtuosity, close vocal harmonies, and a fast, driving tempo. The musical genre took its name from the Blue Grass Boys, and Monroe's music forever has defined the sound of classical bluegrass—a five-piece acoustic string band, playing precisely and rapidly, switching solos and singing in a plaintive, high lonesome voice. Not only did he invent the very sound of the music, Monroe was the mentor for several generations of

Bill Monroe, Father of Bluegrass.
© Dave G. Houser/CORBIS

musicians. Over the years, Monroe's band hosted all of the major bluegrass artists of the 1950s and 1960s, including Flatt & Scruggs, Reno & Smiley, Vassar Clements, Carter Stanley, and Mac Wiseman. Though the lineup of the Blue Grass Boys changed over the years, Monroe always remained devoted to bluegrass in its purest form.

Monroe was born into a musical family. His father had been known around their hometown of Rosine, Ky., as a step-dancer, while his mother played a variety of instruments and sang. His uncle, Pendelton Vanderver, was a locally renowned fiddler. Both of his older brothers, Harry and Birch, played fiddle, while his brother Charlie and sister Bertha played guitar. Bill himself became involved with music as a child, learning the mandolin at the age of ten. Following the death of his parents while he was a pre-adolescent, Monroe went to live with his Uncle Pen. Soon, he was playing in his uncle's band at local dances, playing guitar instead of mandolin. During this time, Monroe met a local blues guitarist called Arnold Shultz, who became a major influence on the budding musician.

When Monroe turned eighteen, he moved to East Chicago, Ind., where his brothers Birch and Charlie were working at an oil refinery. Monroe also got a job at the Sinclair oil refinery and began playing with his brothers in a country string band at night. Within a few years, they performed on the Barn Dance on WLS Chicago, which led to the brothers' appearance in a square dance revue called the WLS Jamboree in 1932. The Monroes continued to perform at night, but Birch left the band in 1934. Ironically, it was just before the group landed a sponsorship of the Texas Crystals Company, which made laxatives. Charlie and Bill decided to continue performing as the Monroe Brothers.

The Monroe Brothers began playing in other states, including radio shows in Nebraska, Iowa, and both North and South Carolina. Such exposure led to record label interest, but the Monroe Brothers were initially reluctant to sign a recording contract. After some persuasion, they inked a deal with RCA-Victor's Bluebird division and recorded their first session in February of 1936. One of the songs from the sessions, *What Would You Give in Exchange*, became a minor hit and the duo recorded another sixty tracks for Bluebird over the next two years.

In the beginning of 1938, Bill and Charlie parted ways, with Charlie forming the Kentucky Pardners. Bill assembled his own band with the intention of creating a new form of country that melded old-time string bands with blues and challenged the instrumental abilities of the musicians. Initially, he moved to Little Rock, where he formed the Kentuckians, but that band was short-lived. He then relocated to Atlanta, where he formed the Blue Grass Boys and began appearing on the Crossroad Rollies radio program. Monroe debuted on the Grand Ole Opry in October of 1939, singing *New Mule Skinner Blues*. It was a performance that made Monroe's career as well as established the new genre of bluegrass.

In the early 1940s, Monroe & the Blue Grass Boys spent some time developing their style, often sounding similar to other contemporary string bands. The most notable element of the band's sound was Monroe's high, piercing tenor voice and his driving mandolin. The Blue Grass Boys toured with the Grand Ole Opry's road shows and appeared weekly on the radio. Between 1940 and 1941, he cut a number of songs for RCA-Victor, but wartime restrictions prevented him from recording for several years. The classic lineup of the Blue Grass Boys fell into place in 1944, when guitarist/vocalist Lester Flatt and banjoist Earl Scruggs joined a lineup that already included Monroe, fiddler Chubby Wise, and bassist Howard Watts. This is the group that supported Monroe when he returned to the studio in 1945, recording a number of songs for Columbia. Early in 1946, he had his first charting hit with *Kentucky Waltz*, which climbed to number three; it was followed by the number five hit *Footprints in the Snow*.

Throughout 1946, the Blue Grass Boys were one of the most popular acts in country music, scoring hits and touring to large crowds across America. At each town they played, the band would perform underneath a large circus tent they set up themselves; the tent would also host a variety of other attractions, including Monroe's baseball team, which would play local teams before the concert began. During the late 1940s, the Blue Grass Boys remained a popular act, landing five additional Top Twenty singles. Numerous other acts began imitating Monroe's sound, most notably the Stanley Brothers.

Flatt & Scruggs left the Blue Grass Boys in 1948 to form their own band. Their departure ushered in an era of stagnation for Monroe. After Flatt & Scruggs parted ways from his band, he left Columbia Records in 1949 because they had signed the Stanley Brothers, who he felt were simply imitating his style. The following year, he signed with Decca Records, who tried to persuade Monroe to attempt some mainstream-oriented productions. He went as far as cutting a few songs with an electric guitar, but he soon returned to his pure bluegrass sound. At these sessions, he did meet Jimmy Martin, who became his supporting vocalist in the early 1950s.

Throughout the 1950s—indeed, throughout the rest of his career—Monroe toured relentlessly, performing hundreds of shows a year. In 1951, Monroe opened a country music park at Bean Blossom, Ind.; over the years, the venue featured performances from a number of bluegrass acts. Monroe suffered a serious car accident in January of 1953, which sidelined his career for several months. The following year, Elvis Presley performed Monroe's *Blue Moon of Kentucky* at his one and only Grand Ole Opry appearance, radically reworking the arrangement; Presley apologized for his adaptation, but Monroe would later perform the same arrangement at his concerts.

Monroe released his first album, *Knee Deep in Bluegrass*, in 1958, the same year he appeared on the country singles chart with *Scotland*; the number twenty-seven single was his first hit in over a decade. However, by the late 1950s, his stardom was eclipsed by

Flatt & Scruggs. Monroe was not helped by his legendary stubbornness. Numerous musicians passed through his band because of his temperament and his quest for detail. He rarely granted press interviews and would rarely perform on television; he even canceled a concert at Carnegie Hall because he believed the promoter, Alan Lomax, was a communist. In the 1960s, Monroe received a great career boost from the folk music revival, which made him popular with a new generation of listeners. Thanks to his new manager, ex-Greenbriar Boys member Ralph Rinzler, Monroe played bluegrass festivals across the United States, frequently on college campuses. In 1967, he founded his own bluegrass festival, the Bill Monroe Bean Blossom Festival, at his country music park, which continued to run into the 1990s.

In 1970, he was inducted into the Country Music Hall of Fame. The following year, he was inducted into the Nashville Songwriters Association International Hall of Fame. Throughout the 1970s, he toured constantly. In 1981, Monroe was diagnosed with cancer and underwent treatment for the disease successfully. After his recovery, he resumed his busy touring schedule, which he kept into the 1990s. In 1991, he had surgery for a double coronary bypass, but he quickly recovered and continued performing and hosting weekly at the Grand Ole Opry. In 1993, the Grammys gave Monroe a Lifetime Achievement Award. After suffering a stroke in early 1996, Monroe died on September 9, 1996, four days short of his eighty-fifth birthday.

Flatt & Scuggs

Probably the most famous bluegrass band of all time was Flatt & Scruggs and the Foggy Mountain Boys. They made the genre famous in ways that not even Bill Monroe, who pretty much invented the sound, ever could. Because of a guitar player and vocalist from Tennessee named Lester Flatt and an extraordinary banjo player from North Carolina named Earl Scruggs, bluegrass music has become popular the world over and has entered the mainstream in the world of music.

Like so many other bluegrass legends, Flatt & Scruggs were graduates of Bill Monroe's Blue Grass Boys. Because of the unique sound they added ("overdrive," one critic called it), Monroe felt let down after Flatt's quality vocals and Scruggs's banjo leads left in 1948. Quickly, the two assembled a band that in the opinion of many was among the best ever, with Chubby Wise on fiddle and Jody Rainwater on bass; a later band, with Paul Warren on fiddle and Josh Graves on dobro, was equally superb. With so many extraordinary musicians and the solid, controlled vocals of Flatt, it's no wonder the Foggy Mountain Boys were the band that brought bluegrass to international prominence. From 1948 until 1969, when Flatt & Scruggs split up to pursue different musical directions, they were *the* bluegrass band, due to their Martha White Flour segment at the Opry and, especially, their tremendous exposure from TV and movies.

Flatt & Scruggs were originally brought together by Monroe in 1945, when they joined a band that also featured fiddler Chubby Wise and bassist Cedric Rainwater. This quintet created the sound of bluegrass and helped bring it to national recognition through radio shows, records, and concerts. After three years with Monroe, Flatt left the mandolinist behind in 1948, and Scruggs followed his lead shortly afterward. The duo formed their own band, the Foggy Mountain Boys. Within a few months, they recruited ex-Blue Grass Boy Rainwater, fiddler Jim Shumate, and guitarist/vocalist Mac Wiseman. Initially, the band played on radio stations across the South, landing a record contract with Mercury Records in late 1948. Over the next two years, they toured the United States constantly, played many radio shows, and recorded several sessions for Mercury. One of the sessions produced the original version of *Foggy Mountain Breakdown*, which would become a bluegrass standard.

In 1951, Flatt & Scruggs switched record labels, signing with Columbia Records. By this point, the band now featured mandolinst/vocalist Curly Seckler, fiddler Paul Warren, and bassist Jake Tullock. Where the careers of other bluegrass and hard country acts stalled in the early and mid-1950s, the Foggy Mountain Boys flourished. One of their first singles for Columbia, *'Tis Sweet to Be Remembered*, reached the Top Ten in 1952, and in 1953, the Martha White Flour company sponsored a regular radio show for the group on WSM in Nashville. In 1955, the band joined the Grand Ole Opry. The following year, they added a dobro player called Buck Graves to the lineup.

Flatt & Scruggs reached a new audience in the late 1950s, when the folk music revival sparked the interest of a younger generation of listeners. The duo played a number of festivals targeted at the new breed of bluegrass and folk fans. At the same time, country music television programs went into syndication, and the duo became regulars on these shows. In the summer of 1959, Flatt & Scruggs began a streak of Top Forty country singles that ran into 1968—their chart performance was directly tied to their increased exposure. The duo's popularity peaked in 1962, when they recorded the theme song to the television sitcom *The Beverly Hillbillies*. The theme, called *The Ballad of Jed Clampett*, became the first number one bluegrass single in early 1963, and the duo made a number of cameos on the show.

The Beverly Hillbillies began a streak of cameo appearances and soundtrack work for Flatt & Scruggs in television and film, most notably with the appearance of *Foggy Mountain Breakdown* in Arthur Penn's 1968 film *Bonnie and Clyde*. With all of their TV, film, and festival appearances, Flatt & Scruggs popularized bluegrass music more than any artist, even Monroe. Ironically, that popularity helped drive the duo apart. Scruggs wanted to expand their sound and pushed Flatt to cover Bob Dylan's *Like a Rolling Stone* in 1968 as well as land concert appearances in venues that normally booked rock and roll acts. Flatt wanted to continue in a traditional bluegrass vein. Inevitably, the opposing forces came to a head in 1969, and the duo parted ways. Appropriately, Flatt formed a traditional bluegrass band, the Nashville Grass, while Scruggs assembled a more progressive outfit, the Earl Scruggs Revue.

Throughout the 1970s, both Flatt and Scruggs enjoyed successful solo careers. In 1979, the duo began ironing out the details of a proposed reunion album, but they were scrapped upon Flatt's death on May 11, 1979. Scruggs retired in the 1980s. In 1985, Flatt & Scruggs were inducted into the Country Music Hall of Fame.

Poised to Shake, Rattle and Roll

This was the landscape of possibilities in America in the first half of the twentieth-century. Black music descended from slavery—through worksongs and gospel, then the blues, and rhythm and blues. White music descended from poor, working class immigrants to America from Ireland, Scotland England, Spain, Germany, and other western European countries—through barn dances, ballads, polkas and breakdowns, then to western swing, hillbilly boogie, and rockabilly. As the people of America mixed, the music mixed as well, and soon this combination would shake up the realms of music and culture with unprecedented force. The status quo structure of popular music and idols in America, that of the squeaky clean, well bred, cabaret suave yet homespun image, would soon be annihilated in the years following World War II. A new music and image reflecting the changing times would emerge with the post-war generation, different enough to cause confusion and misunderstanding in their parents, yet completely evolved out of the music and culture that came before.

It's been said that rock and roll is a great mongrel. There are so many different ethnic and regional influences to be found in the study of rock and roll; from the musicians, the independent record labels who produced it, the disc jockeys that played it, the people who danced to it—all came from diverse backgrounds, and all sought to graft a little bit of themselves onto the tree of music. Looking at the evolution of this true folk music gives us a clear picture of American culture at its grassroots.

Worksheet Assignment: Chapter 2
20th-Century America

1. Any culture that uses a written system of communication is known as a(n)
   _____ tradition

2. Any culture that uses spoken word exclusively as a system of communication is called a(n)
   _____ tradition

3. In African tribal cultures, the person who is the keeper of the comprehensive body of folklore, history, and beliefs is called a

   _____

4. Secret meetings held for the purpose of social interaction and conducted in the deep woods in the middle of the night by the slaves in America were known as

   _____

5. The most important musical aspect of work songs and gospel music is a technique called

   _____

6. Railroad workers who used music as a means of keeping rhythm with the work are called

   _____

7. Any music that deals with topics of God or spirituality are known as

   _____

8. Any music that deals with topics *other than* God or spirituality are known as

   _____

9. When we talk about delta blues, what delta are we talking about?

   _____

10. Hillbilly and bluegrass music is most strongly associated with what region of the United States?

    _____

11. The fastest tempo music of barn dances, a fast dance two-step, is known as a

_____

12. Ballads came to the forefront of American music through the cowboy, who sang to their herds to quiet them at the end of the day in a song form known as

_____

13. On the map provided, circle the region that is most strongly associated with the delta blues.

14. Identify these cities on the map provided
    —New Orleans, La.
    —Memphis, Tenn.
    —Chicago, Ill.

15. Draw a circle around these regions
    —The Mississippi Delta
    —The Appalachian bluegrass region
    —The Western cattle region

16. Identify on the map where are you right now.

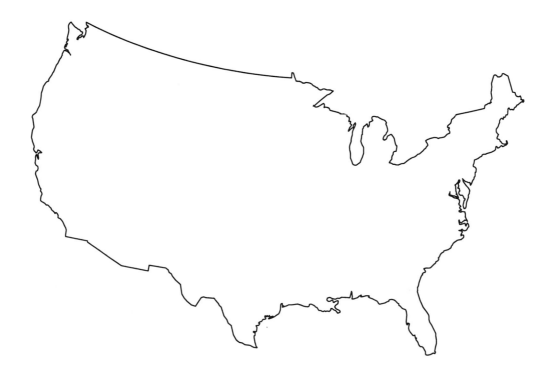

3 The Emergence of Rock and Roll Post War America
The Evolution Will Not Be Televised

The Birth of Rock and Roll

In the years following World War II, although many blacks had served with honor, they came home from the war to find the racist aspects of segregated America had not changed. Although they had fought against one racist regime, they had done so for another. Segregation was the law of the land in many states, and fighting for freedom did nothing to change that. Black radio, nightclubs, restaurants, and dance halls were for black people while white radio, nightclubs, restaurants, and dance halls were for white people. But soon, as a new generation of white teen America grew tired of their parents' hit parade, they started to venture into the waters of black radio and dance halls. Much of white America . . . and some black America just wasn't ready for this cultural shift.

Throughout the first half of the century, musicians were mixing up the various styles they ran across on the road. Blues musicians incorporated country aspects like boogie woogie and twangy guitar, and country musicians incorporated blues aspects like blues form and New Orleans style rhythm and blues honky-tonk and honkers saxophone, and they all incorporated their soulful vocal-based gospel roots from childhood. This climate of all inclusiveness among musicians would eventually lead those who listened to the music to unconsciously question the racial status quo.

There was confusion among the public in the late 1940s and 1950s. There was no television or mass media advertising to show the listener what the musician looked like before they had a chance to decide if they liked the music. Consequently there are many stories of black performers getting in front of white audiences, and white performers getting in front of black audiences, where there is a hush, then unison gasp from the audience. Elvis Presley had a hard time getting airplay at first because people couldn't tell if he was black or white. Chuck Berry had so much country music in his songwriting style that white audiences flocked to see him just to find themselves utterly confused as to why this black man was on stage.

Rock and roll didn't just happen overnight. To mainstream America, it did seem to suddenly appear from nowhere, but it was certainly not the case that one day there was no rock and roll, then suddenly—*blam*—rock was everywhere. This music had been brewing throughout the whole century. From blues from the delta, to electric blues, to hillbilly boogie, and cowboy swing, to big band jazz, to New Orleans and Kansas City rhythm and blues, from east coast to west, if we listen to the music from the late 1940s and early 1950s, it is sometimes very difficult to say "this is now rock and roll" at any specific point.

Certainly rock and roll is in place by the early 1950s. Big Mama Thornton released *Hound Dog* in 1952, and Big Joe Turner's *Shake, Rattle and Roll* topped the charts in early 1954. But before that, in the 1940s, where no one talks about rock and roll, Clarence 'Gatemouth' Brown released *Guitar In My Hand* in 1947, Louis Jordan released *Choo Choo Ch' Boogie* in 1946, and Helen Humes topped the charts with *Be Baba Leba* in 1945. In these songs we find perfect examples of the rock and roll styles as popularized by the now big names of the 1950s: part swing jazz, part hillbilly, part honky tonk, part blues, part gospel, and pure rock and roll. It was fast, danceable, and somewhat taboo for the white teens who were searching for something different than their parents' music. The trouble was, in segregated America, white kids were tuning in to late night black rhythm and blues radio and going to black rhythm and blues dance halls. These kids just didn't care what color the musicians were. If there was fun to be had, then they were going to have it, regardless of the cultural taboos (and laws) of race mixing, or of what their parents had to say about it.

What this really meant was that white teens, for the first time in America, were dancing on the same dance floor as black kids, especially at concerts by such purely energetic and outrageous musicians like The Treniers or Little Richard or Screamin' Jay Hawkins. Rock and roll music, and the dance halls where it was performed, was more instrumental in breaking down racial barriers in America than any other aspect of 1950s society hands down. In fact, the segregation and oppression of black Americans seemed to be getting worse in other aspects of society, especially in the south where opposition to desegregation was feverishly expounded by such groups like the Ku Klux Klan and the Alabama White Citizens' Council. But for the most part, the kids didn't care about color, or segregation or, in some cases, the fear and hatred for blacks that their parents tried to hand over to them. Maybe, and maybe not too, later in life they would learn it, but this was not that time.

In the world of music, there is no black or white. There is only talent or no talent. It simply did not matter, and should not ever matter, what color a musician is. When it comes time to roll the recording tape, there is only one thing on everyone's mind . . . can you "cut the lick?" If you've got musical and hit-making songwriting talent, then no matter what color you are, in the recording studio you are only sound. If you can play, then everyone wants to be your friend. If you don't have talent, then no one wants anything to do with you, and it has nothing at all to do with what color you are or what side of the tracks you came from.

As the rock and roll train gained momentum, and as it started to make record labels more money, opposition to the new rock beat dwindled to a few fanatical voices like those mentioned previously. That is truly where the opposition to rock and roll lost its battle against what they saw as a demoralizing influence. Not in the fact that kids were dancing to it, but the fact that the teens went to the dance, then went out and bought the records.

Rock and roll teens. © Bettmann/CORBIS

Once the major record labels realized how much money could be made from this new music, label after label scrambled to sign as many musicians as they could. The major label executives might not have understood the music or what it meant for American society in the future, but they did know a good business venture when they saw it. Once the mass marketing of rock and roll began, there was absolutely no turning back. The people who didn't like what was happening would have to look elsewhere, like the school-houses in their districts, to inflict their racial authority and view of a whites-only America, for this battlefield belonged to those colorblind musicians and their fans of the era.

Jump Blues and Rhythm and Blues

Whether from New Orleans, New York, Los Angeles, Memphis, St. Louis, or Kansas City, big city musicians started to mix aspects of blues and swing together to create a whole new style called jump blues. Later, the term rhythm and blues would replace that term, but in essence, jump blues and rhythm and blues are the same thing. The primary difference being that rhythm and blues *can be, though is usually not* slow and romantic, while jump blues should make you do exactly what the name indicates; jump, or dance. If it's not fast, fun, and danceable, it's not jump blues.

Other signature aspects can be found in the raucous honking and wailing of the tenor saxophone, the rhythmic drive of the pounding piano, and the heavy amounts of call and response between lead vocalist and the back up vocals, or between the lead vocals and saxophone. These ideas are where rhythm and blues really separates from its sweeter sounding swing-jazz and blues cousins.

In good jump blues, along with raucous and frequently risque vocals, the saxophone solos must have large amounts of aggressive controlled insanity in the playing. Squawks, squeeks, moans and groans, biting down on the reed, and overblowing the instrument were all things to be shunned in proper jazz circles, but the younger rhythm and blues musicians reveled in the raucous crazy sounds available to the tenor sax player. This raucous playing style was actually seen as somehow deviant or perverse by mainstream America, including some jazz musicians. There was a real split over this issue of exactly what was the proper use of the instrument. Some jazz musicians couldn't understand why some talented musician friends of theirs would even want to play that "hillbilly blues." Likewise, those friends couldn't understand why their jazz-playing friends wanted to keep

Bourbon Street, New Orleans. © Jerry Cooke/CORBIS

playing that old style instead of this new, fast and fun, and lucrative trend. The fact is that many jazz and pop musicians were thinking about job security, and there was a strong feeling that this rock infant called rhythm and blues would never last . . . that it was just a fad. Even some rhythm and blues musicians walked both sides of the fence thinking that they had better cover their bets in case the whole rock train derailed. But as more and more teenagers started tuning into the new sound, so did more and more musicians start exploring the possibilities of the new limits on musical acceptability.

The rhythm and blues musicians helped to create a whole new palette of musical colors to choose from. As they explored the limits of their instruments and voices, and showed what could be done, more musicians learned the new techniques, expanded on them, and thus raised the bar for other musicians trying to keep up with the new sounds. This friendly and healthy competition among the musicians facilitated an increase in virtuosity across the board, and did so to a great degree within the formal constraints of the 12-bar blues.

The simplicity of the blues form allowed the soloists a certain freedom to explore the possibilities within a limited structure. In other words, if you're a saxophone soloist, and the time comes for you to solo, you can allow yourself to let go of your training and self-restraint, play whatever flows out, as crazy and uncontrolled as you want, and know that you can swing right back into the rest of the band at the return of the 12-bar cycle. In the 12-bar rhythm and blues style, you can get as lost as you want and still find your way back into the groove with ease. It's not that this can't be done in jazz, but the simplicity of the music's 12-bar form, the very thing that rock music gets a bad rap for in classical and jazz ivory-tower circles, allows for unrestrained freedoms that are uniquely rock and roll.

But rhythm and blues isn't just about the soloists and lead vocals. Getting people to dance is all about backbeat. The rhythm section—drums, other horns, piano, rhythm guitar, and handclaps—emphasizes a strong backbeat, throwing the emphasis on the second and fourth beats of the four-beat meter, which allows the bass and soloists to stress the downbeat. When you listen to jump blues rhythm and blues, and pay attention to what is happening on the backbeat, you realize that the emphasis on backbeat is what gives rhythm and blues its locomotion. That constant stressing, even overstressing, of backbeat at the fast tempos used in rhythm and blues somehow makes you want to move. As jazz evolved away from swing, rhythm and blues kept the dance craze of the 1940s alive through the 1950s, and the unrestrained nature of the music reflected the new unrestrained teen image.

Now think about the timing of this frantic, raucous, unrestrained dance music and it becomes clear why America was ready for it. It began its domination right after a terrifying world war, which came right after an ever inflationary depression era. The country was tired of having to take itself so seriously. As the song says, *"Happy days are here again,"* and Americans wanted to dance away the uncertainties and hardships they had endured during the war. It was simply time to have fun again and try to forget what had just happened, and rhythm and blues was there to supply the soundtrack. Every music has its time (think folk rock in the 1960s) and the time for rhythm and blues had arrived.

The New Romantic Hero: *Rebels Without a Cause*

Was it the right time for the music, or the right music for the time? Probably both. The music was headed in this direction, but the postwar timing was just right as well. When opportunity knocked, the musicians were there to answer the call, the disc jockeys, armed with high power clear-channel stations, were there to play the new beat, and a new generation of teenagers flocked to a music they could call their own. The fact that the teens' parents couldn't fully appreciate the new sounds coming out of the radio just made it all the more appealing. Every generation wants a music to call their own. Something fresh and different from what their parents listen to. But something else happened too in the 1950s—teen marketing. For the first time in America, the teenager became the focus of marketers at all levels. A new teen image emerged based on attitude and reflected in the clothes they wore, cars they drove, movies they watched, and the music they listened and danced to.

Through the 1950s, the image of the leather-clad, duck-tailed biker or dragster with his bobby-socked, pony-tailed, gum-chewing girlfriend at his side was now unwilling to wait for the future to unfold, and willing to question authority to the end. James Dean in the movie *Rebel Without a Cause*, when asked, "What are you rebelling against?", he replied, "What do ya' got?" perfectly captures the restlessness of the 1950s teenager.

Well . . . that was the idea at first, but you can't market movies to teenagers where everyone always dies in fiery car wrecks at the end. The classic image of the romantic hero, bowing to no law, whether man's or God's, was softened quite a bit so that all of the teen movies wouldn't upset parents too much, and throughout the 1950s, what started as the *"Rebel Without a Cause"* image settled into endless scenarios where the rebellious teens turn from their ways and realize that a house in the suburbs, a car, and two kids isn't so bad after all. Just like the movies, there were strong attempts within the music industry to soften the hard edges of rock and roll to make it more marketable to a wider mainstream audience.

Major and Independent Record Companies

Unfortunately for the stability of the music business, throughout the 1950s, and the 1960s, every time the industry thought it had an understanding of rising trends and a firm handle on marketing those trends, new ideas, new performers, and new styles would emerge to upset the balance of power. This is an age when the regional independent record labels dominated the direction of popular music trends. The independent record labels were (and still are) the only labels willing to take risks on new sounds. The major labels had (and still have) a vested interest in promoting music that already had a foothold with the public. The major labels were much less willing to break new ground, whereas the independent record label *had* to try new things in order to hopefully find, or stumble into, a hit making performer that could catapult the label to higher rungs of the ladder and supply them with more financial resources to sign more artists, to make more hit records, to make more money, etc., etc., etc.

Actor James Dean. The rebel without a cause. © Bettmann/CORBIS

The major labels were constantly playing catch-up with the independent labels, sending out A& R (artist and repertoire) men to all corners of the country to keep a grip on the new rock trends. Sometimes though, the major labels would just wait until someone hits it big, then offer large sums to the indie label owner for that artist's contract. To the financially secure major label it might be just "pocket change," but to the indie label the offers allowed more financial resources to promote new artists.

Covers and Crossovers

Covers are the term used for performing or recording someone else's song. Everyone covers songs. That's how songs become traditional and carried through time. Covering someone else's song is usually done in tribute to the originator. Record companies, however, found that they could make a lot of money by having already established pop artists cover authentic rock songs that were charting. What guides this strategy is the idea that given enough promotional support, you could take any good looking, clean-cut, wholesome teenager with a smooth, crooner voice, have them record versions of songs that were already a hit by the original artists, and create a teen-rock idol.

The major label's—cover songs performed by fabricated teen idols—strategy for cutting into the new rock and roll market was a particularly unsettling one to the people who were making and giving airplay to authentic rock and roll. These cover versions of the songs were always tamed down and drained of any authentic rhythm and blues vitality, but almost always outsold the original versions due to the promotion techniques of complete market saturation. In this way, the major labels would pillage the country and rhythm and blues charts, buying the rights to a song for a few hundred dollars from a frequently all too hungry songwriter, then re-recording it by one of the cultivated teen idols, giving the label a top ten, million-selling hit on the pop charts.

Crossover is the term used when a song that climbs high on one chart, like the country and western or rhythm and blues charts, crosses over to another chart, like the Billboard pop charts. It was very common in the 1950s for songs to crossover in many directions as people's tastes for music broadened, whether major or indie produced. Country songs were crossing to the rhythm and blues charts, rhythm and blues songs were on the country and western charts, and both of these were claiming larger pieces of the pop charts. When an independent record label has a song climb into the pop chart Top Ten, it means that the label now has a little more financial freedom and industry credibility to fulfill its vision and mission objectives. When a major label fails to hold those Top Ten spots, it means that someone in New York or Los Angeles gets fired.

The major labels, then and now, are completely dependent on the sales generated by having multiple songs and artists in the Top Ten spots. Major labels are big companies; they have Boards of Directors; they have expensive offices in New York and L.A.; they have many executives on large salaries who each have big expense accounts; and they are desperate to maintain their status as Fortune 500 companies. Their interest in providing the marketplace with proven, formulaic, mainstream product is necessary in order to maintain the heavy cash flow needed to stay a major label. Independent record labels, on the other hand, are small businesses, sometimes family-owned and operated. They have small staffs and little offices; they record their artists in small, little known studios on relatively modest equipment; and though they are also in business to make money, they have a vested interest in recording and promoting authentic sounding and original music.

Radio

Regardless of the where, why, and who of the beginning days of rhythm and blues, the question of how this fire was fanned can be found in the smooth late night radio voices of a few disc jockeys around the country. One of the first disc jockeys to start playing rhythm and blues records on the air was William "Hoss" Allen working at WLAC in Nashville, a 50,000 watt clear-channel AM station. **Clear channel** means that no other station exists on that frequency, which insures a "clear channel" for the might of the power station to broadcast over vast areas of the country. A powerful clear channel station like WLAC was able to be heard in many states in the south and midwest, and the influence wielded by disc jockeys on the air would reach into all corners of those states.

Along with Hoss Allen, Dewey Phillips in Memphis and other disc jockeys across the country got caught up in the new music and gained popularity as the radio voices that brought out the music. Alan Freed, a champion of the vocal harmony doo wop styles, was working at WHK in Cleveland in 1951 when he coined the phrase "rock and roll" for the first time on the air. The term had long been used as black slang for sex, but it didn't have the implication of color that the term "rhythm and blues" did. The phrase caught on, and regardless of its past meaning, or maybe because of it, it could be easily associated with youth. The magic of the radio medium is that it does reach into all corners of society. All you need is access to a radio, and regardless if you're black or white, regardless of what you should or shouldn't listen to, if you wanted to hear the music, you just needed to tune in to the broadcasts late at night.

The man who coined the phrase "rock and roll" on the air was WHK Disc Jockey Alan Freed. © Bettmann/CORBIS

The first disc jockeys that played rock and roll were strongly committed to the authentic sounds of the independent labels. Alan Freed even banned the major label, white cover versions of songs on his radio shows. The network of radio in that period included friendships between the personalities on-the-air and the independent label owners, who were known to personally deliver new recordings to their favorite disc jockeys.

Phil and Leonard Chess of Chess Records did exactly that in driving fresh test-pressings of new songs from their studio in Chicago to Alan Freed in Cleveland, and later in New York. In July of 1954, Memphis disc jockey Dewey Phillips was the first to play *That's All Right Mamma* by a new trio of Elvis Presley, Scotty Moore, and Bill Black. Soon other disc jockeys, who at that time had control over what they played on-the-air, started to pick up on the model of playing recordings of anything new, different, original, and fresh. It was, in fact, the best way, at that time, for a radio disc jockey to gain notoriety, fame, and status as a radio personality.

The independent record labels and the radio disc jockeys fed off each other's enthusiasm for an authentic rock and roll sound. As the decade progressed, this tide started to shift. Radio stations are frequently owned by larger companies, and for most of the disc jockeys a rising pressure began to mount from those above to play songs on the air from a song-list of major label, teen idol cover artists. Some rebelled, some played along, and those few, like Alan Freed, who refused to play along, were removed from the scene.

Early Rock Heroes

There were so many good, innovative, and dynamic early rock and roll acts that it seems unfair to discuss a few representative groups. The best way to really discover the richness and depth of the early rock and roll musicians is not to read about them in a book but to listen to their recordings. With so many labels today re-releasing all of this music, there is certainly ample availability for those who seek it out. From early delta blues to electric to early rhythm and blues to rock and roll unknowns and heroes alike, there exists today an unprecedented depth of collections of this music available on CD. But if we were to pick just one, we probably couldn't find a better example of the sound that is rhythm and blues than The Treniers.

The Treniers

Formed by Alabama-born twin brothers Clifford and Claude Trenier in 1945, the Treniers were signed to Mercury Records in 1947. Their unique saxophone-heavy sound and outrageous stage show helped make them one of the top attractions on the new rock and roll circuit of the 1950s. Not much happened for them on Mercury, and in 1951 they signed with Columbia subsidiary and newly revived OKeh Records in New York City. Their popularity by this time along the New Jersey dance circuit was going strong, and their reputation as a talented, wild, and fun rock act catapulted them to dominance in the exploding rhythm and blues dance scene. They performed *Rockin' Is Our Business* on the Colgate Comedy Hour in 1954, and America started to get its first glimpse of the raucous jump blues style. Their outrageous stage antics included choreographed dance and slapstick moves, frantic call and response screaming, and parody music collages that mixed together other rhythm and blues hit songs.

Their recorded and film versions of *Rocking On Sunday Night* give a glimpse into their fun antics. At the countdown to Sunday they sing, *"Rockin on Tuesday, Wednesday, Thursday, Rockin' on Friday, Saturday, Sunday."* At the word *"Sunday,"* the saxophone player wails out of control for a moment while the singers slap their hands over their ears in mock horror at the sound. The Sax player then slides into a smooth solo over the steady backbeat. He stops his solo suddenly and Claude shouts out, *"Say man, Don't stop now. Let's keep on rockin' right on through to Sunday night."* At which point the sax player takes off on another raucous solo. There's another countdown to Sunday and another raucous solo following, and at each solo the rest of the band reacts in synchronized choreography of mock terror at the honking sound of the sax. All the while, the backbeat handclaps never stop. The infectious beat drives on.

There were so many good rhythm and blues acts during this underground period for rock music that a comprehensive survey of all of the groups would fill volumes. With the re-releasing of all of this rich music in the compact disc medium, there is now unprecedented easy access to nearly everything that was recorded in the early 1950s. However, though the music has been re-released, no one is marketing it today. If you have an interest in this music you have to seek it out.

Listen:	*Rocking On Sunday Night*	**The Treniers**
	Shake Rattle and Roll	**Big Joe Turner**
	Choo Choo Ch' Boogie	**Louis Jordan and His Tympany Five**
	Hound Dog	**Big Mama Thornton**
	Good Rockin' Tonight	**Wynonie Harris**

Risque Rhythm

As previously stated, the term "rock and roll" comes from black slang for sex. The raucous rhythm and blues styles of people like Little Richard are cultivated most predominantly in New Orleans party and strip clubs. Many of the early rock musicians had experience playing in burlesque houses and loose honky tonks, so it is no surprise to find a degree of sexually risque lyrics in the music. The words of rhythm and blues songs had always had suggestive content, but that was tolerated in the music business as long as it was confined to the black community.

Once teenagers started tuning into the late night radio shows in the early 1950s, their parents' concern for lyric content increased and grew into the first of many campaigns against rock and roll. In 1954, there was a national crusade against "suggestive" R&B records. The "that music is gonna' ruin our children" feeling among mainstream white America was an extension of a largely segregated country and the misunderstanding and perceived fear of black Americans that it fostered.

The risque elements of rhythm and blues, however, contained the attraction to the music for many listeners, and, as stated, the songs were tolerated by the music business as long as it remained predominantly in the black community. By 1954, as the forbidden sounds of late night radio drew in more and more teenage listeners, concern among parents grew into crusades against "suggestive" rhythm and blues songs. Risque elements are part of the music and it was not at all uncommon for even quite respectable performers to record an occasional *blue* song. There was an art form to creating double meaning lyrics that stems from burlesque theatre, and a good risque song could mean a hit in the rhythm and blues charts and Broadway musicals alike.

Big Ten Inch as recorded by Moose Jackson is an excellent example of the double meaning and word-play elements of risque rhythm and blues. The thinking behind the double meaning aspect goes something like this: Let's say I'm defending an accusation that this song is just about sex.

"I say, This is a song about 10 inch blues records (*before the 12 inch format, records were made 10 inches in diameter, as well as the trusty 7 inch format*) and if you think that it's about something else . . . well then get your mind out of the gutter."

In this way, songwriters could defend themselves tongue-in-cheek.

𝄞   **Listen:**   *Big Ten Inch*   **Moose Jackson**

The song continues on in the manner for a couple more verses, but you get the idea. The art was being able to loosely hide the true meaning of the song lyrics through use of double meaning. The question "what is the big ten inch?" is quickly answered just as, or just after, the mind has filled in the gap. This is just like the old burlesque and Vaudevillian style songs like *Shaving Cream.*

The singer hangs on the *shh* sound in the word *shaving* just long enough for the listener's mind to fill in what seems to be the obvious rhyme in the fourth line. These are the little tricks that made for good burlesque theater, humorous Broadway show tunes, and risque rhythm and blues.

Just in case you thought this was something only the guys did, another good example of the risque style is *Big Long Slidin' Thing* recorded by blues-jazz singer Dinah Washington in 1954. Though the song never made it onto the radio airwaves, and it's probably pretty obvious why, it was well known underground and contains some of the most creative and clever use of word-play to be found in rhythm and blues music. It also serves as a somewhat blue not so young person's guide to the rhythm and blues ensemble. In the song, she is lamenting her missing trombone-playing boyfriend as the players of other instruments in his band try to *console* her. Now, if someone says it's about something else entirely, you can tell them to get their mind out of the gutter.

But was it really just a bunch of overly suggestive, dirty music about promiscuity, or was it imaginative, fun, and humorous word play on top of some truly fun rhythm and blues music? Or is it even more than that? If we look deeper at this aspect of rhythm and blues, we find a message

Blues-Jazz Singer Dinah Washington.
© Bettmann/CORBIS

woven into some of the song content that exemplified rock and roll's early period. Many of the songs have an "I'm all right—you're all right" attitude underneath the lyric content. The message that "it doesn't matter if you're not perfect—no one is, so let's just have some fun," is one of the most important aspects of rock and roll songwriting that endeared it to so many teens. Just ask Chuck Berry.

One of the risque rhythm and blues songs that captures that idea while carrying an overt sexuality in tongue-in-cheek fashion and another song that never saw radio airplay when it was released was *It Ain't the Meat* by The Swallows. The song puts this message in clear perspective. In the song lyrics, it doesn't matter if you're skinny, or short, or tall, or fat, or whatever you may look like. What matters is how you act and perceive yourself, as well as the understanding that the world is not perfect and neither are you. And if this message can get through and make the listener smile a little too, then certainly no harm is done to the morals of the youth of America.

Musically, *It Ain't the Meat* vamps along to constant backbeat handclaps and smooth backing doo wop vocals behind Norris "Bunky" Mack's deep bass lead vocals.

Listen: *It Ain't the Meat*   **The Swallows**

As the resistance to suggestive lyrics gained fever pitch by the mid-1950s, some performers only added fuel to the arguments against it. ***Toy Bell*** was recorded in 1954 by **The Bees** and sings blatantly of getting various people to play with "my ding-a-ling." There wasn't much double meaning in that, and songs like it were certainly not welcome in the polite society of a Mayberryesque American culture. *Toy Bell* was later recorded as *My Ding-a-Ling* by Chuck Berry in 1972, and received heavy airplay that year. By then, the times definitely had-a-changed.

Roll Over Beethoven

In the glow of postwar prosperity, a growing number of teenagers had simply outgrown the styles of the hit parade of their parents and the war years. They reached out for something different to explore and found a rich treasure of authentic American music that had been evolving out of the blues and hillbilly music.

Neglected for too long, the time had finally arrived for the music of the common people of America to take center stage. The music; the musicians; the thriving performing scenes in places like New Orleans, Memphis, and Chicago; the small independent record labels and their studios; and the disc jockeys had all been there since the mid to late 1940s, but once white teenagers discovered what was out there, rock and roll would rocket to the limelight of not only the recording industry and radio but television and movies as well.

Once rock and roll—rhythm and blues, hillbilly, and gospel based music—did break into mainstream American culture, there would never be a turning back. The new image in the 1950s of what it was to be an American youth, complete with wardrobe, soundtrack, and attitude, prevailed until the cultural shifts of the 1960s—the British Invasion and rising civil rights attitudes to name a couple—when social awareness replaced the largely ritual dance music. That is not to denigrate the music of the 1950s in any way as a catalyst for social change. As previously discussed, this rhythm and blues-hillbilly based music was *THE* most important instrument in tearing down the barriers to racial equality in America in the 1950s. It brought the kids together in ways that were never allowed by cultural and legal channels before. The new 1950s generation dancing together, black and white, for the first time in America. Rock and roll was indeed one of the most important catalysts for social change. In the 1960s, the words would change to unite the many new ideas and voices of that era, but for now . . . it was good that people were just dancing together.

Worksheet Assignment : Chapter 3
The Emergence of Rock and Roll

1. A new style of music emerged from the blues that was faster and danceable. The primary name for this new faster blues music was *rhythm and blues*. The name for the fastest forms of this new style is

   _____

2. The most important rhythmical aspect of rhythm and blues, as well as hillbilly boogie, is the

   _____

3. A new teen image emerged along with these new musical forms. Define three of the signature aspects of this new teen image and marketing.

   _____

   _____

   _____

4. Record labels that are listed in the Fortune 500 are known as

   _____

5. Record labels that are small and have a "do-it-yourself" mode of operation are known as

   _____

6. Recording or performing a song written by someone else is called a

   _____

7. A song that originates in one market but is also popular and profitable in another market is called a

   _____

8. Radio stations that are given the ability to broadcast at 50,000 watts, covering vast areas of the United States and beyond, are called

   _____

9. One radio station in particular was responsible for spreading the sounds of rhythm and blues and the other roots of rock musical styles. Located in Nashville, Tenn., and led by DJ Hoss Allen, what station was it?

   _____

10. Draw a circle around these cities on the map below.
    —Memphis, Tenn.
    —New Orleans, La.
    —Chicago, Ill.
    —New York City
    —Cleveland, Ohio

11. Using a highlighter, highlight the Mississippi River on the map below.

4 Like a Rollin' Stone
The Big Rock and Roll Hayride

As rock and roll progressed through the 1950s, it became obvious to the record companies, both indie and major, that there was money to be made in harnessing the power and vitality of this music. Everyone had their radar out, meaning that labels and promoters knew they could sell this music to a large audience if they could just find the right personalities to deliver it. What was needed was a really good looking white guy who had authentic rhythm and blues feel and style. Big Joe Turner may have shaked, rattled, and rolled, but he was an aging, large black guy. Bill Haley may have rocked around the clock, but he was an aging, large white guy. Though their music was vital, pure, and soaked in authenticity, they didn't have the image that was needed to deliver rock music to the masses. What was needed was slim, trim youth.

The question of just where this sought after rock and roll hero would come from and who would find him was on the minds of everyone in the music business. It became obvious that something was going to break open, but who would be the one, when, and where?

The Rockabilly Model

Though there was vast amounts of rhythm and blues based rock and roll to go around, with horn sections, a raucous lead saxophone player, guitars, and lots of vocal harmony, it would be a completely different style of rock and roll that would ignite the interests of the country and open the door into all of the rock styles. Rockabilly music is a scaled down version of hillbilly boogie, but without all of the instrumental trappings of a large ensemble that country swing and much hillbilly boogie used.

The standard rockabilly ensemble consists of stand-up bass guitar (contra bass) playing a rhythmic slapping style; an electric hollow-body guitar like a Gretch or Gibson, complete with twang-bar, aka. whammy bar; a small drum kit, usually just kick drum; a snare drum; high-hat cymbals; and that's about it. Gone in the new rockabilly sound was the large ensemble environment that included accordion, saxophones, steel slide guitar, and everybody singing.

Rockabilly is a backbeat-oriented, fast 12-bar blues form over a clickety bass playing boogie runs, the guitarist jabbing rhythmic and slide solos here and there, with the vocals soaked in a hiccup diction mid-southern dialect. Rockabilly, though it was not called that yet, is also the style that Elvis Presley was working in when he introduced mainstream America to rock and roll. In fact, rockabilly really starts with Elvis. His style and band instrumentation was emulated by legions of southern whites.

What does this model really mean for rock and roll? For starters, it's small. Only three, maybe four, band members are required. That has multiple impact. A small band can travel much easier than a large ensemble. A small band can also get to know each other much more intimately musically, creating tightness and team precision, as well as each band member's understanding of how the other members think musically. In the rockabilly band we see the emergence of the rock band model: drums, two guitars, and bass. Let's not leave out the piano though, as there were some fine piano "pickers" playing rockabilly style, of which Jerry Lee Lewis led the pack.

Another very important aspect of rockabilly on the emerging rock and roll music scene was that it showed that a few people with a couple of guitars can get together, learn a few songs, and get out there and play the dance halls and honky-tonks. You didn't need to know pedal steel guitarists, accordion players, or horn sections full of musicians to put together a rockabilly band. It proved that anyone could buy a guitar and with a little practice and a lot of ambition, be playing the dance halls and maybe record a few songs that could ignite a career. Presley's scaled down version of hillbilly boogie, built upon the foundation of rockabilly prototype bands like Bill Haley's Comets, became the model for so many.

Once the rockabilly model, transference to a small three or four piece band of guitars and drums, proved itself as a favorite on the airwaves and dance halls, teenagers flocked to the heavy backbeat oriented music, and started saving up to buy that guitar in the window of their local music store. The model of the garage bands, a few people getting together and forming a band in someone's basement or garage, begins with the rockabilly

Bill Haley and The Comets: The best of all worlds. © Bettmann/CORBIS

bands. It has been said that rock and roll was really just a lot of boogie-woogie with some twangin' sanging and guitar. Little Richard claimed that he hit it big once he threw boogie-woogie on top of gospel-blues. It always seems to come back to that term boogie-woogie. From rockabilly to rhythm and blues to gospel, everyone seemed to be throwing boogie-woogie into their own musical experience, and out popped rock and roll.

Haley's adapted rockabilly ensemble proved to be a good prototype for rock and roll: drums, bass, guitars, and saxophone. The accordion and steel slide guitar, a throwback to western swing, would soon disappear, leaving the rock band model at a few guys with guitars and drums, instead of the big-band style ensembles found in much rhythm and blues. After that, the idea that anyone could learn a few chords on guitar and put a band together prevailed and guided the course of rock and roll from then on.

Boogie-woogie is really a style of bass playing over which a musician can work above. The idea stems from a style of piano playing. In the 19th and early 20th-centuries, America was a wild land. Small towns dotted the landscape along railroad lines and early highways, and in each small town there was a honky-tonk or saloon (not to mention bordellos that also hired musicians), and in every one of those was a piano. Piano "pickers" would improvise all night long over ragtime and boogie-woogie left-hand bass lines.

The boogie-woogie style of playing found in rockabilly and Leadbelly alike is a throwback to early American frontier saloon piano playing. Sadly, of all the countless frontier piano players that worked in the rustic pioneer environment throughout America, we don't know any of their names. Much like the early blues from the delta, the chronicle of these musicians went woefully neglected in their own homeland. The legends and romantic images of this environment certainly portray the piano player, but usually it's a comical image of a musician jumping behind the piano for cover as a shootout erupts in the saloon.

The reality is that these musicians were of vital importance to a sense of community in these small but growing towns. There's even a popular saloon sign still found in bars that reads "Please Don't Shoot the Piano Player." Today it's just a humorous sign at the bar, but there was a time when that sign was put up in all seriousness. It would devastate a small frontier town not to have any entertainment in a time before radio, stereos, and television. Suddenly the town becomes quiet without that piano "picker" to supply a soundtrack to their lives. It is true that 100 years ago, most people could get by on at least one instrument, but that meant you had to put a band together. Single piano players, however, have the full spectrum of harmonic and melodic choices available to them, limited only by having ten fingers to play with. Boogie-woogie and ragtime proved to be handy tools to the piano men, whether they lived in the city or out on the frontier.

The key to the piano "pickers'" ability to improvise for long hours is the left-hand playing. In a ragtime left-hand bass, there is octave and chordal bouncing incorporated that gives the feel of two rhythmic instruments in syncopation, while the right hand playfully works melody and harmony above. In the boogie-woogie bass style, the left hand walks through the outline of the tonic root chord then adds the 6th and 7th above tonic, then walks back down. That outline is then transposed to the subdominant (IV) and dominant (V) as needed for use within the 12-bar blues form.

Major   **Minor**

For the added minor 7th, this is commonly known as the **minor blues scale** and can be played in either major or minor key. Another highly rollicking popular boogie bass line requires a bit more dexterity to pull off in left hand only, but the same rule applies; once you learn it in one key, it's just a matter of transposition into the 12-bar form.

The eighth note rhythm is not meant to be adhered to strictly. The offbeats should be anticipated and played just a fraction early to give the line bounce. Over any one of these bass lines can be played raucous saxophone, twangy electric guitar, slick Hawaiian slide guitar, country accordion, bluesy harmonica, breakdown banjo, and, of course, vocal wailing of all sorts. These are just a couple of the boogie bass lines, and there are great amounts of differing adaptations and deviations by the many various musicians who used it. Boogie bass has been around at least as far back as the turn of the twentieth-century, and can be found in all of the styles of rock music in the 1950s.

Like the 12-bar blues, there is much adaptation available to the musician and still maintain the boogie style. And like the 12-bar delta blues and gospel, boogie is handed down from one generation to the next, learned in the honky-tonks, juke joints, and front porches in rural and urban areas wherever people gather to meet. As well, it stems from the music of the common folk of America. Once these styles merge together—blues, rhythm and blues, gospel, hillbilly, country and western—rock and roll is born.

Vocables

Nonsense lyrics are a big part of rock and roll vocals. **Nonsense lyrics** are made up of non-language based vocal words, also known as **vocables**. They make no sense, and aren't supposed to. Helen Humes sang "Be baba leba" in the mid-1940s, and Little Richard sang "A-womp-ba-ba-loo-bomp-ba-lomp-bam-boom" in the 1950s, and "doo-wah-ditty" was yet to come. The term for a whole genre of music, *doo wop*, is a tribute to nonsense lyrics. It might just as easily have been called *sh-boom*, or *boom ba-dop*, or even *wamma lamma ding sh-la la* for that matter. The words, if we call them that, don't particularly mean anything.

Sometimes, though, lyrics that seem nonsensical are, in fact, just incredibly thick southern dialect adaptations. The song *Dad Gum Ya Hide* by Louis Jordan and His Tympany Five is a good example of this, as well as being one the best preachin' gospel based rhythm and blues songs ever recorded. The words "dad gum ya" might be seen as non-sense lyrics until you listen to the song, which is about one guy blasting his friend for being a no good, two-timing loser. The chorus gives us an idea of what is really meant by the title of the song. Hint: Exchange the first letters of the first two words.

The idea of nonsense lyrics may have had a basis in the widespread use of fun devia-tions and adaptations of real language and phrases. They may also have been first em-ployed simply as a means for back up vocalists to supply rhythmic locomotion and preci-sion to the music, a common practice in gospel jubilee show songs, which drew the idea from authentic gospel and work songs before that. To the musicians, rhythmic precision was more important, but if you could playfully twist a few words around in doing so to give a song some wry wit, then all the better.

Frequently, the words of risque songs had to be changed to make them suitable for airplay, and turning the offending words into nonsense vocables was one way of doing that. Little Richard's song *Tutti Frutti* was treated just this way. The original lyrics could be downright pornographic.

New Orleans

New Orleans had long been a crossroads of culture. It is one of America's largest sea-ports, and anywhere there is a crossroads of trade route, there is a vast exchange of ideas. Just like Mesopotamia (land between two rivers) and Mesoamerica (land between two Ameri-cas), New Orleans represents to North America that same status as a gateway and cross-roads of trade. Anywhere you have many people from many lands exchanging goods, they are also exchanging ideas and language, with music being one of those. Also, in a large trade port city, or crossroads of trade, you will find many establishments of entertainment of all sorts to accommodate the many travelers. Any city that wants large amounts of trade business would want to create this atmosphere as a way of attracting the traders. If your life is spent traveling, you tend to look forward to those stops in places with a wild and fun reputation, and cities like New Orleans foster and cultivate that reputation as a promotional strategy to gain more trade and tourism. Every big city today plays into that strategy by hiring highly paid people and creating large committees whose job it is to promote trade and tourism. Some cities promote their sports entertainment, some promote their scenery and location, some promote their stage and show entertainment, some promote their cul-ture. No other city in America supports music like New Orleans.

New Orleans is known as the birthplace of jazz, but so many different kinds of music come from the region that it really deserves a much broader title. Not only does jazz and rhythm and blues evolve there out of the blues, but cajun music from the swamps, Carib-bean music from the islands, and the rich and very funky music of the Mardi Gras Indians who "battle" every year for domination as Mardi Gras kings through their costumes and music all come together in a city called New Orleans.

The rich musical tradition there is very much alive today, as anyone who visits or lives there can attest. The streets of the French Quarter are still very active with the

Street musicians in the French Quarter. © Robert Holmes/CORBIS

sounds of street musicians playing for tips (*busking*), wandering preservation jazz bands, romping cajun music, and authentic rhythm and blues that drifts out of the clubs on and around Bourbon Street.

It was in those clubs that rhythm and blues evolved into being. Some clubs were known for their music, and some clubs were known for other performances, but had live music to accompany the stage shows and fill in between acts. Little Richard sang the blues between stage shows of exotic dancers and transvestites long before he developed his rock and roll style. Up and down Bourbon Street and all around the French Quarter were clubs offering every sort of live music to be found in the South. It is in that "anything goes" environment of a wild-sided seaport town that rhythm and blues was able to sprout and flourish.

J&M Studio

Cosimo Matassa, owner and chief production engineer of J&M Studio on the edge of the French Quarter, was one of the most important figures on the New Orleans music scene. Everyone who was anyone, and a lot of other folks as well, recorded at Matassa's studio. Like Sun Records in Memphis, J&M used relatively simple equipment with very few special effects. Reverb was achieved by using the bathroom or hallway to record vocals. Echo (delay) was achieved by an ingenious series of microphones and pipes. There was not yet available any of the effects boxes and digital toys that musicians have available to them today. There wasn't even multi-track overdubbing (*the ability to record and add new material over previously recorded material*). Everything had to be recorded live in one non-stop take, which means that once the levels on the microphones are set, the band simply performed the song. That performance, without any mixing, effects processing, or overdubbing was what was cut into a record. At that time it wasn't the equipment that a studio like J&M Studio had that lured musicians to record there, but the sound of the studio itself and the reputation of the engineer.

Matassa's father owned two bars side by side in New Orleans. One was a black bar and one was a white bar in accordance with the laws of the time. Each had a jukebox that reflected the bar's racial format, black rhythm and blues, and blues in the black bar, and white country and hillbilly music in the white bar. But when they started to mix the music in the jukeboxes up, it was soon discovered that a lot of white people wanted to play the black rhythm and blues music, and that a lot of black people were playing the country and hillbilly music. The magic of a studio owner like Matassa is that he was able to see the potential for a music that combined the two based on this experience, and was thus willing to spend time and effort where a lot of studios wouldn't.

Fats Domino (b. 1928)

Antoine "Fats" Domino came from the New Orleans culture. He grew up in a musical family and was able to see the business before just jumping onto it. His music has always been seen as an easy, non-threatening introduction into the world of rock and roll. That's a little simplistic however, as Fats' early music is filled with rollicking boogie bass, rocking guitar parts, and raucous saxophone solos.

Fats was one of the classic rhythm and blues crooners with a smooth, articulate voice and rhythmic, but not overly pounding, piano style, like Little Richard and Jerry Lee Lewis. He developed his own easily acceptable version of rhythm and blues based largely on an 8 or 16-bar form that has a lot of the feel of a two-step dance. On top of that, there was the almost always present pounding piano triplet figures in the high end right hand of his piano style. He eventually cultivated his style into a more popular easy rock sound as a way of insuring a life in pop

Fats Domino. © Neal Preston/CORBIS

music, as opposed to a flash in the rock and roll pan that some performers became. It was his own unique sound and it was pure rhythm and blues. When Fats was interviewed in 1955, he said "well, today what you're calling rock and roll is really just rhythm and blues, and I've been playing it for fifteen years in New Orleans."

Fats Domino's strategy worked well for him in the height of the rock and roll craze. He achieved the most commercial success of any of the New Orleans artists and was the biggest selling black musician of that first era of rock and roll. By 1956, Fats Domino had twelve of his songs climb into the top ten R&B charts, and had crossed over to the pop charts with *Ain't That A Shame* and his classic cover of *Blueberry Hill*. Times had changed fast though and just five years later the sound of rhythm and blues was already dated as new styles of rock music filled the charts.

Listen: *I'm Walking*	**Fats Domino off of Louisiana Piano Rhythms (Rhino71568)**

Little Richard (b. 1932)

"Little" Richard Penniman (b. 1932) was born and raised in Macon, Georgia. His up-bringing and his musical training centered on the church. His mother had raised her twelve children to be morally clean and religiously active. After Little Richard found blues and rhythm and blues, he would spend the rest of his life vacillating between rock and roll and the church.

Little Richard was the most flamboyant and outrageous of all the big names of rock and roll in the 1950s. His attention getting antics date back to his teen years, when as one of twelve children, he became given to unpredictable behavior to draw attention to himself. His neighbors may have thought that he was just some crazy kid, but that very same behaviorial pattern would create one of the wildest shows in rock and roll. His show was *so* dynamic that other musicians shunned the possibility of being compared to him. When Little Richard came to perform in a town, no one wanted to follow him up, either on stage that night, or even for weeks after he played.

That's a good indicator of how powerful a performer he was. His vocal style was a mixture of the powerful gospel song styles and vocal calls, mixed with the raucous power and vocal whoops and hiccups of rhythm and blues and hillbilly, with the occasional outright maniacal screams that only he could pull off. Combining those talents along with his piano playing style of fast, rhythmic pounding chords and boogie-woogie bass lines created music that became the hallmark of rhythm and blues authenticity. To anyone who had never seen or heard an authentic gospel and blues based singer perform unbridled and unrestrained, Little Richard came across as the very essence of rock and roll.

He would frequently play the rhythmic pounding with his feet instead of his hands, jump on top of the piano, dress in wild, flamboyant stage clothes, and slide and dance in provocative motions to the beat of the songs. This outrageous stage show wasn't just a stage show, but one of the best promotional strategies in rock music.

Little Richard was keenly aware from his years of work in New Orleans that people love to see a wild show when they're out for a fun night on the town. As word spread of this "wild man that's gone crazy" piano player, Little Richard Penniman had indeed found his way out of Macon and into the history books. But he wasn't just a good stage show performer. If it hadn't been for his strong talents as a songwriter and musical arranger, his name might be only a footnote in the history books, instead of heralding him as one of the prime innovators of this music.

The turning point toward fame for Little Richard came when, after little success from his recordings with RCA and Peacock Records, he sent a demo tape of his rhythm and blues style music to Specialty Records in Los Angeles. In September of 1955, Specialty Records brought together Little Richard and a group of hard hitting, experienced New Orleans musicians for a recording session that would mark a watershed for American music. After a long session of uninspired recording,

Little Richard. © Bettmann/CORBIS

just when the men in the control room were beginning to wonder about their decision to bring this together, Little Richard and the band broke into the song *Tutti Frutti*, an obscene, risque rhythm and blues song Richard sang in the clubs. They cleaned up the lyrics and recorded rock and roll history.

Lucille was the one song of Little Richard's that was most endeared to himself and a song that he played in every performance of his career as a reminder of where he came from. Richard relied on *Lucille* anytime he felt unsure of himself with an audience. The song rocks with the strength and power and rhythm of the railroad engines that it is musically depicting. As Richard says it, "Where I grew up there wasn't anything happening except for the roosters crowing and the trains going by." The driving rhythm and power of the drums, saxophones, piano, and bass pulsate in emulation of locomotives streaming down the line. The sounds of the south that he grew up in are woven into the song.

Richard's vocals style on the word "Lucille" illustrate the coy sexuality of his musical experience. On the last part of the word, his voice slides up (*glissando*) to the very top of his range and then keeps going right through the roof. It almost seems like his vocal slide disappears not because he runs out of voice, but because he sings right out of our hearing range. This vocal hiccup style, where a male vocalist begins a word or phrase in their normal voice range, then slides quickly up into their falsetto range, particularly at the end of a vocal line, is found throughout 1950s rock and roll. Elvis Presley (*Anything from the Sun recordings*), Buddy Holly (*Peggy Sue*), Big Joe Turner (*Shake, Rattle and Roll*), and Jerry Lee Lewis (*Whole Lotta Shakin' Goin' On*) all used it, to name just a few representatives. On both sides of the rock fence, whether you came from a predominantly rhythm and blues or rockabilly style, this vocal hiccup was used to great effect in the music. Little Richard was one of the best at it. He could go higher, faster, and deliver it with more gospel authenticity than anyone else had dared try.

The Originator

Little Richard was also one of the best and most prolific songwriters. Almost everything he wrote and recorded became a Top Ten hit, and everyone, from Elvis Presley to Pat Boone to Donald Duck, covered Little Richard songs. In that time, this was done frequently without even notifying the songwriter. Suddenly a song you may have written was now a hit for someone else.

What happened was that the musicians did not have the business savvy that the record people did, and they would sign away the rights to a song for relatively little money. The record company would then take the already proven song and have their top stars record it, most often far outselling the original version. The laws better protect the songwriters today, but in that period, once you sign away the rights to something you created, the law stands against you no matter how fraudulently you believe the company acted. That's what happened to Little Richard and to so many black *and* white musicians in the 1950s.

Though Little Richard certainly never received all the money due to him, when his music was covered by the latest stars of the hit parade, people would hear the song, know it was a cover, and frequently want to hear the original. This would lead them right back to Little Richard and the power of authentic rock and roll. The larger cultural picture here is that though the white performers and their record companies who covered and sold Little Richard's compositions (and many others) benefitted from the loopholes in the laws, and frequently left the originator of the work holding nothing, by being white, the performers who covered Little Richard's material helped to open the door for Little Richard and other black performers into the mainstream white American culture.

White Spectators

Another even bigger cultural aspect of a performer like Little Richard, and of rhythm and blues music in general, is that in a time of legal segregation, his music helped to bring the races together. At that time period, blacks and whites were not allowed to dance together. They weren't even allowed on the same dance floor. At the dance halls, if there was a black performer, blacks were allowed on the first floor dance floor, while whites had to go sit in the "white spectator seats" balcony. But when a dynamic and outrageous performer like Little Richard hit the stage and started screaming, hooting, and banging on the piano, the white kids would jump from the balcony, and to the horror of the segregationist society, black kids were suddenly dancing with white kids. The kids just wanted to dance, and they didn't care who was black or who was white, and they hadn't yet learned the hate of racism.

At first, there was some very strong opposition to rock and roll for this very reason. The chairman of the Alabama White Citizens Council even went so far as to declare "This music is a means by which the white man and his children can be driven to the level with the nigger. If we choose to call that Communist ideology, then I think we hit it squarely on the head." In some people's view, rock and roll had made the jump from ritual dance music to a communist plot. As stated earlier, those views would soon become fundamentalist cries in the wilderness as rock and roll became big business in America and as people realized that there just wasn't that much to be feared in this teen music. It was a fun night out and that was about it, and Little Richard led the pack.

In Little Richard, we see the model of the true rock hero that could do it all. He was a dynamic performer and showman. He was a prolific and proven hit-making song composer. He was a great recording and stage musician who could relate to the other musicians (except when he got tired of waiting for guitarist Jimi Hendrix and closed up the tour bus and left, leaving Hendrix behind in New York City to fend for himself—itself a fateful story that would later help change the course of rock music). Little Richard had the keenest sense of self-promotion. In the end, he is a great musician, performer, showman, composer, and promoter—Little Richard could do it all.

Memphis: Sun Records

Up the Mississippi River from New Orleans, Memphis was also a thriving music city after World War II and into the 1950s. The city was rich in both black and white gospel, southern blues, country, western, and hillbilly traditions. All of this diverse musical vitality would start merging together in the 1950s to change the face of music in America. This is where the merging of rhythm and blues with hillbilly took place to create rockabilly. When people first heard of Elvis Presley, Scotty Moore, and Bill Black, they called it rock and roll, but it was pure rockabilly through and through.

A musical environment fostered by Sam Phillips, radio engineer, and owner and chief engineer of the Memphis Recording Service, blossomed to record the rich heritage of black music in the region. Not many of the people of Memphis had much use for the records Sam Phillips was making. The largely white population was raised on country hillbilly and western swing music. Though he knew that the black blues and rhythm and blues he was recording had a vitality to it that could "make a noise," he also knew that he was a white engineer recording black music in a predominantly white neck of the American woods.

Like J&M Studio in New Orleans, Phillips' studio made use of relatively inexpensive recording equipment and makeshift reverb and echo effects with tremendously high impact on the music industry. Once it caught on with the public, everyone, including the major label studios, wanted that sound and spent a great deal of money trying to recreate it technologically, but never could. Also, again like J&M, it was the acoustics of the studio itself and the daring experimentation of the engineers that created the authenticity to the sound of the recordings. The record producer would replace the recording engineer in importance in the 1960s, but there is absolutely no doubt that credit for all the great musical sounds and studio reputations belonged to the engineers who built the studios and experimented with what could be done.

Sam Phillips kept recording rhythm and blues musicians, sensing the new musical trend in the air. He had a number one rhythm and blues hit in 1951 with *Rocket "88"* by the Ike Turner band. The success of that record gave Sam Phillips the initiative to start the Sun Records label. His commitment to recording authentic black rhythm and blues was impeccable, and he is responsible for recording some of the best early work of blues giants like Muddy Waters. In his own words, "I always thought at that time in history, that if I could find a white southern boy, we just might be able to do a few of the things that I knew it would take a long time to do," he was talking about the strong resistance to black music that dominated the music business in America.

His strategy of shifting all of his energy away from recording black blues and rhythm and blues artists and toward recording white rockabilly artists, once he had unleashed Elvis Presley to the world, is often attacked. But once Elvis wandered in off the street to record a song for his mother's birthday, *My Happiness*, and once the first recording sessions in July of 1954, just meant to be a tryout to see what Elvis could do, with Scotty Moore on guitar and Bill Black on bass eventually yielded the vibrant hit covers of *That's All Right* and *Blue Moon of Kentucky*, Sam Phillips was so inspired and reawakened by the sound of rockabilly and the impact of Presley's musical and performing style that he never dwelt on what might have been had he stayed in the rhythm and blues genre. That one recording session

Elvis with Bill Black on bass.
© Bettmann/CORBIS

had changed American music so dramatically that many credit it, arguably, as being the actual day rock and roll really started.

After Sam sold Elvis off to RCA Records, he kept the rockabilly ball rolling by recording and producing such artists as Jerry Lee Lewis, Carl Perkins, Johnny Cash, Roy Orbison, and a host of less famous rockabilly performers. He had turned over the reins of blues, and rhythm and blues to other labels like Chess Records and Specialty, who were wholly embracing efforts to record black musicians, in order to focus on a sound and style that he could call his own.

Elvis Presley (1935-1977)

America was simply not ready for Elvis Aaron Presley when he broke into national attention in 1955. His defiant attitude and wild gyrations on stage were an affront to the good, clean, moral boy scout image of American youth. But here also, the image was just that, something Elvis cultivated in mirroring the portrayals of youth that his movie heroes James Dean and Marlon Brando had developed in *Rebel Without a Cause* and *The Wild One*, respectively. The duck-tailed hair, the leather jacket, the sneer, and the irreverent attitude were all developed by Elvis for his own image out of these inspirations. The image belied the truth as it turned out as Elvis was in reality someone very dedicated to virtuous family and moral character from his upbringing.

The one thing that Elvis did have and didn't hide was unrelenting ambition and a desire to break the cast set for him by the fate of his birth into a poor family, and in doing so, he became the most influential character in creating mass market appeal for rock and roll. He was able to walk both sides of the fence as far as his image goes. On one hand, he was cocky and defiant to authority figures and looked the part, on the other hand he could easily portray himself as a wholesome, spiritual, polite, and innocent good ol' boy that you could take home to meet your parents.

Elvis Aaron Presley was born in Tupelo, Miss., to poor parents. His twin brother, Jesse Garon, died at birth, and his mother pampered her only child as he grew up. His parents moved to Memphis in 1948 in search of better times, and Elvis' fate seemed destined for a hard-working life. After graduating from high school with a reputation as an introverted kid who sat in the back of the class, or quietly alone off somewhere with his guitar, Elvis took a factory job and it seemed that his life was cut for him far away from the fame he would actually achieve. When Elvis did find his stride at Sun Records, his music reflected an exuberance and playful extrovert who was realizing for the first time that destiny and fate aren't always what they seem.

After high school, Elvis started hanging out at Sun Records and the Beale Street honky-tonks in Memphis, soaking up all the music that was a part of the city, from blues and gospel to rhythm and blues to hillbilly boogie and bluegrass to the Grand Ole Opry. He started shopping for clothes at black-owned stores that catered to flamboyant styles, dressing in shocking pink, green, red, and gold outfits and trendy suits.

His first sessions with Sun Records with Scotty Moore and Bill Black were really just a tryout of what he could do. The only reason that his first recordings there, *That's*

Alright Mamma, originally written by Arthur 'Big Boy' Cruddup, and *Blue Moon of Kentucky*, originally written by Bill Monroe, included only Scotty and Bill was that Sam Phillips had only called them in, as opposed to a whole band, to sit and see what talent the young Presley possessed.

As Scotty Moore tells it, "It wasn't intended to be a session at all. That was the reason only Bill and I were in the Studio. Sam just wanted to see what he sounded like on tape. Then we were taking a break . . . and all of a sudden Elvis started singing a song, jumping around and just acting the fool, and then Bill picked up his bass and he started acting the fool, too, and, you know, I started playing with them. Sam had the door to the control room open. I don't know, he was editing tape or doing something, and he stuck out his head and said, 'What are you doing?' and we said, 'We don't know.' 'Well back up,' he said, 'try to find a place to start and do it again.'"

Sam recorded what was taking place in his studio, and at the end of the song, *That's All Right*, he knew he had found his man. Sam asked Elvis what else he had in that style, and Elvis cut into a raucous, supercharged version of the bluegrass hit, *Blue Moon of Kentucky*. Again, Sam Phillips was blown away by the sounds coming out of his studio. *Blue Moon of Kentucky* was done originally by its composer, bluegrass legend Bill Monroe, as a slow waltz (triple meter). The Elvis version shifts the song to a fast duple meter with heavy backbeat emphasis. It was a truly ingenuous interpretation and adaptation of the song. Again, Phillips was stunned and elated by what he was hearing. What had started as a workout session to see if Elvis could sing ballads, had turned into a seminal moment for rockabilly and rock and roll.

In 1955, Elvis was named the Billboard up and coming country and western artist. Everywhere that Elvis performed he was met with both bewilderment and adoration. Radio stations refused to play his music at first because no one could tell if he was black or white, rhythm and blues or hillbilly. But at the shows, Elvis won over every teenager who saw him, especially the girls. Elvis would sing standing up on the balls of his feet and rocking up and down and all around. It all began quite innocently as an extension of his own excitement in the music, but soon he realized that the girls were rushing the stage and falling all over each other to get a better look at the handsome spectacle bouncing, shaking, and shimmying on stage. Realizing a good stage strategy when he saw it, Elvis started to develop and embellish the movements until he had become one of the most popular and controversial figures in music at the time. It wasn't just the teenage girls that were deeply affected by what Elvis was doing in the studio and on stage; just about every musician who came along in the years after Elvis broke rock and roll to the world wanted to emulate the performer in their music, style, and attitude. Some very big names in rock music, from Buddy Holly to Eddie Cochran to John Lennon to Mick Jagger, and far beyond, credit Elvis Presley with making them want to chase their rock and roll dreams.

After Elvis had signed on with RCA Records through his new manager, Colonel Tom Parker for $40,000 (RCA made over ten million off of Elvis in that very next year), the company had toned down the maniacally fervent performing and musical style that Elvis had created in order to make him a more marketable commodity in the mainstream marketplace. Elvis desperately wanted that superstardom and went along with the image change. After his term in the army (1958–60), Elvis chased his own dreams of being a movie star (making 33 films between 1956 and 1972), and eventually ended up the last years of his career as a Las Vegas showman and Hollywood actor. The vitality and raw energy of the early Sun recordings would never be regained, but the impact of those early recordings on American culture and music can never be overstated.

If it hadn't been for Elvis Presley, maybe someone else would have come along to play that role, and maybe not. The argument that the times change regardless of the specific names breaks down when we're talking about the influence of Presley's early recordings. His personal role in the development of rock and roll is so strong that it is not at all certain that rock and roll would have ever

Elvis performing in the "great comeback" show of 1968. © Bettmann/CORBIS

broke into the mainstream without his character. He had broad popular appeal in audiences both black and white, and male and female, which plays heavily into his ability to become an overwhelming commercial success. After his time at Sun Records, on the credibility of those early recordings and performances, Elvis became the very personification of rock and roll, and along the way, he became an American icon. There would certainly have still been rock and roll, but its impact on American culture and music certainly would not have been the same without him.

There's just one other point about Elvis that needs to be made; the fact that Elvis was from the common people from start to finish and needed their approval and adoration. Common folks still gather every year on his birthday at Graceland to proclaim the fact that "he was one of us." His "great comeback" television special in December of 1968 showed a revitalized black leather clad, trim Elvis, still cocky and energetic. For this show, originally slated to be a Christmas special with Elvis singing carols and gospel tunes, he reunited with Scotty Moore and D.J. Fontana for a concert of rip 'em up rock and roll in front of a live audience.

Elvis set the pace for the night when he opened the show by coming out on stage and proclaiming, "If you're looking for trouble, you've come to the right place." Elvis took that show very seriously as his comeback to the people. He sweated and worked hard in the performance, and it was obvious that Elvis was not riding on any past laurels.

Although he did perform many of his early hits, he had been isolated from live audiences for years in his Hollywood movie star quest, and now he wanted his fans to know that he was still a part of them. He also wanted to know that those people still loved him. That 1968 show gave America a glimpse of the greatness that once was, still was, but would never be again.

Jerry Lee Lewis (b. 1935)

Another one of Sam Phillips' discoveries was a brash, young piano player nicknamed "The Killer." His real name is Jerry Lee Lewis, and he was born and raised in Ferriday, La. After Phillips had already become known for breaking new talent, first Elvis, then Carl Perkins and his rock anthem *Blue Suede Shoes*, he turned his focus on a new talent who arrived at his doorstep after selling enough chicken eggs for gas for the trip to Memphis. This came after Jerry Lee was thrown out of the Southwest Bible College where he was studying to be a preacher along with his cousin, Jimmy Swaggart. Jerry Lee's offense that sent him back to playing bars and honky tonk juke joints was teaching the choir how to sing gospel songs in a honky tonk boogie style.

Lewis first worked at Sun Studio with Sam Phillips' assistant, Jack Clement. After some regional success with a cover version of Ray Price's *Crazy Arms*, Clement was working with Lewis in the studio one day and, after some hours spent working on some other material, the engineer told Lewis to just play whatever he wanted. Lewis and his band broke into a song he learned while staying in Memphis in 1956. He was hanging out at a club called the Wagon Wheel when he heard some guy on stage swing into *Whole Lotta Shakin' Goin' On.* Jerry Lee claimed that he learned the whole schtick that night; the song, and the act that went with it, with its talking section about "that's it, stand there and move real slow, now turn around a little for me. . . ." *Whole Lotta Shakin' Goin' On* ignited Lewis' career when Sam Phillips heard it and signed Lewis to the Sun label.

Jerry Lee's music jumped straight to the top of the charts, and many thought that here was the guy that would be the next Elvis. People loved his curly blond hair and country boy looks, and his attitude. His raucous boogie style and quickly developed stage act of controlled pandemonium drew in large crowds of people who had grown to expect new sounds and acts.

Jerry Lee Lewis. © Bettmann/CORBIS

Jerry's stage show was even more frantic and unpredictable than Little Richard's. Here was a guy that didn't just climb up on the piano. He gave his patented sneer and leaped on top of it like a panther. He was such a hard pounding piano player in performance that there was an element of uncertainty as to just what was going to happen. Piano benches and chairs flew through the air as Lewis leaped from a sitting position to an aggressive standing position so he could pound even harder on the instrument. The evolution of the proto-punk outrageous pandemonium that was Jerry Lee's stage show was an unexpected find for him. He was actually quite introverted and stage shy at first. But once he found his act, he never looked back.

He was on his first tour with other Sun artists Carl Perkins and Johnny Cash. They noticed how shy he was on stage and told him to face the audience and "Make a fuss." That next night, Lewis exploded into the act that we all know as Jerry Lee Lewis. Attacking the piano, standing up to play, jumping on top of the piano, and, of course, that "Killer" sneer. His attitude from then on was irreverent and cocky, but strangely, tempered with southern politeness in interviews, very similar to Elvis.

As Jerry Lee topped the charts in the late 1950s, he demanded that he be the headliner on any concert listing. In one show when he was on with Chuck Berry, who was also at the time a million-seller at the top of the charts, and Alan Freed as emcee, Lewis was told by Freed that Berry would be closing the show that night. After some words with Freed about the issue, Jerry Lee reluctantly abdicated his top spot. He hit the stage and fervently blew through his set list with the energy of a mad man. Then on the last song, *Whole Lotta Shakin'*, Lewis grabbed a can of lighter fluid and dowsed the inside of his piano, threw a match on it, and walked off stage, telling a stage hand, "I'd like to see any son of a bitch follow that." That was a full decade before Jimi Hendrix would shock the world by doing the very same thing to his guitar at Monterey.

Jerry Lee was the first of the real punks, two decades before anyone even thought of the punk rock attitude, which actually endeared him to rock and roll fans all the more. Everything was going tremendously well for Jerry Lee. As stated, he was so dynamic a stage presence there was even talk of him being the new Elvis. Then the walls came tumbling down.

In 1958, with two of his songs charting in the England Top Ten, Jerry Lee embarked on a tour of England. Unfortunately he took with him his thirteen-year-old wife, Myra, who also happened to be his cousin. The press quickly pounced on the "child bride," once they realized she was not his daughter.

He came home to America to find that his skyrocketing career was in ruins. His songs dropped off the charts immediately. Without the airplay, big concert shows, and television appearances, Jerry Lee quickly faded from public view. He tried desperately to keep some momentum going, but it was all for naught in the face of his blacklisting from pop music. It wasn't until 1967 that Lewis was able to revive his career, but this time as a country music singer.

He eventually reached a truce with the industry over his blacklisting and launched a new career singing country music, with, of course, his old rock and roll hits added into

Jerry Lee and Myra Lewis. © Bettmann/CORBIS

the live performances. Jerry Lee had twelve songs climb into the Top Ten country charts between 1968 and 1973, but he never stopped singing the songs that built his reputation as "The Killer."

Chicago: Chess Records

Chicago is best known for the rise of electric blues. So much so, in fact, that another term for electric blues is Chicago blues. The most important of the Chicago record labels was Chess Records. Owned by Phil and Leonard Chess and started in 1950, Chess was an independent company focusing on recording the Chicago blues artists. When the new rock and roll sounds started to take hold, the Chess brothers were there waiting to help make it happen.

Chess records had been leasing some of its artists in the blues, and rhythm and blues genres from Sun Records, and had a good sense of how to know a hit sound. If it was new and fresh sounding, then they knew they had a hit. Chess Records developed a curious, but wholly grassroots way of deciding on what songs to release. The Chess brothers would play freshly recorded songs loud enough to be heard at the bus stop outside. Then they would watch the reaction in the little old ladies and others waiting for their bus. When they saw a positive reaction, meaning they watched for toe tapping and swinging to the music, they knew they had a hit.

Bo Diddley (b. 1928)

In 1955, the Chess brothers heard a fresh sounding guitar player with an infectious primal beat and rushed to record him. His name was Elias McDaniel, born in McComb, Miss., but everyone knew him as Bo Diddley, a name the Chess brothers tagged on him. His family moved to Chicago when Bo was a young lad. Bo started out playing violin, but when his sister bought him a guitar for Christmas one year, it would change Bo's life forever, and help influence the course of rock music for years to come. So many musicians emulated the rhythmically pulsating guitar style Bo Diddley had developed.

His biggest influence on other musicians is as a guitar player who was tirelessly creative, innovative, and above all, rhythmic. Bo always maintained that "I play the guitar as if I was playing the drums. That's the thing that makes my music so different. I do licks on the guitar that a drummer would do." He was also not afraid to experiment with music, incorporating latin percussion instruments, electric violin, and a true rarity in that time for rock music, he had a female bass player. His rhythmic power chording on guitar was a model for not only other musicians in the late 1950s, but carried over through the 1960s in bands like the Rolling Stones, and even beyond, into 1960s hard rock and 1970s punk rock. Every rock musician knows the Bo Diddley rhythm.

Bo had a hit on Chess in 1955 with his self-named song, *Bo Diddley*. *I'm A Man* followed it into the Top Ten R&B charts. Though Bo never really chased superstardom, being more content to just make good rock music, his impact on how rock music evolves in the years after outshines so many of the superstars of his era.

	Listen:	*Bo Diddley*	**Bo Diddley**
		I'm A Man	**Bo Diddley**

Chuck Berry (b. 1926)

St. Louis born Chuck Berry was another of the high-impact guitarists of the first era of rock music. He is, arguably, *THE* most influential rock guitarist until Jimi Hendrix comes along in the late 1960s. His style of mixing a heavy amount of hillbilly and country music over the blues form directly influenced, through his records, the developing styles of the likes of Keith Richards, George Harrison, and John Lennon. His guitar style is a tribute to all the great hillbilly boogie and western swing guitar innovators, tempered in a blues feel and wrung through with rhythm and blues delivery.

While Chuck Berry was playing in a blues and rhythm and blues trio led by Johnny Johnson in St. Louis in 1953, he gradually became the focus of attention in the trio with

Chuck Berry. © Bettmann/CORBIS

his strong country feel and stage antics with the guitar. The famed blues man Muddy Waters saw their act when they toured to Chicago, and sent them on their way to visit Chess Records.

In 1955, Chess Records released Berry's remake of a country song called *Ida Red*, renamed *Maybellene*. The song became one of the first rock and roll songs to garner national attention. It has a bouncy, playful, and novel feel to it in a classic country style, not boogie-woogie, but the simple bluegrass style bass line bouncing between tonic and dominant with Berry's guitar supplying solo jabs and rhythmic backbeat. As a matter of fact, there was so much backbeat in the *Maybellene* recording session that the Chess brothers were beating the down beat with drumsticks on phone books just to help emphasize that there *was* a downbeat. Berry's music had so much country feel to it, that when he was first starting to tour, white audiences, expecting a white country singer, would let out a collective gasp when he walked out onto the stage. (Remember, this is a time before television brought their faces into every home.) Other hits soon followed after *Maybellene*. *Roll Over Beethoven* in 1956 and *Sweet Little Sixteen* in 1957.

Beyond his energetic guitar playing, the words to Chuck Berry songs are really what endeared him to teen audiences. His singing and diction was clear and forceful. His song topics of cars, school, and young love made sense to a teen audience. As Chuck tells it, "I said, now why can't I do as Pat Boone does and play good music for the white people, and sell as well there as I could in the neighborhood . . . I wrote about schools, and half of the people have cars—I wrote about cars, and mostly all of the people, if they're not now, they'll soon be in love, and those that have love, and are out of love, remember love, so write about love. So I wrote about all three and I thought hit a pretty good capacity of the people."

Indeed he did. His songs convey a message of "I'm OK. You're OK. and it's OK to be young and kind of dumb and ugly, because we all are." This is exactly the kind of message that teenagers, endlessly staring in the mirror wondering if the world sees them as pretty or ugly, need to hear. Berry's music drove home the idea that being young is a good thing and that there is no need to grow up too fast.

Everything was going great for Chuck Berry until late 1959. While "sweet little sixteen" may have been OK, sweet little fourteen definitely wasn't. Berry was sent to prison for violating the Mann Act (transporting minors across state lines) when a girl he had picked up in Texas and put to work at his club in St. Louis went to the police after he fired her. Berry spent three years in prison, and upon his release hit again with the aptly named song, *No Particular Place To Go,* in 1964. In the 1960s, however, music was changing fast. Berry never really reclaimed the glory he enjoyed in the 1950s, except for the complete adoration from the blues and rhythm and blues revivalists.

The postscripts on all of these artists are not to be taken too critically. Many of the 1950s rockers had a lot of trouble keeping afloat as the 1960s rolled in and music continued to evolve at breakneck speeds. The true magic and power of their impact on music, and American culture and society, lie in their music when in its prime. Berry's songs reached out and gave the American teenagers a sense of belonging to something. His guitar style influenced every guitarist who heard it, and his attitude of fun and frolic within music and life was a message the youth needed in their uncertainty of coming of age.

Listen:	*Maybellene*	**Chuck Berry**
	Johnny Be Good	**Chuck Berry**

Buddy Holly (1936–1959)

Other regions of the country were erupting with their own regional versions of rock and roll. Buddy Holly and the Crickets came out of Lubbock, Tex., big fans of Elvis Presley and the upbeat rockabilly style that was erupting along with and part of rock and roll. But to call the Crickets only a rockabilly band would be a grave injustice to them. True, they could play rockabilly right up there with Elvis and Carl Perkins, but there was a much more ingenious and theatrical aspect to the Crickets than just rockabilly.

In the short time between 1957 and 1958, Buddy (Charles Hardin Holley) saw seven of his songs chart into the Top 40. Holly and the Crickets had a skyrocket success story. Formed in high school, the Crickets signed with Decca Records to do country music. Those recordings did nothing for the band, and Decca let them go. They quickly resurfaced in a studio of producer Norman Petty, who later became Holly's manager, in Clovis, N.M. to record some new material.

The results, including a version of *That'll Be the Day*, were good enough to get them on New York indie label, Coral-Brunswick. It wasn't that they didn't have material for Decca (the first recording of *That'll Be the Day* was recorded there), but that the production was so drenched in echo and unbalanced mixing of the instruments that they were deemed not commercially viable.

Once released from Decca, and given the chance to work in the studio with a kindred spirit in Petty, 1958 was a good year for the Crickets. They saw chart success with the songs *Peggy Sue*, *Oh Boy*, and *Maybe Baby*, among others.

Buddy Holly and the Crickets. Michael Ochs Archives.com

Buddy Holly was influential in the 1950s as well as the 1960s in so many ways. He was doing things on his own in the late 1950s that became standard in the 1960s. He was one of the first rockers to perform a repertoire of mostly all of his own compositions. He was also the first to overdub doublings of vocal and guitar tracks, and he was the first to popularize the solid body Fender Stratocaster guitar. Before Buddy, almost everyone played the hollow body electric guitars built by Gretch, Gibson, and others.

And that voice . . . that voice changed *so* much of the way music was sung in the 1960s. He had the vocal hiccup down to a patented science. His sweet use of falsetto and yodel-ish yips and whoops that swing from his low baritone range, into his soft mid-range, then up into high falsetto before glissing back down in the baritone range is unparalleled in rock music. But more than that, there's a definite sense of vulnerability, youthful passion, and love yearning in his vocal style. It's mostly a quite childlike or feminine touch that he incorporates that gives it that sense. His word usage also reflects a childlike nature. With song titles like *Oh Boy!*, *Maybe Baby*, and lyric usage like in *Peggy Sue* when he slips into a feminine voice and sings in a childish rhythmic patter, "Pretty, pretty, pretty, pretty, Peggy Sue." He was particularly influential to the British Invasion bands who were just starting to form. John Lennon, Paul McCartney, Ray Davies (Kinks), and others followed Buddy's lead in experimenting with the possibilities of the voice as an instrument, instead of just something you use to yell out the words.

What endeared him most to teenagers, besides his childlike vocal style and ingeniously simple instrumentation and arrangements, was that his songs were all about an optimistic and innocent love. What better way to relate to kids in high school than to sing about their number one concern.

The Day the Music Died

Buddy wanted to take his career into new directions. He had a good sense of the changing trends in music, and moved to New York City to go back to the drawing board and reinvent himself. But touring was lucrative, and he set out on one last tour with his new band, including the now outlaw country legend Waylon Jennings on bass. It was

February 2, 1959, when Buddy, Big Bopper Richardson, and Ritchie Valens boarded a small charter plane in Clear Lake, Iowa en route to their next tour stop. The rest of the band members took the tour bus, including Buddy's friend, Waylon, who was going to ride on the plane, but then let the rising star Ritchie Valens have his seat at the last minute. The winter storm was intense, and Buddy's plane went down in a farm field, killing everyone on board. Many rock historians and fans alike consider this moment to be the definitive end of the first era of rock and roll. Some people even argue that rock and roll itself dies completely within the next year. That's a hard-core view of things, but a view that should be considered. After 1959, music changes. There is certainly *rock* music that continues to evolve, but whether there was any *roll* left in what was being produced in the early 1960s is debatable to say the least.

	Listen:	*Everyday*	**Buddy Holly and the Crickets**
		Peggy Sue	**Buddy Holly and the Crickets**
		Well . . . All Right	**Buddy Holly and the Crickets**

Screamin' Jay Hawkins (1929–1999)

Jalacy "Screamin' Jay" Hawkins was born in Cleveland, Ohio, in 1929. He built a reputation as the wildest show in rock and roll. And he lived up to that reputation, hands down over all others who would try to outdo him. His signature song, recorded on the OKeh label in 1956, *I Put A Spell On You* has been covered by so many musicians that it's hard to keep count, including Van Morrison (*Them*), Creedence Clearwater Revival, The Animals, Nina Simone, Pete Townsend (*Who*), Audience, Leon Russell, Brian Ferry (*Roxy Music*), and The Crazy World of Arthur Brown. Jay's own version of the song is by far the most energetic and maniacal of any. They even had to edit out much of his low moaning and bellowing because it was too obscene for radio.

Jay was born to a mother that was constantly on the hoof. Of his childhood, Jay said, "My mother had four children by different men. She wasn't much of a mother. She would have a child and drop it off at an orphanage. I was raised by a tribe of Blackfoot indians who took me out of the orphanage when I was 18 months old." His adopted parents encouraged and cultivated music in the young Jalacy. By the age of six he was playing the piano. In his teens he would pick up the saxophone as well. Screamin' Jay spent his teen years playing the Cleveland rhythm and blues nightclubs, developing his musical style. In 1950, Jay started to realize that he possessed a tremendously deep and powerful voice, and began serious voice lessons in his quest to fulfill his dream of becoming an opera star. It was that first voice teacher who gave him the "Screamin' Jay" name.

In 1951, Jay headed off to Korea to fight communists, but when he found himself suddenly sharing a foxhole with a live grenade, Jay scampered out of the hole *almost* in time to avoid the explosion. His injuries were enough to bring an end to his military career, and he soon found himself back in Cleveland playing music.

Screamin' Jay's macabre stage show had been described as the "voodoo fright show." He wore outrageously colored or fake animal skin clothes, capes, hats, suits, and shoes. He used fireworks, flash pods, and anything that wouldn't burn the theatre down. He loved to use stage props in his show like a stand up comic pulling endless props out of a bag, only Jay's props were things like rubber snakes, worms, spiders, coffins, shrunken heads, and his always present and faithful chain-smoking friend, *Henry—the Skull,* whom he would sing to.

The center of Jay's stage show was a coffin that Alan Freed, who was somewhat managing Jay, bribed him into singing from on stage for the first time in 1957 at the Paramount Christmas show in New York City. Jay wanted nothing to do with the idea, but Freed kept laying down hundred dollar bills until Jay reluctantly said, "Show me the coffin." He used a coffin from then on in his stage show. One time at a show at the Apollo Theatre in Harlem, the Drifters locked him in the casket, almost suffocating Jay. He rocked the casket off the stand and smashed it open, then chased the Drifters out of the theatre screaming obscenities. The audience thought it was all planned and loved it. Jay was banned from renting coffins by the National Casket Co. because they thought he was making tasteless fun of the dead, so he had to buy his own coffin if he wanted to keep the act. He would be brought out onto the stage inside the coffin by pall bearers, then as the music began, he would leap from the coffin screaming. "I used to lose half the audience when I leapt out of my coffin," says Jay.

Musically, Jay fit the bill of the voodoo fright show there as well. He is the first rocker to make serious use of the dark minor key to help create the fun yet morbid atmosphere he sought. His style was firmly entrenched in black rhythm and blues. The songs *Alligator Wine* and *Feast Of the Mau Mau* are perfect examples of the dark, jungle voodoo atmosphere he loved to create on stage, with jungle sound effects and howling monkey sounds as backdrop for his powerful grunting lyric delivery and honking tenor and baritone saxophone rhythms.

Jay always had a few surprises up his sleeve, and his recording of *I Love Paris* must have shocked more than a few people. It would certainly be considered downright politically incorrect today. It starts out sounding just like a Broadway

Screamin' Jay with his faithful companion, Henry, the Skull. Michael Ochs Archives.com

musical number, and a very good one, at that. The operatic quality of his talented voice is clearly evident in this song. Listening to it, one can just imagine a major label representative hearing it and thinking he had found the next big Broadway star. That would last only until Jay gets past the first verse and chorus, which is followed by Jay basically just making fun of different national stereotypes, first Germany (*"ach tung-zoogo zacha dooba . . ."*), then China (*"bing dong-hung dong deedle . . . "*), then Africa (*"I saw Mau Mau kissing Santa Claus"*), then finishes off on the French (*"Oui, Oui ah suerrr, mesuer- achh ahhh . . ."*), then swings back into his opera voice to finish off in the big chorus of *"I Love Paris . . ."* Was that the limit to which Jay could be offensive and still make you laugh? Well, not even close.

To hard core fans, a night with Screamin' Jay just wasn't complete until he performed *Constipation Blues*. A song that would make any FCC representative swallow his gum if he heard it on the airwaves. I'll leave it to the reader to seek this one out, but be ready to laugh until your sides hurt when you hear it. The baritone saxophone and Jay's voice are used to tremendous effect to paint the musical picture.

Jay's timing in this effort couldn't have been better. Fright shows, horror, and monster movies were coming out of Hollywood in record numbers, and teenagers were going to drive-in theaters in record numbers to see them. Seeing Screamin' Jay Hawkins perform was like seeing a cryptic horror movie live on stage, but it was always tempered with tongue-in-cheek humor and a spirit of fun. Screamin' Jay only recently passed away, in Paris, of all places, and it was certainly refreshing to see that he had not been forgotten. Now, if only the Rock and Roll Hall of Fame would acknowledge this giant from their own backyard.

Listen:	*I Put A Spell On You*	**Screamin' Jay Hawkins**
	I Love Paris	**Screamin' Jay Hawkins**
	Feast Of the Mau Mau	**Screamin' Jay Hawkins**

Duane Eddy (b. 1938)

The Twang Bar legend Duane Eddy was born and raised in Phoenix, Arizona. Like the other musicians we've discussed, once Duane Eddy gets done creating his own version of rock and roll, there's no turning back for those who hear the sounds. Musicians have the ability to change the landscape of possibility by their innovation and experimentation with sound and form, and Eddy's impact can be seen in the quantities and quality of countless garage bands from the 1960s.

The genius of the Duane Eddy style of guitar playing is his simplicity. He's not a chordal player, but cut more from the mold of the great guitar musicians of cowboy swing and country with a keen understanding of the blues and rhythm and blues, which makes perfect sense considering where he lived. He was a single line picker who could wrangle a uniquely "open road" sound out of his instrument. He was also a master of the twang

Duane Eddy: The Twang Bar Legend.
Michael Ochs Archives.com

bar—a steel bar connected to the bridge that allows pitch bending by loosening or tightening the strings. The effect is most powerful on the lowest strings of the guitar. There was also the always present vibrato and reverb effects that sweetened the sound all the more.

Duane Eddy started out by playing lap-top steel guitar in country bands around Phoenix, all the while developing a more serious commitment to guitar in his desert isolation. He's best known in the category of instrumentalists, meaning music with no words, or music for music's sake. In 1957 he recorded his first instrumental, and a year later, when he was only twenty years old he rocketed to the top of the charts with his song, *Rebel Rouser*, an anthem for hot rodders and motorcyclists alike. This was music you could drive to, which also makes sense since the only real excitement in Arizona in the late 1950s was tearing up the miles of open highway in suped up roadsters

That one song, *Rebel Rouser,* almost by itself established the institution of the garage band. Kids heard it and said to themselves, "I bet I can do that." Guitar teachers all over the country were luring in new students with radio ads that proclaimed, "Now YOU can play the guitar like Duane Eddy," at which the teacher would sign them up for lessons, get them to buy a Gretch guitar, complete with twang bar, teach them to play *Rebel Rouser* and a couple of rhythm and blues rockabilly songs and send them on their way. That was Eddy's magic, that people would hear his music, its simplicity, its strong and well defined single note playing, especially in the low register of the instrument, and know that with a little practice they could play that way too. He made rock and roll accessible to the common teenager on a performing level. He was thus a favorite hero of music store owners all over the country who were selling those teens their first guitars.

 Listen: *Rebel Rouser*   **Duane Eddy**
               Tiger Love and Turnip Greens
               Peter Gunn

End of an Era

The adventurous and innovative independent record labels, the musicians who worked there, and the radio stations that played their music had cut new paths in popular music trends. The new teen image and attitudes toward the society they would inherit helped reshape the landscape of possibility. The music would draw the races together on the dance floor for the first time in America, though with great resistance, and illustrate the possibility that the end of a racially segregated society, at least legally, was around the corner. The civil rights movement of the 1960s owes a great debt to the musicians of the 1950s for being the first to break cracks in the stone walls of resistance to free speech and racial equality.

A series of events in the late 1950s nearly silenced the authentic nature of rock and roll forever. Elvis went into the army, and never regained the power and creative energy of his Sun recordings. Little Richard, never fully convinced of his calling to either the church or rock and roll, vacillated between the two; starting in 1958 when he dropped out of rock music (the first time) to pursue a career as a preacher. Chuck Berry went to prison for transporting a minor across state lines. Jerry Lee Lewis' career was cut short by the sensational scandal of his marriage, though he did revive that career later in country music. The Payola scandal brought down one of the radio voices most dedicated to authentic rock and roll, Alan Freed, who was convicted of commercial bribery, and died four years later, a broken man. Carl Perkins' career was cut short, also revived later in country music, when a car crash on tour injured him seriously and killed one of his band members. Good looking rockabilly hero Eddie Cochran had also died in a car accident. And the one that hurt the most was the death of Buddy Holly and Ritchie Valens in a tragic plane crash.

The music industry felt, with good reason, that it had a tiger by the tail, and may have been looking for ways out when these events presented themselves. In the music, the musicians, and the attitudes people saw in their own children, there seemed to be too much independence and questioning of authority for most Americans who had been brought up in the "children should be seen and not heard" school of parenting. The music industry was looking for ways to tone down the true rebellious image of rock and roll. When Buddy Holly and Ritchie Valens died in the plane crash, Fabian and Paul Anka were brought in to finish the tour. A squeaky clean new image was cultivated by the music companies to reassure the parents that they were indeed in control. The new artists that replaced the old ones were prim and proper enough to bring home to meet the parents. The 1950s had ended just like it began, with wholesome, safe, watered down music and performers meant for consumption by the mainstream of America.

By the end of the decade, the vitality and raw energy of rock and roll had been drained out, the regional flavors silenced, the individuality stifled, and the image and attitude washed over with clean cut, nonthreatening teen idols whose music pretended to be rock and roll. The end of an era had arrived, but no matter how the trends of popular music fluctuated, the influence and impact of the musicians discussed here could not be diminished. There would be new vitality and freshness in time, but the creativeness and innovation that took place in American music in the 1950s would never be repeated in quite the same way. To any real musician the music and attitude of these early legends is just as valid today as when it came out. We're still learning from the examples they set.

Worksheet Assignment : Chapter 4
Like a Rollin' Stone: The Big Rock and Roll Hayride

1. The electrified version of hillbilly music is called

_____

2. The romping bass lines from hillbilly music were incorporated into early rock and roll. The term for this style of bass is called

_____

3. Early rock and roll utilized a vocal style called nonsense lyrics. These lyrics had imaginative made-up words that we call

_____

4. Though this southern port city is known as the birthplace of jazz, it also had primary importance in the emergence of rock and roll. What city is it?

_____

5. What kind of cities have the widest open exchange of ideas?

_____

6. Street musicians in big cities often made their living by performing for the public on the streets in what is called

_____

7. The recording studio in New Orleans operated by Cosimo Matassa, where Fats Domino and Little Richard recorded, is called

_____

8. Little Richard, though a talented performer, is most highly regarded for his

_____

9. In the segregated Southern United States, the law of the land dictated that the races could not share the same dance floor. The area where the white patrons were allowed (legally) to watch black rhythm and blues performances was called

_____

10. Sun Records is located in

_____

11. Name two performers who recorded at Sun Records.

_____

_____

12. Chess Records is located in

_____

13. Name two performers who recorded at Chess Records.

_____

_____

14. Circle and identify the cities of New Orleans, Memphis, and Chicago on the map below.

15. Highlight the States of the Confederacy.

5 Space Is the Place
Framework of the 1960s

Hyper-Industrialization

In order to really comprehend the depth of change in America in the 1960s, we need to take a thorough look all around the landscape of possibility. A comprehensive view of American culture and society in the 1960s is necessary in order to comprehend the motivating factors that contributed to the atmosphere of change in the music.

The 1960s exploded with new ideas and attitudes in all parts of American culture, from the Civil Rights movements, to science and technology, to spirituality, to the war in Vietnam, to the massive paradigm shift brought about by the fact that this was the decade that we humans took our first baby steps off of our planet earth, and in doing so, made our application for cosmic citizenship. Rock music of the space-age generation united these ideas and the people involved into a new view of who we were and where we were going.

In the 1960s, America entered what is known in anthropological corners as **hyper-industrialization**, which is really the ideas of industrialization slipped into high gear and transformed from a high understanding of factory production and technology to a high understanding of scientific production and technology. The 1960s was also a time of visionaries: the Berkeley political radicals, the hippies, President John F. Kennedy, Martin Luther King, Bobby Kennedy, NASA, and other scientists. It was a time when anything seemed possible, when every day brought new innovations and new ideas into our lives. American society began a metamorphosis, like a butterfly emerging from its cocoon.

Change was in the air, both east and west, as the world underwent fundamental shifts in social viewpoints. It was the best and the worst of times all rolled up together. Every new idea and change was reflected in the music of that 1960s generation. In the entire history of the human species, there had never been such a deep and thorough shift in how we perceive ourselves, our relationships to each other, to our planet, and our place in the universe, as in this decade.

There was a paradigm shift in the complete psyche of the human race so fundamental that it is still not understood completely, and still not comprehended by the mass of the common people, or those in control of the levers of the industrial, political, and social machines. It was a time when the common people put their own hands on the levers in attempts to guide the machines in new directions of equality and world order. A time when the young people of America, who would soon inherit the system, were utterly repulsed by what they saw in the structures of society throughout the land and sought to change it.

Every Day Brings Something New

Innovations in technology in the 1960s broke open at a pace that could hardly be comprehended, even by the people who were innovating. Some of the innovations were good for American society and some weren't. There were fundamental scientific break-throughs in our understanding of electronics, communications, industry, medicine, science, aerospace, and computer technology, as well as the social upheavals that changed America, and the world, so deeply. It was a time when people were open to new ideas in social aspects because their ideas about technology were also being rewritten.

There was so much new technology being introduced in our daily lives that people could more easily accept, or at least have an open mind about, the accompanying new ideas in culture and social order. Television, though around in the 1950s, but not in every household, now was a regular part of American life and introduced in color for the first time to the general public. Microwave ovens made their debut to mass American markets, quickening the pace of daily life. Toaster ovens, contact lenses, dishwashers, Hi Fi stereos, and FM radios all contributed to the general idea in common people that the future, as seen by science fiction writers of the past, was finally here making every aspect of our lives easier and more convenient. The phrase, *"You can't stop progress,"* was probably the most popular cliche of the period.

But it was exactly that mindset that allowed people, who were amazed on a daily basis at all of the new technology in our lives, that also allowed them to view the social changes of the period with a more open mind as well. The revolutions in technology facilitated the revolutions in social change for the common people.

If we list the innovations of the 1960s, we can see just how much change was brought about in this arena and how important those changes were on the psyche of Americans. Along with the microwave and stereo FM radio, satellites were being launched into the Earth's orbit that would completely change the landscape of communications around the planet. Laser technology, the ability to compact light into a highly powerful package, made its debut as well. The space race was responsible for so much new innovation that it is truly difficult to put it all in perspective, even today. The impossible was actually happening. Men were walking in space, not just going out there in sealed capsules, but actually opening the door and stepping out into the void of space. Earth and the Moon are considered a binary planet system by cosmologists. Soon astronauts would be walking on our sister planet. The human race had taken their first steps out of the incubator of earth and ventured into the unknown.

It's very easy to take these technological advances for granted, but if we look around at American life in the mid-1950s, compared against American life in the mid-1960s, we see just how far we had come as a species in such a short amount of time. But also in the 1960s, there was an outcry from the white teenagers and college students that it was also time to catch up in other areas as well, like Civil Rights, the plight of the poor, and U.S.

The UNIVAC computer (circa 1955) had paved the way for the computer revolution of the 1960s. © Bettmann/CORBIS

foreign policy. With all the new technology, we still couldn't "stop the wars, make the old younger, and lower the price of bread." But that, too, would change as people took to the streets in unprecedented numbers to rally for black rights, women's rights, and stopping an unpopular war.

The most far-reaching effect today of the technological revolution of the 1960s was, by far, the advent of the computer revolution. The UNIVAC was one of the first computers. It filled a whole room, and yet didn't even possess close to the abilities of the average PC today, but was so instrumental in changing the face of America that its potential will probably not be fully explored for centuries, or even millennia, to come. Computer technology is growing so fast today that its innovators and adherents are seen as a priestly class, much like the Greek Ionian scientists (who invented the scientific method still in use today and figured out the ideas of evolution, planetary movement, and the laws of

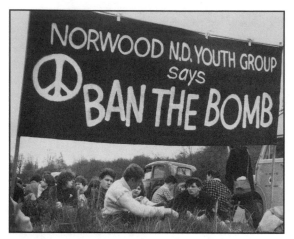

Nuclear Bomb Protesters. © Hulton-Deutsch Collection/CORBIS

nature 500 years B.C.) and those who worked at the Library of Alexandria before the last ones were brutally murdered and their knowledge and books burned by the church in the 5th-century A.D., beginning a thousand years of intellectual darkness and an embracing of mysticism. Computers and their influence on all the other aspects of 1960s technological advancement (hyper-industrialization) began the human species down a path of knowledge and perception that was unprecedented. Within our grasp now seemed the ability to evolve into high-technological civilization.

The Cold War

While there was so many silver linings to American society of the 1960s, there were also dark clouds that hung over all of the people of earth, the darkest of which was the nuclear bomb and the threat of a full scale nuclear exchange between the United States and the U.S.S.R. (A very real possibility even today. The cold war may be over, but the warheads are still active and poised for a strike. If you think there's not one aimed at a big city near you anymore, think again.) The strange cuteness of cold war America in the 1950s, with catchy little songs for school children to sing, masked a truly macabre reality of American life. The classic *Duck and Cover* song was distributed to schools, movie houses, and television broadcasters by the Defense Department to teach children what they needed to do in the event of a nuclear attack. Grade school classrooms included the exercise of practicing for a nuclear attack, and the black and yellow nuclear fallout shelter signs were a familiar sight on any solid brick or stone building with a basement. One government propaganda cartoon depicted a singing turtle encouraging children to sing along with the lesson of the day.

We all must learn what we need to do—You and you and you and you
> Duck and cover
Now, kids . . . what are you supposed to do when you see the flash?
> Duck and cover.

The atom bomb was certainly not new in the 1950s and 1960s. America had unleashed the terror of igniting a nuclear furnace above human heads to end World War II. But now the stakes had been raised considerably. Thermo-nuclear hydrogen bombs had been developed that made the atom bombs dropped on Hiroshima and Nagasaki look like firecrackers. They possess a thousand times the power of those earlier bombs, and, in fact use an atom bomb as a detonator for the thermo-nuclear hydrogen device.

Developed in the 1950s, and refined and honed to an exact science in the late 1950s and 1960s, with the thermonuclear device the human race gained the power to completely annihilate all life on earth. We now had the power to bring to a grinding halt 4 billion years of evolution. This realization obviously should not sit well with any generation about to inherit the system, and the psychological impact of such a thoroughly horrific threat certainly plays into the mindset of the generation who grew up singing *Duck and Cover*.

Even the scientists who had developed the atomic bomb technology in the 1940s were horrified at its use and potential. Robert Oppenheimer, principle architect of the atomic bomb, and a man who tried desperately to stop the development of the hydrogen bomb and *any* use of this harnessed stellar power against humans, was deeply worried about its use by the military. After witnessing the utter destructive power of the atom bomb, and later the hydrogen bomb, Oppenheimer solemnly quoted Hindu scripture, "Now I am become death . . . the destroyer of worlds."

The threat of the atomic and hydrogen bombs played a large role in the atmosphere and attitudes of people during the 1950s and 1960s. Some would even argue that the loose and playful attitudes were a direct result of this weapon. That people were unconsciously saying to themselves, "I better have fun now, because tomorrow the world may end." The possibility was not imagined. It was, and still is, very much a part of life on this planet. Today it is much more of a silent giant, but if just one hydrogen bomb is detonated over human heads, the resulting nuclear exchange will forever silence the collective voice of humanity. As scientist Carl Sagan put it, "There would be no more big questions, and no more answers. No descendants to remember us and be proud. No more voyages to the stars. No more songs from the Earth. Maybe the reptiles will evolve intelligence once more. Perhaps one day, there will be civilizations again on Earth. There will be life, there will be intelligence, but there will be no more humans. Not here. Not on a billion worlds."

This is the world climate that the musicians of the 1960s grew up in, so we should find it no surprise when their music reflects a distrust and reviling of the older generations that gave birth to the ultimate bringer of death. The peace and love generation of the 1960s had good

Bikini Island takes a hit. © CORBIS

reason to rebel against the previous generations that gave humanity this weapon of ultimate hate.

The Space Race

While the atom bomb may represent a dark cloud, the space race would be the conduit through which humanity would, for the first time in the history of life on earth, realize a fundamental truth that it had tried to hide from for hundreds, if not thousands, of years. Though America's work to put men in space was a military effort loosely disguised as a scientific exploration, when we finally got to the moon, the result transcended far beyond what anyone had even thought to anticipate. The results of which reverberated through American music in so many songs about space: *Eight Miles High, Space Oddity, Set the Controls for the Heart of the Sun, Interstellar Overdrive, 2,000 Light Years From Home,* to name just a few examples. Far beyond that, it helped to create an atmosphere that we could do anything and go anywhere we wanted to if we could just cooperate, take care of each other, and harness our technology for peaceful purposes.

Go Fever

President John F. Kennedy was the man responsible for igniting this fire in the minds of Americans. On May 25, 1961, just three weeks after Alan Shepard had flown the first

On November 21, 1963, President John F. Kennedy gives his space speech on the day before his death. © CORBIS

American flight into space, Kennedy gave his immortal "Before This Decade Is Out" speech to congress. This is the speech that gave birth to "Go Fever," a phrase the astronauts gave to this command given by their commander-in-chief. The now famous speech included Kennedy's declaration, "I believe this nation should commit itself to achieving the goal before this decade is out of landing a man on the moon and returning him safely to Earth."

After visiting the NASA launch facilities on November 18, 1963, to view the progress of work on the Saturn rockets and meet with the Mercury 7 astronauts at Cape Canaveral, Florida, Kennedy gave a speech on the very day before he was assassinated. In the speech, he told a story of two Irish lads who ran through the countryside, and when they reached a high fence, they would throw each other's hats over the fence so that they would have to climb the hurdle to get their hats back, then proclaiming that this nation had "thrown its hat over the fence of space." The speech gave Americans a sense of goal and adventure. The next day, Kennedy was dead, making "Go Fever" an even more important mission to the astronauts and the nation. The time line had been set.

Apollo

"Go Fever" became a metaphor for America. The Apollo program, the missions to land men on the moon, was the best and the worst of times for NASA and makes for a perfect analogy for America in the 1960s. America was moving so fast into the Civil Rights era that there was no time to digest all the changes to social structure. There were so many good things about the 1960s. People were standing up to be heard and exploiting the American system of democracy. They were starting to question long-held racial and gender biases and discrimination. They were starting to understand that the system is no good if everyone was not included. And they started to realize an urgency to take care of each other and the planet. But it was simultaneously the worst of times. The backlash came down hard from those that didn't want to see this happen. Riots tore at the fabric of society. Protests over free speech, black rights, and particularly the war in Vietnam had turned into violent confrontation between the protesters and

The First NASA Astronauts: The Mercury 7. © Bettmann/CORBIS

Saturn V: Rocket to the Moon.
© Bettmann/CORBIS

the establishment-backed armed police forces. Blood flowed in the streets of America over these issues, and it seemed that the nation was tearing itself apart.

For NASA, the worst of times came in 1967 with the preparation for the first Apollo flight. In a disaster that nearly ended America's space effort, three astronauts, Gus Grissom (one of the original Mercury 7), Ed White (the first American to walk in space), and Roger Chaffee (who took the spy plane pictures of the missiles arriving in Cuba, igniting the Cuban Missile Crisis) had all died on the launchpad when a fire broke out in the cockpit during a routine test. A spark ignited the 100% oxygen atmosphere inside the capsule. It ignited like a blowtorch, and within a couple of minutes, all three were dead.

The best of times, for NASA, the nation, and the world, came on Christmas Eve 1968. NASA had gotten word that the U.S.S.R. was planning an attempt to circumnavigate the moon, and decided to send their next flight out to the moon, go into lunar orbit, and return home. That flight was Apollo 8, and it was, by far, the most daring move ever attempted in the space program. No one, not America or the U.S.S.R., had yet left the Earth's orbit. Now NASA would send three men into deep space. If they missed the moon, they would forever orbit the sun. If they achieved their goal, the space race was effectively over, as landing on it would then be just a matter of time.

When Apollo 8 reached lunar orbit, the main goal of the mission was to take pictures of the moon for researching future mission landing sites, but when they came around from the far side of the moon, they saw Earth rising in the lunar horizon. They scrambled for every camera and started to take pictures of the view, one of which was made into a stamp in 1969, called simply, Earthrise. NASA wanted the astronauts to do something appropriate for their Christmas Eve live television broadcast from lunar orbit. 1968 had been a bad year for the nation. Martin Luther King and Bobby Kennedy had been assassinated, and the mayor of Chicago had sent police thugs into the streets during the Democratic National Convention to violently confront student protesters. Anti-war and black rights protests had resulted in many bloody confrontations with police in cities all over the country, and riots over these issues were tearing America apart.

The year couldn't seem to end too soon, and the nation's future never seemed so uncertain. But all of the tragic events of 1968 seemed to disappear for one night when Apollo 8 broadcast the image of Earth from deep space. There was our planet looking so fragile and silent suspended in the complete blackness of space. The world, not just America, stopped what they were doing to see this incredible image accompanied by the astronauts reading the beginning words of *Genesis*. For the first time in the history of our planet, humanity had been able to see itself and Earth in this light; fragile, silent, and alone. The astronauts closed their broadcast with the words, "From the crew of Apollo 8, we close with good night, good luck, a merry Christmas, and God bless all of you . . . all of you on the good earth." We had gone to explore the moon, and had accidently discovered ourselves and what we really were. The impact of that moment in time will reverberate in us forever.

Earthrise photo taken by Bill Anders on the Apollo 8 mission, December 24, 1968. Digital image © CORBIS; Original image courtesy of NASA/CORBIS

Social Movements—Civil Rights

The Civil Rights movement of the 1960s began when students protested the actions of McCarthyism, and soon became a free speech issue. The campus of the University of California at Berkeley erupted into political activism, much to the dismay of university administrators and the Governor of California, Ronald Reagan. The administration tried to portray the protesters as alienated malcontents on the fringes of society, when, in fact, the protesters were some of the nation's best students at one of the nation's best universities. They were actually more tied into the system that they protested than anyone else in the country. They believed in the constitution so fervently that they were willing to seriously jeopardize their futures in order to create the change that was needed.

Once the issues of free speech had been settled on the campus, the student protesters took a good look at the rest of the system that would be handed to them and were repulsed by what they saw in the social structures throughout the land. The issues of black rights, women's liberation, and the most vital of these issues, America's involvement in Vietnam came streaming to the forefront of political activism. This would become the rubicon of the Civil Rights Movement. Once the anti-war movement gained some momentum and brought people into the streets, there would be no turning back. For the first time in

Anti-war protesters burning their draft cards. © Bettmann/CORBIS

human history, there was a repulsion towards aggression by the people of the aggressor nation. Marches were held in Oakland to try to shut down the military induction center, and soon this fire spread throughout the country, literally, as draftees began publicly burning their draft cards in protest.

The turning point for the anti-war movement came not because of the radicals' protests, or sit-ins, or when the protest songs were sung or received airplay on the rising, yet still underground, FM format radio stations. Those things did indeed bring the issues into public view, but when the soldiers themselves started to come home from the war and tell people about the horrors of what was going on in Vietnam, and when the mothers of killed and wounded soldiers began to speak up at the rallies as well, then people started to listen.

It was one thing to discredit radical student activity, but quite another thing altogether to discredit the soldiers that had returned from the war or the mothers who had seen their sons come home in body bags. Though the war

Women's Liberation brought the issues of Civil Rights into every home.
© Bettmann/CORBIS

would continue until the mid-1970s, once these events came into public view, national public opinion would gradually shift the tide away from aggression and toward a gradual, but complete, withdrawal of American soldiers. The many songs recorded, released, getting national airplay, and being sung in solidarity in the streets that expressed anti-war and Civil Rights perspectives gave the people involved in the movements the courage to continue their beliefs and the spirit to fight on for justice, just as songs of inspiration, patriotism and courage had done during the American, French, Russian Revolutions, and the American Civil War.

Listen: *For What It's Worth*   **Buffalo Springfield**

Last Name ______________________ First Name ______________ ID Number ________

Worksheet Assignment: Chapter 5

Space Is the Place: Framework of the 1960s

1. The ideas of Industrialization, transformed and adapted to high technology, are known as

   ____

2. A massive shift in the fundamental way people look at or understand some aspect of life is known as a(n)

   ____

3. Name three newly introduced technological aspects of life for the average American in the 1950s or 1960s.

   ____

   ____

   ____

4. The Cold War is a reference to the nuclear arms race between

   ____

   and

   ____

5. The same two entities were also involved in another race that opened the door to exploration in ways that could not be comprehended at the time. That race is known as

   ____

6. The NASA metaphor used to explain the extreme ups and downs of American society in the 1960s is called

   ____

7. The collective name for the various 1960s movements for social equality is the

   ____

8. Give an example of "the best of times" for American society in the 1960s.

_____

9. Give an example of "the worst of times" for American society in the 1960s.

_____

10. What singular event of the 1960s gave the brightest glimpse of hope to a nation tearing itself apart?

_____

11. Highlight the States of California and New York on the map below.

12. Circle and identify these cities
    —San Francisco
    —New York City

6 The Early Sixties

Part 1

Surf Beat

When the statement is made in so many rock documentaries, "As the fifties drew to a close, a series of events took place to *nearly* silence rock and roll forever," and is then followed by a discussion of Elvis in the army, Jerry Lee and his child bride, Little Richard and the church, and Buddy Holly and the plane crash—the *nearly* that is put in the sentence can only point in one direction . . . west. The American west coast, particularly southern California, was largely unaffected by the events at the close of the 1950s that shook up the rest of the country's music scene. The west coast had been brewing its own underground scene that plays a direct and utterly vital role in the direction of real, grassroots rock music.

In the late 1950s and early 1960s, while the radio stations around the country were filling the airwaves with over-produced, formulaic pop music by contrived rock-star idols, the collaboration and close friendship between Leo Fender and Dick Dale was about to introduce the next era of rock music. Not only did Dick Dale introduce the idea of a fast, hard-driving, heavy metal guitar sound in his introduction of surf rock to the world of music, but he was also the first musician to have the ability to play it loud—*very loud*.

Having Dick Dale, southern Californians were blissfully ignorant of the authentic rock void that the rest of the country endured until the British youths revived authentic blues in England and then in its home, America, in 1964, (with the exceptions of James Brown, what was happening at the Stax Records and Fame Recording Studio, and a few other bright stars of true rock grit that made high marks on the charts, ie., *Louie Louie* in 1963). In fact, the very week before the Beatles claimed the number one spot on the Billboard Album Chart in February of 1964, the album they displaced for that spot was The Singing Nun. Not exactly hard driving rock and a perfect indicator of the direction the major labels preferred.

To southern Californians, however, who were packing 4,000 people per night for months in a row to see this "crazy maniac on guitar," this paradisiacal world of endless summer days of riding the surf and sun worshipping, and endless nights of dancing in beachside dance halls and around beach bonfires to a hard rock sound that was uniquely their own, was so far removed from the rest of America that they may as well have been on another planet.

Dick Dale and Leo Fender

The technological advancements that allow a guitarist to perform at a seriously high level of volume simply had yet to be worked out yet in the early 1960s. The whole concept of playing seriously loud was not really in the musicians' mindset, mostly because the best amplifiers of the day were low power amplifiers (5 to 20 watts) sold by Sears and Roebuck. The concept of loud, as in 100 watt or higher amplification, had still not been explored or exploited by rock and roll bands until Dick Dale met Leo Fender in the late 1950s. Together, they would help redefine every single bit of authentic rock music of the 1960s and beyond. Not only did Dale perform through the very first 100 watt amplifier in the late 1950s, he did so on a new breed of guitar, the solid body Fender Stratocaster, and in doing so, greatly helped to popularize the instrument.

Dick Dale (Richard Monsour) was born in Boston, Mass. on May 4, 1937, and moved with his parents to southern California in 1954. His father was Lebanese-born and introduced him to Middle Eastern modes and rhythms at a very young age. His parents fostered a musical environment as Dick was growing up, and he taught himself to play every instrument he could get his hands on. He never received formal training on any instrument, instead preferring to rely on his natural musical talent to guide his playing style on whatever instrument he picked up.

Today, Dale expresses tremendous pride in being able to make inborn talent alone work for him. Statements like "I don't know what I'm doing now, so why should I confuse myself?" and "I can't even play a scale! Who cares? But I can play every instrument there is and make a sound, and it comes from my soul." When told that if he played guitar the right way, he'd be the best guitarist on the planet, he replied, "Why fix it if it ain't broke?" These statements give an insightful view into the kind of grassroots musician that Dick Dale is.

Most impactful on the future surf guitar king was the drums and particularly the exotic, trance-like jungle drum playing of Gene Krupa. Dale still professes at every opportunity, "Gene Krupa was my first hero that I listened to on big band records, and he was why drums became my first instrument." When Dale switched to the guitar, he simply transferred everything he learned on the drums to guitar. In the same spirit as Bo Diddley, Dale plays the guitar as if he's playing the drums. Dick Dale's guitar style is, above all else, rhythmically driven. He keeps his frantically fast-tempoed songs rhythmically tight by employing a constant double-picking style he learned from his father's Middle Eastern influence, adding to that Middle Eastern melodic modes over frequently used minor keys (a darker quality than the standard major keys).

The most unusual aspect of Dick Dale's guitar playing, however, is that he played it upside down and backwards, meaning he turned a right handed guitar around to match his left-handedness, and left the strings the same, which placed the high strings near the top and the low strings near the bottom. Jimi Hendrix, a big fan of Dick Dale's music and frequent attendee at Dale concerts, not only played the instrument the same way, but would later get the same fluttering effects that Dale got through double picking by utilizing a heavy amount of trill. Dick Dale's combination of double picking with slow slides down the length of the guitar neck (glissando) gives his music a feeling of being under water, a natural effect reflecting Dale's own preoccupation with the ocean and surfing. Dale also owned lions and tigers, as well as just about any animal he could rescue from circuses and zoos, and you can hear the evening roars of his lions in the intros to many of his songs.

Dick Dale started out his stage career playing country hillbilly and western music in Boston. When Dick Dale's father noticed his strong innate talent, he moved the family to California, eventually starting the Del-Tone record label to release his son's records to the public. As Dale became more and more involved with the southern California surf and beach scene, he drifted away from rockabilly and started developing a style all his own . . . surf rock. In the

Dick Dale. Michael Ochs Archivs.com

late 1950s, Dick Dale and his father discovered an abandoned big band ballroom in Newport Beach called the Rendezvous Ballroom, capable of holding 4,000 people—an unheard of size for a rock audience at that time (even the big stars of the 1950s were still only playing for hundreds at a time). They went to the city's officials to get a permit to use it for live shows and were met with strong resistance against "the devil's music." The Dales were unrelenting and persuasive, and the city allowed the permits only if everyone who came wore a tie. Deal done, they bought boxes of cheap ties and handed them out to the barefooted, swim shorts clad surfers who showed up. Word spread fast and within weeks they went from a small handful of Dales surfing friends to a packed house of 4,000 every night to see Dick Dale and the Del-Tones. Dick's father, seeing the potential, went around to other southern California towns to secure dancing permits for more shows. In a short amount of time, Dick Dale had all of southern California listening to his fast, maniacal, and completely original surf beat music.

In the age of fabricated teen pop idols, and overproduced "teen symphonies," Dick Dale and the Del-Tones were the vanguard of a new way of looking at grassroots, authentic rock music that has far-reaching impact right on up to today's heavy metal and hard rock styles. Some of the attendees at Dick Dale concerts included The Ventures, The Righteous Brothers (who, at that time, were performing some very authentic rock and roll themselves), Jan and Dean, some young lads who would become The Beach Boys, and one of Dale's biggest fans, Jimi Hendrix. Hendrix even dedicated the song *Third*

Stone from the Sun, from his *Are You Experienced* album, to his hero after rumors had circulated that Dale was dying of cancer (he beat it) in 1966. Hendrix dubbed in the line, "You'll never hear surf music again" at a whisper, in tribute to the impact that Dale's music had on Hendrix's playing style. *Third Stone from the Sun* is also the only instrumental that Hendrix ever recorded in the studio. Considering how much of an impact Jimi Hendrix had on music, and still has, that's a pretty strong testimonial to the tremendous importance of Dick Dale and his surf rock guitar.

The large crowds Dale was playing before presented a problem in that their bodies were absorbing too much of the sound of the band (large crowds muffle a band's sound substantially). This is where the relationship between Dale and Leo Fender fully blossoms. Fender had given Dick Dale his first Stratocaster guitar and Fender amplifier. Dale kept blowing up the amplifiers trying to fill the big ballroom with sound. Fender kept giving him amps, and Dale would promptly blow them up by overdriving them. Finally Leo Fender went to see Dale perform at the Rendezvous and realized why he needed more volume when he saw the unprecedented number of people at the show. The result of the collaboration was the first high-power amplifier. Dick Dale still uses the amplifier that Fender built especially for him, a package containing two 15 inch JBL speakers powered by a 100 watt output transformer amplifier. Fender then marketed the amplifier as the Fender Showman Amp, which quickly became the dominant amplifier on the market, and in doing so, pushed rock and roll into the next era of loud, heavy metal rock.

Together, Dick Dale and Leo Fender changed the way rock music was played—fast, aggressive, and loud . . . VERY LOUD! (Dale still encourages his audience to wear earplugs while refusing to turn the volume down.) Fender and Dale also worked together to develop the first reverb unit. At first, Dale wanted it to create a warmer, rich full sound to his voice. Fender obliged with what became known as the Fender Tank Reverb, and it didn't take long for Dale to plug his guitar into it instead of the microphone.

Dick Dale had not only introduced a wholly new style of music based on Mid-East modes, performing styles, and rhythms combined with big band jazz drumming and rockabilly back beat, but he had pushed on the boundaries of possibilities with the first high-power amplification and a faster action, thinner necked, solid body guitar to carry rock and roll music into the age of hard rock. Today, Dick Dale sees himself as the "Johnny Appleseed" of grassroots, authentic and soulful rock music. As of this writing, he still maintains an aggressive touring schedule to bring the sounds of authentic rock music to all who will listen.

Dale is still performing his maniacal, energetic, and youthful brand of music decades after the artists, pop idols, and producers who dominated the music market of the early 1960s have been long forgotten except by historians and oldies radio stations. He's been around longer than the Rolling Stones and Bob Dylan, the only other nonstop rock acts from the 1960s that are still going strong. Dick Dale's music is as much alive today as it was in the 1960s, not only because people like Hendrix emulated him, but because he's actually still out there performing. He truly is the Johnny Appleseed of authentic rock music as he continues to inspire legions of guitarists through his live performances and relentless touring the world over.

Listen:	*Let's Go Trippin'*	**Dick Dale and the Del-Tones**
	Miserlou	" "
	The Wedge	" "

The Ventures

Though there were many musicians who imitated the Dick Dale surf guitar style, and also many musicians who wanted to play grassroots rock as a backlash to the over-produced music of the hit parade, the most popularly successful of these groups was the Ventures. The Ventures were founded in 1960 in Seattle, Wash., also home of the Wailers, the Viceroys, and the Sonics. They hit it big rather quickly, releasing Top Ten hits *Walk—Don't Run* and *Perfidia* that same year. The Ventures cultivated a surf rock sound that was at once smooth and popularly accessible, while maintaining the authentic feel of surf beat in much of their music.

The Ventures were capable of playing both smooth and mellow surf beat, and twisted and disturbing sounds as well. *The Ventures In Space* album is loaded with some of the most hard-edged, demented instrumentals found anywhere in music (listen to *The Bat*), while their hit singles like *Walk—Don't Run* and *Perfidia* are some of the most accessible instrumentals in music and received some very heavy airplay nationwide. The Ventures had a similar element to them as Duane Eddy; their music was frequently so simple and direct sounding that it also helped to inspire teenagers nationwide to learn to play guitar.

The Ventures released over 50 albums in their career, never gaining a million seller, but every album sold over 100,000 copies, giving them a long and consistent stand as performers. Their style of accessible yet authentic sounding surf rock, while not as consistently hard-driving and gritty as Dick Dale, allowed them to pour any musical style into their surf cauldron. They took songs from such genres as blues, doo wop, R&B, hillbilly, science fiction movie themes, television themes, bosa novas, calypso, soul, and put their stamp on it. This ability to transform any song style into their own unique style allowed them unlimited material for all of those albums. The Ventures were also great explorers of musical elements, frequently employing minor tonality and other melodic modes, utilizing whatever studio tricks were available for atmospheric effect and framing it all in a sound that was uniquely the Ventures.

The Ventures enjoyed a very long, uninterrupted musical career, performing and touring from their inception in 1960 into the 1990s. Unlike Dick Dale, who did put vocals in some of his songs, the Ventures were a purely instrumental unit, which plays heavily into their high popularity in places like Japan and the Netherlands (where there is currently a surf beat revival in full bloom). Without words in their songs, there is no language barrier to prevent listeners from non-English speaking countries from relating to the music. It was pure music for music's sake, sacrificing vocals in exchange for the ability to create intense musical moods. Without vocals, the Ventures became rock and roll for the world.

Listen:	Walk-Don't Run	The Ventures
	Telstar	" "
	The Bat	" "
	War of the Satellites	" "

Other Surf Beat Essential Listening:	Moment of Truth	The Surfaris
	Latinia	The Sentinals
	Wipe Out	The Surfaris
	Pipeline	Chantay's
	Surfin' Bird	The Trashmen

Surf Beat Revival

Today, at the beginning of the 21st-century, the surf beat style of rock is enjoying a dramatic revival from musicians who are once again fed up with over-produced, fabricated pop idols and formulaic, cookie cutter "alternative rock" bands, which are neither alternative nor rock. Thanks to the efforts of people like Dick Dale, who feel a lifelong mission to dispense the sacrament of authentic grassroots rock music, new legions of converts are walking away from the turntables, the drum machines, the digital keyboards and effects processors, the loops and sampling machines, and re-embracing the authentic styles, techniques, and analog instruments and amplifiers used by the surf rockers of the 1960s.

Link Wray

At the same time that Dick Dale and Leo Fender were laying the groundwork for the hard rocking 1960s, there was one other guitarist working at the same time in a very different part of the country that would have a strong impact in his own way.

Though not a part of the west coast surf scene, Link Wray was a highly innovative guitarist who developed his own style of instrumental hard rock in the late 1950s that was also very influential to the rise of menacing hard, heavy, and loud rock music. A full-blood native American, Wray was born and raised in North Carolina, and relocated to the Washington D.C. area with his brothers Vernon and Doug to form Link Wray and The Lazy Pine Ramblers in 1955. In 1958, with another brother, Ray Vernon, as producer, the now renamed The Ray-Men released the song *Rumble* on Cadence Records, and in doing so introduced the **power chord** to the world. A power chord is a hard, forceful, and full strumming of the guitar at high volumes. Other people had used the technique, but when *Rumble* climbed to number 16 on the national Billboard charts, the raw unrestrained nature of the style captured the imaginations of younger guitarists who would soon follow.

Rumble is a slow, dirge instrumental that sounds like dark, menacing strip music. Archie Bleyer, who owned Cadence Records, gave the song its name because his daughter thought it sounded like the rumble scenes from *West Side Story*. The song became associated with big city street gangs simply due to its title, and (a song with no words) was actually banned from radio airplay in big city markets, including New York City, for that reason alone. *Rumble* has no real melodic line, except for a couple of turn around bridges back to the beginning of the song's form; instead, it relies completely on the rhythmic force of Link's power chords.

Other Link Wray songs from the same period, the late 1950s and early 1960s, reflect the same style, but at different tempos, peppered with uncomplicated searing, high-pitched guitar solos. The song, *Raw-Hide* (no relation to the television show theme), released in 1959 as an Epic Records single, uses the same power chord style in a fast, pounding, guitar driven rhythm and blues style instrumental. Link never really gained much fame after *Rumble* was released, but the damage had been done. Pete Townsend, guitarist of The Who (who still holds the Guinness world record as the loudest rock band ever), summed up the impact of Link Wray when he said, "If it hadn't been for Link Wray and *Rumble*, I would have never picked up the guitar."

Studio Production in the Early 1960s

By 1960, the hard edges and raw power of rock and roll had been eradicated by the major label music industry and were replaced by formulaic producers and songwriters, using interchangeable performers as recording artists. It may not have been hard-edged rock and roll, but it did open doors into production techniques and new technologies that would trickle down to the smaller independent studios and allow future rock musicians access to new recording abilities. When musicians go into a recording studio today, they take for granted the technology and recording techniques that surround them, though a line can be drawn from the high tech studios we use today right back to the music producers of the 1960s; and even more so, right back to Phil Spector.

Phil Spector and The Wall of Sound

Phil Spector had almost single-handedly reshaped the essence of the producer. No one, then or now, has ever shown the passion and drive of a self-made producer like Phil Spector. He was, simply put, the most unrelenting and daring producer of the time, a strategy that made him a millionaire by the age of twenty-one. When Phil Spector heard something in his head, he just did not stop until his vision was captured completely and clearly defined on tape.

Using the term "clearly defined" to describe what Spector did musically may seem a contradiction, as his approach to recording music was anything but. The whole essence of Spector's production style, known as the **Wall of Sound**, was to pack a lot of musicians, including not only standard rock and roll instruments, but also orchestral instruments like strings, brass, and timpani, into a relatively small studio. Then microphones were placed on all of the instruments. The mics for the violins would pick up not only the violins, but all other sound as well, a fraction of a second later. Likewise, the mics on the pianos (he used three of them at the same time) would pick up the pianos, and a fraction of a second later, the drums as well. When the musicians started playing, the sounds and rumbles of the other instruments would hit the ceiling and bounce into far away mics on the other side of the studio, again, a fraction of a second later.

Spector would also use **multitracking** (mixing together multiple recorded tracks) to fatten up the sound by essentially duplicating, even tripling, the already recorded tracks of the rhythm sections. When Spector came up with this ideas of using large ensembles combined with large numbers of microphones displaced all over the studio, combined with multitrack mixing, the Wall of Sound was born, or as Spector himself put it, "That's the sound of gold."

Phil Spector reshaped the sound of pop music in America in the early 1960s, with his girl group phenomenon, Ronnie and The Ronettes' *Be My Baby*, and a fleet of other number one pop hits, including *Da Doo Ron Ron* by the Chrystals and *You've Lost That Loving Feeling* by the Righteous Brothers. The performers were largely interchangeable, as the driving popular force of any Spector-produced song was Spector's production, the Wall of Sound.

No other producer had ever captured the potential of authentic rock music and turned it into a popularly marketable product like Spector did, but in doing so, he also exposed the limits of his production style. Just how big of a sound can you create before it becomes too big? How many pianos, how many drum sets, how many orchestral instruments can be packed into a song before popular tastes shift away from them? Phil Spector's music was a vital exploration into the possibilities of the recording studio, but a shift back to authentic rock music performed by authentic, blues-based rock bands and individual musicians would dethrone the true king of pop music. After the British Invasion of 1964, Spector never regained the music industry authority and dominance he once claimed. The rules were being constantly rewritten, and the musical and cultural shifts of the later 1960s would usher in yet another new era in rock music.

Brian Wilson and The Beach Boys

Another of the extremely powerful forces in American music and production style in the early 1960s was Brian Wilson, founder and dominant figure for the Beach Boys. Taking their inspiration from the surf music scene of southern California, the Beach Boys popularized the ideals, youthfulness, and fantasy of surf culture to mainstream America. Up until the Beach Boys, kids in the rest of the country didn't really know about the surf culture lifestyle that was daily life for the southern California teenager, with the exception of the few authentic instrumental songs that gained national airplay. For the rest of America, authentic, instrumental surf rock didn't really *tell* them what was happening there. Though that music made complete sense to those who were a part of the culture, if you didn't live there, the instrumental surf beat was just another curious fad in rock music. But once the Beach Boys put the lifestyle into words and set those words in lush vocal harmonies on top of vaguely surfy music, America caught the "go west, young man" bug. Suddenly there were teenagers in the Midwest attempting to realize the surf cult fantasy.

Many would be so swayed as to make the move out west to be a part of it. This really isn't that surprising if you think about it, or if you're from the Midwest. The Midwest is cold a great amount of the year. There are no palm trees. There are no bikini clad girls or muscle boys. When the sun is shining in the Midwest, it's an event that makes the lead story on the nightly news. And probably most important in the eyes of Midwestern teenagers faced with the view of the southern California surf culture is that they would look around at their own lives, see their fathers sweating out a life in factories and other blue collar labor jobs, and see themselves in ten years if they didn't make some kind of change. Remember that this was a time when the idea of picking up completely and settling in a new land wasn't so foreign in our minds. A lot of midwestern teenagers were first or second generation Americans, meaning that their parents or grandparents were immigrants to America—people who had given up everything to start a new life in the New World.

Remember also that this was a time when people could still travel the country safely, quickly, and adventurously by simply sticking their thumbs out as they stood at the side of a highway (though a piece of cardboard with your destinations written boldly on it would get you a ride a lot faster). When the Beach Boys became popular nationally, California never looked so good in light of the options available to a kid trapped in small town, Midwestern America. If the people that run California had conspired to come up with ways to get Americans to move there, they couldn't have come up with a better promotional strategy than the Beach Boys.

The Beach Boys formed in 1961 in Hawthorne, Calif., a suburb of Los Angeles. As teens, they hung out at the beach concerts and ballrooms and absorbed the sounds, attitudes, and terminology of surf culture. They practiced and developed a vocal ensemble style based on 1950s vocal harmony groups like the Four Freshmen. Later, Brian Wilson would also list Phil Spector, and particularly the Ronettes' song, *Be My Baby* as prime inspiration for his arrangements and production style. Signed to Capitol Records, they released *Surfin' Safari* in 1962, which climbed into the Top Twenty, then *Surfin' U.S.A.* in early 1963, which put them in the Top Ten and catapulted southern California surf culture to the forefront of attention in the national music scene.

With vast popular support, Brian Wilson was able to guide the band into different musical directions by wrestling the job of producer away from a company-assigned studio producer. Now writing or co-writing the songs, performing them, and producing them as well, Brian Wilson had achieved an unprecedented position in rock and roll. Before this watershed in rock music, the popular music industry was set up so that there were always different people for each of those different roles. There are many cases of rock musicians who sang the songs they composed, like Little Richard, Chuck Berry, and so many others, but never did they produce them as well. Likewise, there were songwriters who produced their own songs when recorded by other musicians, like Lieber and Stoller. Wilson, however, had broken through a barrier that was built like a brick wall. Within a few years, when the psychedelic music scene stole the west coast spotlight, it was not at all uncommon for bands to produce or co-produce their own work in the studio.

The Beach Boys' popularity just kept getting higher and higher, until they finally claimed the number one album spot in the country in December of 1964, with *Beach Boys Concert*, but attitudes were changing fast in the music trends by then. In a sign of times and things to come, the Beatles had already beat them to that number one album spot by ten months. *Meet the Beatles!* not only claimed the number one album spot in February 1964, but *The Beatles' Second Album* (May 1964), *A Hard Day's Night* (July 1964), and *Something New* (October 1964) all charted for the Beatles into the Billboard Top Five Album Chart before *Beach Boys Concert* did. In 1966, in their struggle to maintain a strong presence on the charts, the Beach Boys released *Pet Sounds*. The album was a huge success critically and really showcased the talent of a studio producer Wilson had become. Though it did chart into the Top Ten, American tastes were headed in yet different directions; but not so overseas in England, where *Pet Sounds* earned the Beach Boys the title of best group of the year, beating out the Beatles on their home turf.

Eventually, they mostly gave up trying to keep up with the quickly changing music trends of the late 1960s and early 1970s and focused instead on polishing up their live show, getting top billing at the large festivals and stadium shows, but they did so playing the music that made them famous, which was sounding quite nostalgic by the mid-1970s. Exactly like his hero Phil Spector, Brian Wilson would also see his dominance in the American music scene dwindle in the face of the British Invasion, psychedelia, and hard rock. But whatever is said about Brian Wilson, don't forget to add the word "successful."

Part 2: Rebirth of the Blues

British Invasion

The British Invasion was really two distinctly separate musical events. One was the Beatles, a band, and their producer who was more like an accomplice, who would musically evolve so fast in such a short amount of time that there simply is no comparison anywhere in the history of American music. The other was everyone else. Out of the everyone else there were two camps as well: one, the authentic **blues revivalists** like the Rolling Stones and the Yardbirds (who would eventually spawn Led Zeppelin—one of the most blues dedicated hard rock bands of the 1970s) and the other, the more pop sounding and ever cute plethora of pop-idol Beatles imitator bands, like Herman's Hermits.

The question of how the British Invasion happened, and how a bunch of British youths were able to overtake and overwhelmingly dominate the American rock music market is often hotly debated. The **Cultural Inferiority Theory**, one of the dominant theories in rock history circles, states that due to the growing sense of social upheaval, including the assassination of President John F. Kennedy in November 1963, and the brewing Civil Rights Movement, Americans had a "cultural inferiority complex" in the early 1960s, and that because of this inferiority complex, the American music market was ripe for the picking by foreign (but not too foreign) bands and performers. This theory certainly possesses some credibility. The assassination of JFK certainly did bring an adverse effect on all the people in the country. Even people who were six years old and in first grade at the time JFK was murdered remember it as the day all the grown-ups walked around crying. There is no doubt that in the 1960s America had never seemed so unsure of itself since the Depression and the American Civil War before that.

But, historically, when the chips are down, and a feeling of national pride and patriotism reawakens the people, it's a song that becomes the rally cry. For exactly the same reasons that would make a people ripe for lack of confidence and insecurity comes the rebellious spirit to rise above it all. Thus, the hard times and uncertainty would also make America ripe for a grassroots, favorite son or song to emerge, if there was one to emerge. Whenever and wherever in the world there has been a revolution in the last few centuries, there was always a song, songs, or a style of songwriting associated with the movement; a song that arises from the feeling of nowhere to go but up, as the downtrodden gather their strength and courage to act. *Yankee Doodle* during the American Revolution, *La Marsellaise* and *La Compatnole* during the French Revolution, *Battle Hymn of the Republic* for the North and *Dixie* for the South in the American Civil War, and the *Internationale* during the Russian Revolution are all prime examples of how a song can rally a people to action in the midst of an uncertain future.

The rally cries in America in the 1960s would soon come from so many musicians, but in the early 1960s, rock music wasn't yet associated with the Civil Rights Movement. It was not yet the true voice of the people, but instead, for the most part it was still just the voice of youthful ritual dance culture. It did help in bringing the races together in the 1950s, but it did so unconsciously. Soon though, in the latter part of the 1960s, songs would indeed bring the common people of America together. *We Shall Overcome*, *Feel Like I'm Fixing to Die Rag*, *Power to the People*, *Give Peace A Chance*, an even *Yellow Submarine* (three of those written by Brits), all became anthems sung en masse at protests against the Vietnam War and rallies for civil rights reform. How can a people who came predominantly from the lowest sectors of European society suffer a mass inferiority complex? Americans already knew they were the mongrel of the world and have always reserved a great sense of pride in that status. The grassroots people of America have always had a full understanding that they were the refuse and downtrodden of all the other countries of the world, and that together, all these different people were the ones who actually built and defended this country.

Antonin Dvorak even tried to tell American musicians to pay close attention to the grassroots music that was emerging here at the end of the 19th-century. Dvorak was a European composer who came to America in the 1890s to take a job in New York City as the Director of the National Conservatory of Music in America, teaching university composition students the fine art of western music composition. In the three years he was in America, Dvorak spent the summer months traveling to and living with an immigrant Czech community in Iowa, teaching the young ones music. Remember, this is a time of horseback travel, so an adventurous trip from New York to Iowa would take weeks. Along his travels he absorbed gospel and Negro spirituals, blues, work songs, jazz, hillbilly, cowboy, and especially Native American music. He then would return to New York and teach his students that everything they needed to create a whole new music all their own was already here, as opposed to going off to Europe to study the classic masters. Dvorak then composed a symphony to fully illustrate the potential of what he heard in American music. His *Symphony from the New World,* composed in 1893, is heralded today as the model of that potential. Every single Hollywood western movie that ever came out pays tribute to that symphony and what it stands for. Simply listen to the *Symphony from the New World*, then listen to any western cowboy movie soundtrack, and the emulation is unmistakable.

However, the serious art music establishment of the collegiate system was not set up to send their students onto excursions into the backwoods, plains, and deserts of America, but to lock them up in the ivory towers of the east coast colleges or send them off to study the classic masters in Europe. Dvorak raised the ire of the establishment with his insightful view of the American landscape of possibility. He was promptly sent back home to Czechoslovakia (to be fair, he wanted to return home too) but, here again, the damage had been done.

Here was one of the world famous top name composers of the day telling Americans that their own raw and energetic grassroots music had extreme validity. If there is a long-standing national inferiority complex, it's not in the grassroots people, but in those guardians of the ivory towers who never left the big cities, or traveled the land to see what America was really about. When those who thoroughly embrace European culture are exposed to grassroots music, it is easy for them to look at a scruffy hillbilly playing a violin with a sawed down bridge, and playing the instrument tucked into his or her stomach, sawing away at breakneck tempos and not quite hitting the right pitches, as deprived of culture. From that vantage point it's easy to look down, an age old conflict and misunderstanding between classes. Ironically, it is a conflict that was exposed by Mozart and Beethoven, whom the ivory tower guardians hold up as idols.

There is another theory that we should consider in answering the question of how the British Invasion could happen. The **Theory of Contrivance** states that American youth had become overly accustomed to, or were simply tired of the lush, overproduced pop sounds, the contrived squeaky clean, respectable pop idols, and the soft-rock folk music that overtook authentic rock music in the early 1960s. There's certainly nothing wrong or bad about that music, it's just that the pendulum had swung back. That American youths were yearning for a little bit of authentic, hard-edged, and unrestrained grit and mud from the delta can be easily understood when compared against the bubblegum sounds coming out of the "ivory towers" of pop production of that era. Watch a movie of the Beatles performing in 1964 and compare that performance style against the Beach Boys at the same time period. The Beach Boys stand there quite politely, with nice clothes and properly trim hair, and deliver their music with that same polite and non-threatening style. The Beatles, on the other hand, had relatively long hair, played their instruments aggressively, and shook their heads all around while screaming into the microphones. When they took the stage, the energy and unrestrained performing became infectious to the audience. Even Brian Wilson said of the Beatles, "Suddenly we looked like golf caddies instead of rock stars." The Beatles simply performed with an energy and vitality that Americans hadn't seen for a few years.

The exact same argument can be used to explain the popularity of James Brown in the black community during the same period. When you saw Brown perform, you knew you were seeing something unrestrained and authentic. It was infectious, and it threw a glaring light on how much quaint, disposable consumer music there was out there, exposing the pop market hit parade for what it was, formulaic, contrived, and void of any real affinity to the common people. Once you heard James Brown, you would listen to what was being called soul music on the radio, and something just didn't jibe. And, worse yet for the major pop market, once you saw James perform, you certainly couldn't go back to viewing music, and even life, the way you used to. Performers like these show the rest of us what it's like to live on the edge, and what it means to do something full-throttle. How can these types of performers not steal the show?

Think of it this way. Who's going to have the biggest impact and get the most applause at the circus, the overly colorful and happy looking clown who juggles some balls and falls off his bicycle, or the shimmering, silver-clad trapeze artists who breathtakingly tempts fate, hovering alone in the spotlight high above the crowd's heads? The clowns may warm our hearts and make us laugh, because we can easily see a little bit of our own commonality and absurdity in them, but the lone trapeze artist takes our breath away, because in them we see the daring and certain intent that inspires individual dreams and action. We don't all become trapeze artists, but it's good to see that it's somewhere inside of us to be if we choose. Seeing that kind of intense, full-throttle performance can only inspire us as individuals. When these ideas are put to sleep, especially in the extroverted world of show business (let's face it, if you're an introverted music performer in any genre, you've picked the wrong career), as had been done in the early 1960s by the music industry in their mass marketing strategies, and are then reawakened, they awaken with vengeance and furor.

The Beatles, though not blues revivalists, and the Rolling Stones were just the vanguard of the invasion. Through the hole that they blew open in the American lines poured a revival of the blues and creative spirit that would shake the walls of rock music with the force of an earthquake, completely transforming, yet again, the musical landscape of rock and roll. From this point on, authentic blues music would regain its historical importance in the eyes of musicians and would become the dominant formal and interpretive factor in authentic hard rock music. That's a big way of saying that suddenly musicians wanted to understand and play with the intensity and soulfulness of the American blues man. It's not surprising that the musicians wanted to explore and expand on the blues, but that the American public wanted to hear it was a bit of a surprise for the industry and the musicians alike.

The blues revival movement explored the improvisational and formal possibilities within the framework of the blues, and there were literally hundreds of bands associated with it, but only a few stayed true to their blues quest, most opted for a shift into a more pop oriented sound and image. The great ones remained close to the blues. The Rolling

Stones, Led Zeppelin, and Pink Floyd all evolved the language of rock music dramatically, pushing on the boundaries of what could be done, yet always maintaining a root essence of soulful blues and gospel in their music. They also were able to transform it into something new and fresh enough to make them all very successful, long after all the others had gone.

These sorts of bands didn't gain that kind of long lasting fame because of promotional strategies, though they were all certainly very good at self-promotion in their individual ways. There's something in their music, something that moves people emotionally. Without that music, no amount of promotional support can sustain the fan support that they enjoy. Long careers can, however, be sustained with enough corporate promotional support by having artists reinvent themselves to match the pop market trends as they age, but bands like the 'Stones, Led Zeppelin, and Pink Floyd built an intensely loyal fan base on their commitment to authentic, full-throttle performances and solid, creative, and imaginative songwriting and musicianship. They consequently did, and still do, have large corporate promotional support, but as the old saying goes, "It don't mean a thing if it ain't got that swing."

Once the blues revivalists reintroduced America to the blues, so many American musicians would follow their lead as well. Suddenly, being able to **jam** (improvising over a versatile formal structure) meant something. The British musician's term for jamming was **rave-up**, but it meant the same thing, which was basically that they would get a song started, then improvise and explore the ability of their instrument and talent over a repetitive rhythm section of just bass, rhythm guitar, and drums. After about twenty minutes, or sometimes much longer, of improvising and exploring, everyone clicks back into the song for an ending, all based on the blues. The people who danced to this music as well just wanted to, or needed to just dance all their frustrations out of their system. Suddenly, understanding where the mud of the Mississippi delta came from became important. Suddenly, the authentic voice of black America was again being embraced by young, white musicians and used as a stepping stone into new musical directions.

When the British Invasion happened, the bands swept to the top of the charts so fast, and displaced so many other American musicians, that there was a sense of shock among the Americans, like there had been some kind of catastrophic accident. It was obvious from the energy and excitement generated by the British bands that this wasn't just an overnight fad—that the Beatles represented something much larger. The Beatles had been called, "four Elvis Presleys" by the press, and maybe that says it all.

The British Invasion also motivated the American musicians out of complacency as they struggled to keep up with the changing trends. It also polarized the American music marketplace in a racial way. Black musicians were receiving heavy amounts of crossover airplay until then. Once the Brits came, there seemed to be a shift back to a sense of black music for black people and white music for white people. Not necessarily a bad shift, as, in the former system, a performer like James Brown was too raw for the major consumer market.

The invasion did displace many black performers who were recording highly produced songs written by hired songwriters, but it also allowed an authentic, hard-edged performer like James Brown to finally receive deserved attention because he was so far to the left of what the current hit parade's music was all about. Brown's music was so identifiably black that he was one of the only musicians untouched by the shift in focus. This was not the case for the black musicians recording music for the white marketplace, who saw almost every hit song drop off the charts. Once James Brown finally came into focus in the black community, he spilled over into the community of black and white musicians, and soon many would follow his lead into a wholly new style of music called funk. These periodic shifts and sense of competition, while they may or may not be good for individual artists, are vital to the life and vitality of rock music. If music starts getting too silly and contrived, there's always the threat that a new Elvis will come along and abruptly change the rules.

One more point about the British Invasion in general is something of food for thought. Think about the birth dates and geography of the musicians of the blues revival. So many of them had been born into the midst of the most brutal world war in human history. In their most formative years, Hitler was unrelenting in his attempt to bomb the life out of them. Then, after the war, as they were growing up, the hard life and industrial labor of rebuilding an utterly devastated country, both of its cities, and of its men lost to war, was the scenario that they emerged from. Maybe reflected in not only the shear loudness and raw edge to much of the music's feel, but certainly on much deeper levels as well, like the story portrayed of human nature and the darkness of insanity in Pink Floyd's, *The Wall*, with its intense imagery and analogy taken right from the World War II battlefront. *The Wall* was released in 1980. Pink Floyd formed in 1964. The story of *The Wall* took sixteen years to come out. It's worth listening to.

The Beatles

What can possibly be said about this band that hasn't already been said? The history of the Beatles has been so thoroughly documented in such extreme detail, told and retold so many times, that much of the extreme detailing hardly needs repeating here. But there are some very significant aspects of the Beatles, both culturally and musically as a group and as individuals, that warrant our attention.

When the Beatles rocketed to public attention in 1964, it seemed as if they had come out of nowhere, but by that time they had been performing together for seven long and hard fought years around England and Germany. Also, by the time they got to America, they had already developed their own musical style, but had done so over those seven years out of emulation of the early rock pioneers like Chuck Berry, Elvis Presley, and Little Richard. There were many bands like them, but through good management, and their relationship with their producer, George Martin, they had set themselves apart from the pack.

There were some early changes in personnel before the Beatles settled into their familiar fab four lineup. At the heart of the Liverpool band was the team of John Lennon (1941–1980) on guitar and Paul McCartney (b. 1942) on bass, who would soon become one of the most potent songwriting teams in music. Next in the lineup is guitarist George Harrison (b. 1943) who came into the band under the sceptical eye of Lennon, but soon would become one of the premier lead guitarists in rock music. Lastly is drummer Richard Starkey aka. Ringo Starr (b. 1940), whose steady rhythmic flow gave the band the solid and steady beat and backbeat they needed to step into the world of professional musicianship. There were a couple of other performers in the group before they settled into this line up. Stu Sutcliffe, a close friend of Lennon's, played guitar and bass, or at least posed with it as he couldn't really play, but looked good on stage. (He would die of a hemorrhage in 1962 due to a head injury sustained when the Beatles got beat up by some street punks in Germany.)

The Beatles, who had the earlier names of Johnny and the Hurricanes, the Nurk Twins, and eventually the Silver Beetles, settled on the misspelled Beatles by 1960. They frequently performed without any drummer at all, until Pete Best joined the group in 1960. Under Brian Epstein's management, the Beatles signed a one-year, four-album contract with EMI Records. Once Brian Epstein got them working with classically trained producer George Martin in the studio to create those recordings, Martin convinced them that

The Beatles: John Lennon, Paul McCartney, Ringo Starr, and George Harrison.
© Bettmann/CORBIS

Pete Best just didn't have the rock-steady beat needed for professional performances and studio work. Martin told Lennon and McCartney that they could use Pete on stage if they wanted to, but that he would bring in a different drummer for the recording sessions. That drummer, Ringo Starr, became their full-time drummer in 1962.

Their early days playing the clubs of Liverpool, England and Hamburg, Germany would toughen and season them as musicians and performers. They stayed in windowless back rooms, played for very little money. Any notion of superstardom was the farthest thing from their view of the future, as it was with all of the British Invasion bands. Success came at a high price, if at all, for these groups.

The Beatles' career can be viewed in four different periods. The **first period** was from their inception in 1960 until their first trip to America in February 1964. Here they learned to play rhythm and blues and rockabilly-based rock and roll music and developed as seasoned performers and musicians. It also includes the instillation of the songwriting team of Lennon/McCartney, and the unique appearance of a band that wrote their own songs. There was no leader of the pack in their imagery. A look at those early album covers shows the image of a real band in the truest sense; four equal members. This is also when George Martin was instrumental in getting them a recording contract.

The **second period**, the Beatlemania years that started with their arrival in America in 1964 until their last live public performance in August of 1966, was spent constantly touring and trying to survive Beatlemania. This is musically their "yeah, yeah, yeah" period, when their music was hard-driving, straight rock and roll, with nothing too thought provoking in the lyrics, with the exception of their first forays into iconoclasm with songs like *I'm a Loser*, and, of course the release of the album *Rubber Soul*, with its first strong indications that the Beatles were quickly evolving musically. With the release of *Rubber Soul*, it became apparent that they would not just keep playing the music that had made them famous. This was entirely unprecedented in the history of rock music.

Their **third period**, from the release of the *Revolver* album in 1966 until, and including the release of *Sgt. Pepper's Lonely Hearts Club Band*, the most critically acclaimed album of their career, was a time when they experimented

Producer George Martin. © Hulton-Deutsch Collection/CORBIS

heavily both with music and with life. Once they had stopped performing, a very wise move on their part, else Beatlemania would have literally torn them to shreds, they were able to focus on the abilities of the recording studio. Many people see this period as their most vital. With George Martin guiding the way, the Beatles incorporated into their music just about every instrument and every recording trick known to man. They used Bach trumpets, harpsichords, string quartets, sitars, and such studio effects as tape splicing and **backmasking**, the technique of playing prerecorded tape on the playback machine backwards.

The albums from this period are the high-water marks of what they were able to accomplish in the musical environment of experimentation that George Martin fostered. Of particular importance were the watershed events of the release of the song *Tomorrow Never Knows* on the *Revolver* album in 1966, and most importantly, the release in 1967 of the most impactful album of their career, *Sgt. Pepper's Lonely Hearts Club Band*. The other album from this period, *Magical Mystery Tour* in 1967 was a further perfecting of their explorations into studio production, and though it typically gets panned by historians and critics, some of the songs, like *I Am the Walrus*, *Strawberry Fields Forever*, and *Penny Lane* contain a richness of sound and seasoned quality that outshines *Sgt. Pepper* in many ways.

The **fourth period**, from 1968 until their official announcement of break-up in 1970, contains some of their best work as rock and roll musicians. This was also the period that gave indications that the Beatles might not be around as a band much longer. By the time they were recording material for *The Beatles* album, they were drifting far apart in individual visions of where they wanted to take their own personal lives. *The Beatles* double album (known popularly as the *White Album*) in 1968, was critically seen as disorganized and lacking any sense of direction, although it contains some of their hardest-hitting music and hardest-hitting lyrics to date.

This period also contains their largest selling single ever in *Hey Jude*, and the albums *Let It Be*, produced by Phil Spector and released as their last album in 1970 though it was recorded before their previous album release, and their true swansong album, and the last one they recorded together, *Abbey Road*. It does seem oddly fitting that the song *Let It Be* was released last, almost as a message to their millions of fans. They still worked with George Martin during this period, but gradually the direction of the music definitely heads straight back to their rock roots, this time funneled through their now extremely developed sense of musicianship and studio production. The penultimate song on their last recorded album, *The End*, segued (one song progressing nonstop into another) directly from the songs before it, *Golden Slumber* and *Carry That Weight*, is the Beatles at their purest, hardest-hitting rock and roll best, as if they wanted this to be how they would be remembered. In 1970, they called it quits and went out with as big a bang as when they came in.

The key to the Beatles' success was not just their music and performing talent, which was phenomenally large, but equally in their management by Brian Epstein, and the experimental production environment fostered by George Martin. Without George Martin, there would not have been the kind of musical growth that the Beatles had. The Beatles did have a natural magnetism toward experimenting with sound, but without Martin to help cultivate that attraction, they would not have had the availability of resources and depth of musical and technical knowledge to grow in that direction. With Martin as their overseer, they became like little kids playing in a candy store of sound. Eventually, as each of them drifted in different musical directions, John and Paul gradually stopped writing songs together, bringing in the other members of the band to record their individual compositions.

The Beatles' strongest qualities were their musical evolution and highly developed understanding of music, and their willingness to take chances with lyric content. Lennon's frequently iconoclastic and/or Salvador Dali-esque approach to lyric writing pushed hard on the boundaries of what could be written and still sell. The lyrics of Beatles' songs after the invasion years are full of word play and childlike playfulness in their imagery and metaphor use.

Lucy in the Sky with Diamonds, which will forever be associated with the acronym LSD whether Lennon intended it or not, is a prime example of how imagery could be set in rock music, and of how much the Beatles influenced other musicians to experiment with lyrics as well. This was definitely not *Teen Angel*, *Surfin Safari*, or even *I Want To Hold Your Hand*. The Beatles proved that it was OK to explore and experiment with the elements of lyric composition as well as those of musical composition, and proved it was OK to make people think.

The Beatles made their mark in music history by knowing that history and becoming familiar with the history of other music genres as well. Not only did they use orchestral instruments in creatively unique ways, they introduced westerners to many world instruments, music, and idealogy in their explorations in each.

After the death of manager Brian Epstein in August of 1967, the Beatles started their own record label, Apple Corp., Ltd., and announced that they would manage themselves. Though the company was not successful in the long run, it was an adventurous move for a group of young musicians to seize control of their own destiny in this way. This can only be expected from a band that in every step of the way rewrote the rules. When *Hey Jude* came out in 1967, radio was geared toward the three minute song format. It was unheard of to release a seven minute song, yet *Hey Jude* not only received heavy airplay, it was their biggest selling single ever.

In the end, the Beatles had payed a heavy price for all that unexpected vitality. Their timing was perfect for the era, but the era was fading. One by one, they all walked away from the band, only to be talked back into playing by Paul. When Paul no longer wanted to play that role, releasing his first solo album in 1970, the Beatles, the greatest and most influential pop rock band of all time was no more. In their parting shot, the band that had come so far to leave their mark on music and culture gave one final thought to their friends and fans—"let it be."

The Rolling Stones

The 1950s belonged to Elvis, the 1960s to the Beatles, and the 1970s to Led Zeppelin, but the whole rock and roll train belongs to the Rolling Stones. They are the survivors, the kings of the hill, and they did it embracing authentic blues every step of the way. The songwriting team (and friendship), of Mick Jagger and Keith Richards is the longest running in the history of rock music, and no band will ever have the kind of long lasting and far reaching impact on real rock music as the Rolling Stones.

The Rolling Stones were the spearhead of the blues revival, first in England, then in America. Their commitment to authentic delta and electric blues was actually typed up by cofounder Brian Jones in a Rolling Stones' mission statement early in their career. Even the name of the band was taken from the title of a Muddy Waters' song. They had built up a thriving blues scene in England, and when they came to America, the void that they left behind was quickly filled by others wanting to play the blues. Also when they

The Rolling Stones: Bill Wyman, Keith Richards, Mick Jagger, Brian Jones, and Charlie Watts. © Bettmann/CORBIS

came to America, their blues-based pop songs, and pop image would be transformed into what would again become the very essence of rock and roll; sex, outrageous rebellion, and full-throttle performing, after Mick Jagger first saw James Brown in concert. They would also make excursions to the Meccas of American blues and soul music, Chess Records in Chicago and Fame Recording Studio in Alabama.

The Rolling Stones and the Beatles were constantly compared to each other, with one main difference. The Rolling Stones portrayed an image of a bad-boy version of the Beatles. While the Beatles had cultivated a good guy image, and enacted damage control when they got bad press or a bad light was shed on the band, the Rolling Stones were busy staging outrageous publicity stunts to expand their naughty image. There's the famous airplane movie where the band members are carrying around a naked young lady; or the televisions thrown from hotel balcony windows; and the tour announcement press conference, where they told all the press to meet inside of a hotel in New York City.

Ron Wood and Mick Jagger. © Neal Preston/CORBIS

Knowing that their fans would not be able to get into the press conference, they set up stage on a flat bed truck and pulled up in front of the hotel playing *Jumpin' Jack Flash* to the utter delight of their fans who were gathered outside and to the utter befuddlement of the press who were inside. They then drove around New York City performing for the people. There's also the attitude, completely irreverent and cute at the same time. Mick Jagger came across as a cute, lovable kid who needed a good spanking. Without the great music to back up their outrageous publicity stunts, no one would have cared. But they did have the music to back them up. Jagger and Richards, as a songwriting team, were able to develop a style that kept getting more popular with every album they put out. Regardless of how popular they became, they always maintained an edge and raw vitality to their music and irreverent performances that belies their immense songwriting talent and understanding of what it takes to write a hit song.

By far the most important aspect of the Rolling Stones is that they just keep going and going. They've been at it nearly 40 years, and they still show no signs of letting up.

Though bassist Bill Wyman did recently retire before their Bridges To Babylon Tour of 1999, the rest of the band still performs with an energy and enthusiasm that many twenty-year old musicians would do well to study.

In fact, when the Stones were preparing for the Bridges to Babylon tour, all the press they were getting was making much fun of their age. Talk show hosts peppered their monologs with jokes about wheelchair access to the stage and tour sponsorship by Preparation H and Depends Diapers. The Stones certainly had the last laugh. At the beginning of the show, an overhead video was shown of the band members clad in black leather outlaw trenchcoats walking toward the audience. The dramatic stormy music swelled to a high volume, and out from the back of a very large stage ran a man at full speed clenching a guitar. At the middle of the stage he jumped into the air and slid the rest of the way on his knees to the very front edge of the stage, stopping just short of going too far, as he hit the introductory power chord of their first song of the night. That man was 55-year-old Keith Richards. For the next two and a half hours they performed nonstop, as if they were teenagers. The also 55-year-old Mick Jagger never stopped running around to every corner of the stage, its ramps and runways as he delighted the fans with one Rolling Stones hit after another.

The raw energy and irreverence is there more so today than ever in their careers. It even seems like the older they get, the more they enjoy snubbing their nose at conventional wisdom. The old adage about mellowing with age bears absolutely no impact on this band and even trembles under their shadows. Mick Jagger and Keith Richards are not going to get off the stage until they are carried off. And even when that happens, their status as the greatest pure rock band to ever take the stage is as solid as the earth itself.

The line up of the band has stayed pretty much consistent through their history, with a couple of exceptions. Original bassist Bill Wyman's (b. 1936) retirement is the most recent. Except for that, the position of rhythm guitarist went through a couple of changes in their early days, but the line up has been unchanged for almost 30 years. Mick Jagger (b. 1943) on vocals, Keith Richards (b. 1943) on lead guitar, and Charlie Watts (b. 1941) on drums have been there since the beginning as well. Cofounder of the band, Brian Jones dissolved into drug abuse and was booted out of the band in 1969. He died shortly thereafter of drug abuse, though it was officially listed as death by misadventure when he was found drowned in a swimming pool. In the period that Jones was in the band, the Stones released a catalog of hits that just wouldn't quit. Replacing Jones on guitar was Mick Taylor, catapulting the band into what many fans still think of as their most vital period, an amazing statement considering all of the hit songs they had under their belt up to that point. Taylor left the Stones in 1974 to pursue a solo career, a move that he still has a little trouble validating in press interviews. After Taylor left in 1974, Ron Wood, who was playing with Rod Stewart's Faces, became the third, and last, rhythm guitarist for the band.

One of the Rolling Stones' strongest impacts, besides convincing thousands of teenagers to start a band, was Jagger's iconoclastic lyric writing. Jagger has consistently taken shots at long-standing social mores, drastically distancing themselves and their fans from the previous generation. The song *Mother's Little Helper* in 1966 illustrates the schism between generations, with it's opening line of "What a drag it is getting old." From the very first line to the end, this song stabs ruthlessly at adult complacency and the tools used to achieve it.

Listen: *Mother's Little Helper*   **The Rolling Stones**

Ouch! But Jagger didn't stop there. After they had solidified their status in rock music with such tremendously popular hits as *I Can't Get No Satisfaction* and *Get Off Of My Cloud* in 1965, *Let's Spend the Night Together* in 1967, and the immortal *Jumpin' Jack Flash* in 1968, they released the *Beggars Banquet* album in 1968. Most of the songs on *Beggars Banquet* are pure delta blues, electric blues, or country influenced songs with little deviation from their authentic intent, with the exceptions of the rocking *Street Fighting Man*, *Factory Girl*, and their ultimate iconoclastic work, *Sympathy for the Devil*.

In *Sympathy for the Devil*, Jagger takes on the acting role of portraying human evil, sometimes called the devil, or Satan. He even took flack from people who couldn't see the obvious metaphor at work, claiming that Jagger thought that he himself was the devil. The song lyrics detail some of the darkest moments in human history, using first person association. Jagger, portraying the devil, or evil, is saying in essence, I was there when this bad thing happened, and that was me when that bad thing happened. His point is obvious, that evil comes from the hearts and minds of men and women, not gods or demons, and that it happens because we allow it to happen by not standing up against it. "I shouted out, who killed the Kennedys, when after all it was you and me." Interestingly, after the disastrous events that took place at the Rolling Stones' Altamont concert at the end of 1969, where four people lost their lives and band members from Jefferson Airplane were beat up at the hands of Hell's Angels, the Rolling Stones refused to perform *Sympathy for the Devil* for six years.

Controversy aside, there is no diminishing the Rolling Stones' influence on rock music. Mick Jagger was the first real punk. In the early 1970s, as future punk rock musicians were learning how to play hard, no frills rock, they did so by playing covers of Rolling Stones' songs. Their songs were musically simple, but had such strong hooks built into them, and a properly irreverent attitude that they made perfect learning tools for young rock musicians. Unlike the Beatles, who developed such complex production qualities that their music seemed untouchable, the Rolling Stones music was completely accessible to young musicians. All you had to do was learn the I-IV-V progression in a handful of keys and you were well on your way to learning their songs. Plus it was almost all guitar, bass, drums, and vocals, with a few seemingly misguided treks elsewhere, unlike the Beatles who evolved to such a point that they couldn't even perform their own material live if they wanted to.

Sure they influenced countless future musicians, and sure they struck at hard-hitting social commentary in their lyrics, but when all is said and done, the reason for their immense fame still comes down to the fact that the ever youthful Rolling Stones don't get older, they just get better, and they do it by maintaining a close relationship with authentic American blues. Peel away the layers of finely honed rock writing style, and there you'll find the blues. Maintaining a direct link to the roots of rock music has served them well, and secured a very high place for them in the history of this music. When all the others have disappeared or faded into solo careers of constant reinvention to keep up with trends, the Rolling Stones just keep rolling their stone. How long can they go? This author is willing to bet there's still at least one more tour in the new millennium. If Mick Jagger and Keith Richards still breathe, there's always one more tour.

Other Significant Voices of the Invasion

Them

Led by George Ivan "Van" Morrison, Them formed in Belfast, Ireland. Born into a family of blues-playing parents, and a life in industrial post-war Ireland, Morrison could relate to the plight of the American blues man, thus the music made a perfect match to express himself. Van Morrison was one of the most vocally intense and raw singers to come out of the blues revival.

The first release for Them, *The Angry Young Them*, in 1965, contains some of the most powerful music of the era. On songs from that album, like *Mystic Eyes* and *Baby, Please Don't Go*, Morrison's voice communicates an urgent sense of anger and intensity that is a direct relative of the music of bluesmen like Son House. Yet on his sultry versions of Screamin' Jay Hawkins' *I Put a Spell on You*, and T-Bone Walker's *Stormy Monday Blues*, Morrison croons, moans, and scats like a seasoned, if gruff sounding, jazz singer. But for full-throttle, pure power, anger, and raw intent, listen to *Gloria*. The pulsing repetitive three chord progression is a perfect example of a good rave up form. It's laid back when it needs to be to make way for the vocals, then builds to a frantic rhythmic frenzy.

The Animals

Led by Eric Burdon, the Animals added more anger and attitude to what was coming out of the blues revival. Burdon's voice on the Animals' recordings harkens back to the early American blues men, with a proper edge and raw power dictated by the style, while also having the ability to lay back and croon a bit in the softer sections, just to explode again when a song builds to a fever crescendo. The Animals knew how to write a hook into a song, unlike many of the revivalists that are now forgotten in time. They weren't around very long as a band, but the impact of a few songs will carry their name into the history books.

The Animals were also adept at iconoclastic lyric content in songs that made it into the charts. The important thing about that ability is that, it's one thing to write a song about some social absurdity or injustice (Frank Zappa made a whole career out of it), but quite another to frame it musically so that it garners heavy airplay and is heard by the masses. The British Invasion bands not only did this, but were the first to do it. Nobody in

American music was taking shots at the industrial military complex, or really, at any of the social ills of the world until the British bands came over. Then everything exploded. Suddenly everyone in music was a social commentator. The west coast groups associated with psychedelia and the civil rights and anti-war movements would take much credit for opening people's eyes, but it was actually a scruffy bunch of British bohemian street urchins left over from the remnants of Hitler's attempted annihilation of England that introduces the idea of serious social commentary in popular music.

The Animals' song, *Sky Pilot*, is a seven-and-a-half-minute long stab at not just the futility of war, but also the absurdity of the idea of divine providence in war, searing not only in its words, but even more so in the musical setting. Burdon delivers the first verses in a normal musical setting like any song. This is followed by a full two minutes of collaging the music into the sounds of a battle, complete with bomb explosions and dive-bombing planes, and ending with a pan out of the war scene as the sounds of bagpipes pan in. The battle is over, and now the calming music of a string quartet over the original beat portrays a sense of the calmness and sadness of post-battle shock. Throughout this part of the song, a battle is fought, ends, and the quiet remnants of war lay before you. The last verses are sung over this setting, and the song gradually builds to its original fever rock pitch as the chorus is sung over and over, gradually fading away to nothing on the repeated last line, "never reach the sky."

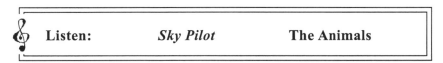

Listen: *Sky Pilot*   **The Animals**

This kind of in-your-face commentary was simply not popular when it came out in 1968. Though the song has a very catchy hook to its melodic line, which would get it airplay, when you got around to listened to the words beyond the "sky pilot" chorus, there was a hard-hitting message directed at the establishment. This song, and a few others like *For What It's Worth* by Buffalo Springfield, were direct shots across the bow of the industrial military complex. Many would follow this lead as the war in Vietnam, and opposition to it escalated throughout the 1960s.

The Animals also utilized a unique strategy to gain a foothold in the marketplace, and a place in the hearts of ev-

The Animals. © Hulton-Deutsch Collection/CORBIS

ery garage band. Their cover version of *House of the Rising Sun* is a slow, haunting tribute to the roots of the music. It came about when the Animals were booked onto a Chuck Berry tour. Knowing that all the other bands on the bill would try to out-rock Chuck Berry (a futile effort if there ever was one), the Animals decided to perform a song that would be unique in the show, or as Burdon put it, "The audience would remember the one song that was different." Their version of *House of the Rising Sun* is certainly that. The organ and guitar slowly arpeggiates up and down in the dark D minor key, and Burdon's haunting vocals portray a sense of distance as he sings about "the ruin of many a men" at a place in New Orleans called the "House of the Rising Sun." The Animals also did a version of Screamin' Jay Hawkin's *I Put a Spell on You*, helping to place it in the standard repertoire of blues revivalists.

Yardbirds

The graduate school of rock guitar, the Yardbirds emerged in England from the vacuum created by the Rolling Stones' success and subsequent departure to bigger markets. In live performances, they would play extended rave ups in classic blues songs, improvising for hours on hypnotic electric blues rhythms. In the studio, however, the band tried for pop market success in songs like *For Your Love*. The pop side of the Yardbirds would chase away their innovative first guitarist, Eric Clapton, in 1965, into other more purely blues based projects like John Mayall's Bluesbreakers and Cream.

Their next lead guitarist, Jeff Beck, was building up his own reputation as a blues guitarist with the Tridents when he was asked to audition for the Yardbirds. He came into the audition, where there were a roomful of guitarists hoping for their chance for fame, played a few authentic blues riffs, and the rest of the guitarists were sent home. Beck pushed the group into a period of innovation and success with his experimental approach and heavy use of special effects like feedback, reverb, and distorted fuzz tones to his guitar playing.

But soon another guitarist would join the Yardbirds that would lead them in yet newer directions. When Jimmy Page joined the band, first as a bassist, then as a second guitarist, his extreme talent gave even Jeff Beck an inferiority complex that wouldn't quit. Beck had a nervous breakdown on stage during their first tour with Page in the lineup, smashed his guitar and walked out of the group. The Yardbirds continued on with Jimmy Page as their lead guitarist. Page had already been using his patented violin bow on the guitar technique, most associated with his work in Led Zeppelin, to go along with his virtuosic fingerboard talent and plethora of special effects.

In 1968, Page formed a new band after the Yardbirds split up, first calling it the New Yardbirds. Legend has it that Who drummer Keith Moon had seen one of their first performances and commented to the band members, "That's going to go over like a lead zeppelin." Now they had a name that fit their slow, plodding distorted and soulful blues sound. Though the term was first associated with Jimi Hendrix, Led Zeppelin would soon become the very embodiment of heavy metal music. They would dominate the authentic rock music scene in the 1970s like the Beatles dominated the 1960s, and Elvis Presley in the 1950s, and inspire yet more legions of musicians and bands to follow.

The Yardbirds had delivered to the world three of the premier, hardest playing and highly talented guitarists in rock music of the 1970s. The Yardbirds were the classroom where Clapton, Beck, and Page learned and developed their craft of blues-based electric guitar, their sense of direction for their own individual careers, and their stage presence. The Yardbirds weren't around very long, but their influence with Clapton, Beck, and especially Page on guitar echoed strongly into the 1970s as each formed their own projects and solo work.

Listen:		
	Gloria	**Them**
	Mystic Eyes	**Them**
	I Put A Spell On You	**Them**
	House of the Rising Sun	**The Animals**
	Sky Pilot	**The Animals**
	I Put A Spell On You	**The Animals**
	Train Kept A-Rollin'	**The Yardbirds**
	For Your Love	**The Yardbirds**
	I'm A Man	**The Yardbirds**

Worksheet Assignment: Chapter 6
The Early Sixties

1. What genre of rock music became the growing fields for hard, aggresive rock music in the early 1960s?

   _____

2. What region of the United States was the home to this new style of music?

   _____

3. Who were the two people—one musician and one instrument maker—who combined forces to facilitate the shift to loud rock music?

   _____

   and

   _____

4. What was the innovation they arrived at to create this shift in rock music?

   _____

5. Dick Dale introduced a fresh world music element to rock music by incorporating

   _____

6. The British Invasion was based most dominantly on a musical movement that reached back into the historical blues roots of American music. This movement is called the

   _____

7. The Beatles arrived in the United States, opening the door for all the other bands of the British Invasion, in February of

   _____

8. Name the dominant songwriting team in the Beatles.

   _____

9. Name the dominant songwriting team in the Rolling Stones.

_____

10. What band of the British Invasion is the ultimate survivor in rock and roll, outlasting every other band or performer right up to today.

_____

11. What band of the British Invasion later evolved into Led Zeppelin.

_____

12. What ocean did the British Invasion bands cross to come to the United States to perform?

_____

13. Identify on the map the surf rock region of the United States.

7 From Soul to Funk
The Revolution Will Not Be Televised

Soul music is a simple mix of sacred gospel music with rhythm and blues. Or least that's how it started. In time, though, soul musicians would evolve their music into unforeseen new directions just as many of the other musicians did. Music must evolve, else it becomes a dead language ready for its place in a museum. Soul music has its beginnings in the 1950s with Ray Charles, and developed further in the early 1960s by Solomon Burke, Wilson Pickett, and other musicians mixing in heavy amounts of gospel feel into the established rhythm and blues format. Their preaching vocal style came directly from the pulpits of America's black churches. Soul came about by musicians taking music they had grown up singing on Sunday mornings, replacing the sacred lyrics with secular ones, and dressing up in flashy clothes to deliver it in concert. Style was everything to soul and funk performers. The clothes, the hair styles, the synchronized stage moves, and the call and response preaching style was all part of the music. Gospel music styles are so dynamic that not much real musical change is needed to transform it into a mass marketable product. The energy and fervor in authentic soul and funk music are such that it would be a substantial challenge to witness it performed live and not get up and dance.

That is the genre of soul music as it was used as a term to describe a certain style of black music in the 1960s. But there is another way at looking at soul music that is the root of why it was used as a term to describe the specific musical style.

The essence of soul music is a way of celebrating being alive, and flows directly from the spirit of the brush arbors, getting out and letting your voices be heard. Soul is a feeling, and way of performing, and certainly wasn't invented in the 1960s. Sun House, Leadbelly, Mammie Smith, Muddy Waters, Little Richard, Elvis Presley, the cowboys, the hillbillies, the railroad workers, and the sharecroppers all sang with soul. Beethoven was a virtual bottomless pit of soul. Listen to Mozart's *Requiem* and try to defend it as lacking soul. Palestrina and Victoria, composers from the Renaissance, wrote such beautiful, soulful music, that someone would have to be made of stone to not be moved by it emotionally. Soul is not a divine gift to any single people or person. It is a part of being human. It is not black or white, Christian or Pagan, young or old. To sing or play or compose with soul means that the performer or composer has learned the highly-valued ability to emotionally move us as listeners. To speak to our hearts and humanness through music is what soul is all about.

When we say that somebody has a lot of soul in their music, we are really saying that they have learned to speak the language of music. This is the true measure of a musician. Many people call themselves musicians without having an inkling as to how to effectively communicate in the language of music. It is exactly the same in the new age movement of today. Many people call themselves shaman without having the slightest clue as to what it actually means. It has been said of soul music, "you know it when you hear it," as if it's some indefinable entity. But soul is definable, as has already been done in this book. Three words says it all, full-throttle performing. Whether it's playing music, climbing mountains, running a marathon, acting on stage, or walking a tightrope high above the circus crowd, when we witness a full-throttle performance, it moves us emotionally, and inspires us individually to do the same in our own lives. Performers with soul, that is to say people who perform at full-throttle, without holding anything back, raise the bar not only for themselves, but for the rest of us as well.

It is often said of child prodigies that no matter how naturally talented they are, they'll only get better once they develop some soul, which is another way of saying they need to experience more of life before they can realize their true potential. Prodigies have not yet

The Dreamer: Martin Luther King, Jr. © Hulton-Deutsch Collection/CORBIS

developed soul. It comes with the experiences of living life. The good times and bad, the happy moments and sad, the triumphs and defeats of our quests, the gaining and losing of love, the emptiness of loss and the fullness of achievement all play into our lifelong development of soul. And as soon as you realize this truth of soul, there is also the realization that there are probably not enough years in life to achieve the fullest potential of it. The ability to perform at full-throttle comes in direct proportion to the acquisition of soul and is a lifelong quest for any true performer in any realm.

That's the essence of soul as a performing style, separate from the idea of soul as a music genre, which we will get to shortly. There is, however, a third way to consider the idea of the soul movement we should look at before we get into some of the music. When soul music emerged in the early 1960s in the work of musicians like Otis Redding, Aretha Franklin, and especially James Brown, the overriding factor that drew people and other musicians to it was a feeling that making a statement of identity was more important than crossing over into white markets.

This feeling, reflected in the music, was a part of a renewed sense of black pride in America. James Brown would be the man to pen the rally cry for the black rights movement in his song, *Say It Loud—I'm Black and I'm Proud*. But African Americans weren't the only ones fighting prejudice and stereotypes, and the effects of this popular song would travel into the psyche of other traditionally downtrodden nationalities as well. There was a message for all the diverse ethnicities in America that is as American as apple pie and democracy itself: no matter where you come from, or what your beliefs are, be proud of who you are. The idea of celebrating ethnicity, so common today in America with Greek fests, hillbilly fests, Italian fests, Irish and Celtic fests, and every other nationality that makes up this country, was not popular before this time. In fact, most immigrant parents wanted nothing more than to hide ethnicity so that their children would more easily assimilate into the melting pot of American society. Other ethnicities in America began to realize the treasure of their heritage as well when the black rights movement manifested itself into public view.

Soul as a music genre evolves out of the rhythm and blues styles popular in the 1950s, adding in a heavy amount of gospel feel to the vocal production. Musically, soul music does break from the traditional 12-bar blues form. Some of the most soulful recording by Aretha Franklin and James Brown are actually one chord songs for the most part, with maybe a chordal shift in the chorus sections. The emphasis is not placed on harmonic progression, but on rhythmic locomotion. *Chain of Fools* by Aretha Franklin is one of the most funky and intense songs from her early years, yet never changes chords. The song is driven entirely by the pulsing rhythm section and driving bass line, but there is not one chord change in the whole song. The 12-bar form is certainly used in soul, but is not a necessary element.

If we trace it back through time, the sequence goes from soul, back to rhythm and blues, to blues, to gospel, and into early Negro spirituals and work songs. In every one of these music forms, the common factor is the driving rhythm. 12-bar blues is used in some of them, obviously in blues, and rhythm and blues, but in early gospel recording from the

1920s we hear no harmonic changes, but rather a build up to a frenzied pace on one, or maybe two, chordal shifts. The element that they do share is driving rhythm. That is not to say that the music is all fast-paced, as slow blues is just as rhythmically forceful in the right hands, as the music of Sun House or Muddy Waters attests.

The real innovations in the transformation of rhythm and blues into a definable soul style can be found in the work of a specific studio, a specific record label, and a specific group of musicians. The new direction of music is guided not by big city labels and performers who traditionally take market advantage of new sounds without really grafting anything new onto the tree of music, but by a grassroots movement. In the case of soul music, that movement points straight to independent labels Atlantic Records, Stax Records in Memphis, and Fame Recording Studio in Muscle-Shoals, Ala.

Booker T and the MGs

Before the Fame studio came into the picture after a falling out between Atlantic Records' producer Jerry Wexler and Stax, Booker T and the MGs slowly formed as studio musicians working in Memphis. The Stax technique, later transferred to Fame, was to have a house band record the basic tracks of a song, then bring in the vocalist to record over those tracks. The most interesting aspect of these early Stax recordings with Booker T and the MGs that lead to the soul sound is the mix of the individual musicians within the band, half of which were black with strong roots in rhythm and blues and gospel, and half of which were white with strong roots in hillbilly, country, and white gospel. They all loved the blues. That paints a simplistic picture, however, as we must consider the regional influence on these musicians growing up in Memphis. The black musicians were exposed to the dominant country sounds of the city, while the white musicians were exposed to blues, gospel, and rhythm and blues as well.

The nuture effect resulted in musicians well-versed in all these forms of music, regardless of their own ethnicity. The essence of being a musician requires a form of colorblind rebellion. A musi-

Booker T and the MGs. © Henry Diltz/ CORBIS

cian should only care about the concerns of whether a song moves emotionally or not. What color the performer is just doesn't matter if the sound coming out makes you want to hear more. The only thing a true musician sees is musical talent.

When the Stax musicians were growing up and learning music, they learned all of the styles because that's what they were exposed to, regardless of racial identification. The sounds from "the other side of the tracks" has an alluring quality mostly because it sounds new and different from what was heard in the home. That's the kind of environment that allows a band like Booker T and the MGs to emerge. Many people have never heard of Booker T, but they have heard of Otis Redding, Sam and Dave, Aretha Franklin, and Wilson Pickett. As the house band at Stax Records, it was Booker T and the MGs that backed up every one of those legends of soul on their most vital recordings. They were also Otis Redding's band when he performed live at the Monterey Pop Festival.

The song they are probably best known for is *Green Onions*, which climbed to number three on the charts in 1962. The smooth rhythmic and repetitive feel of Booker T's organ style provided a hypnotic quality over which the other band members could fill in and around. The band would truly hit their stride in the latter half of the 1960s, both as Booker T and the MGs, and as Jerry Wexler started bringing in singers like Wilson Pickett to record with them as the house band at Stax. When Pickett's *In the Midnight Hour* did well, Wexler found himself looking for a new studio over a dispute and bad feelings with Stax, who barred Atlantic artists from recording there. The studio where they moved production to was Fame Recording Studio in Florence, Ala.; known by the name of a neighboring town, Muscle Shoals.

Against all conventional wisdom, that's how real soul music came about. Pickett remembers traveling for the first time to Muscle Shoals to record at Fame. He describes his own shock as a tall white hillbilly looking man picked him up, telling him that they were going to make some funky records. Then he was driven through the Alabama countryside to the Fame studios. Wilson was shocked to see sharecroppers picking cotton in a field right across from the studio. Then he met the band, a group of white musicians who looked more like truck drivers than soul musicians, and cut some of the hardest-hitting soul sounds ever recorded. Out of that environment came such cutting edge soul hits as *Mustang Sally*, *Funky Broadway*, and *Land of 1,000 Dances*. Pickett brought the fervor of the climactic points of church music into the spotlight. His songs drive hard from beginning to end and are best played when you're in the mood to dance hard.

Jerry Wexler would also bring Otis Redding and Aretha Franklin to work with the Booker T and the other Fame musicians. Out of those sessions, soul music was refined into an identifiable style that departed from the pure dance beat of Wilson Pickett's hits. Pickett's best songs are fast, driving introductions into the direction of funk music, while Otis' and Aretha's music is more laid back at times, leaving room for dynamic emotional crescendos, a technique taken right from the church service in which they grew up.

Booker T and the MGs, and the other musicians who worked at Fame, had grown up exposed to the many different musical forms around Memphis and the South. They not only had the experience and ability to play any style in its pure form, but had taken all of the styles and mixed them together as well. The story of the emergence of soul music seems entirely appropriate considering that the first era of rock and roll skyrocketed to public attention as a result of musicians doing the very same thing.

Listening:	*Green Onions*	**Booker T and the MGs**
	Kinda Easy Like	" "
	In the Midnight Hour	**Wilson Pickett**
	Mustang Sally	" "

Otis Redding

It was in the artistry of Otis Redding that the transformation from fast-paced dance-based soul of the Wilson Pickett style to a slower, but more emotionally powerful, soul takes place. His raspy voice could deliver the conviction of the true gospel style and still maintain accessibility to the general public. Otis created his own version of soul music. His intensity and emotional output in performance is unmatched, with the possible exception of James Brown. When you saw Otis Redding perform, just like Brown, you knew you were seeing someone functioning at full-throttle. He held nothing back.

Redding was also consciously aware of his showmanship. He intentionally gave up every bit of himself knowing that that's what people really wanted to see. He would strut the stage and frequently get so excited when a song built up to a crescendo that there was always an element of unpredictability to his performances.

Redding also wrote a great amount of his own material that he had substantial success with, but would not be around to see the impact of it when it was recorded by other artists. His relationship with Booker T and the MGs allowed Otis the free working studio environment to develop as a songwriter. It also created one of the hottest live combos in music when Otis teamed up with Booker T and the MGs to use them as a live back-up band. By 1967, there were already available 100+ watt amplifiers, and those could be wired in series to create even more power. Rock music was getting

Otis Redding. © Bettmann/CORBIS

quite loud by the time the Monterey Pop Festival took place in 1967. Booker T and the MGs played through little 30 watt Sears amplifiers, yet they electrified the festival's summer of love hippie crowd simply by performing at full-throttle. It would have been very hard to top that performance in its excitement had not there been the arrival of a new artist who was busy creating his own version of rock and roll that would again change the path of the music—Jimi Hendrix.

Otis also enjoyed great success on European tours as a result of the popularity of blues and gospel music there. Nearing the end of 1967, Otis Redding was poised to break into the national scene in a big way. His Monterey performance swayed many people over to his musical style and intense energy on stage. If he could win over the flower children, he could sell in the mainstream market and maintain his intense authenticity. Unfortunately for the voice of authentic soul music, Redding died in a plane crash on December 10, 1967, forever silencing one of the most unique and innovative musicians of the era.

| Listening: | *Respect* | Otis Redding |
| | *Try a Little Tenderness* | "   " |

Aretha Franklin

Known as "Lady Soul," Aretha Franklin was the daughter of one the best known and vocally powerful radio preachers east of the Mississippi, the Reverend C.L. Franklin, and her music reflected that same power. In her role popularizing soul music, she has also become somewhat of an American icon. She was associated strongly with the civil rights movement. The vitality of Aretha Franklin begins with her association with Jerry Wexler and Atlantic Records. Before that time, she was under contract with Columbia Records, which didn't really know what to do with her talent. She had recorded a number of soft jazz-oriented songs, but nothing of any true intensity. Her time there did teach her self-restraint, dynamics, and musical discipline that was not a hallmark of most soul singers. She would use that experience in creating a sense of controlled exuberance

Lady Soul: Aretha Franklin.
© Bettmann/CORBIS

in her singing when Wexler placed her in the Fame studio environment. In 1966, her contract with Columbia had run its course, and Wexler immediately signed her to Atlantic. The next stop was Muscle Shoals and the Fame studios where she was finally able to unleash the fierce power and sensuality of her voice.

Her first recording for Atlantic in January of 1967 was done at Fame with the house band backing her up. The band was taking a break when pianist Spooner Oldham was messing around a little at the piano, and started playing a slow and simple two-chord gospel lick. The rest of the band started playing into the feel that Spooner had started. Aretha began singing to it in true gospel form, the band worked out a few changes, and *I Never Loved a Man* was recorded. Wexler knew he had a hit. The recording session ended on a bad note, however, when Aretha's husband got into a fight with one of the musicians. Wexler brought Aretha to New York to record a B side for *I Never Loved a Man*. Aretha and her sisters recorded *Do Right Woman* in that session.

Aretha would never return to record in Muscle Shoals, but Fame musicians were subsequently brought in for recording sessions in New York City. When the record was released it was a huge popular success. The public, tired of the girl group, teen pop sound, and Motown's overly slick productions, embraced the power, ferocity, sexuality, and intensity of Franklin's music as if a light had been turned on in their own souls. Once you heard Aretha singing on that first album on Atlantic, you immediately knew the difference between mass market-produced artists and authentic soul musicianship. Her years of gospel experience were perfectly woven into a style that was part church, part street, and pure rock and roll.

Other chart-topping songs from this period *Respect*, *A Natural Woman*, *Chain of Fools*, and *Think*, placing her at the top of the heap of soul music within a year of her first album release. Aretha's music and her clear voice on these early recordings give the feeling of a spirit flying high, which was a perfect accompaniment to the renewed sense of black pride associated with the Civil Rights Movement of the late 1960s. Her powerfully fierce voice was also a new model for women in an age of women's liberation. She completely blew the image of the little teen bad girl out of the water with her mature, bellowing gospel intensity, and in doing so, redefined the image of young American womanhood. Now instead of the coy, perky, and alluring bad girl, Aretha's voice redirected how an authentic female voice should, or at least could sound in the arena of male-dominated rock music. However, only one other female vocalist from the same period, Janis Joplin, had shown the same authentic intensity and strength. Why only one? The answer might seem overly simple here. It's not easy to do.

The end of the extreme vitality coming out of the Fame studios came sadly and unexpectedly with the assassination of Martin Luther King Jr. After his death in 1968, black musicians slowly stopped coming to Muscle Shoals to work with the white studio musicians at Fame. There was a seriousness in the air that struck straight at the heart of what was happening in music. Even the colorblind musician felt a bit betrayed and isolated from their studio brothers when the Dreamer had died. The black musicians even knew deep down that their white friends in music weren't involved in racial hatred, but when

King was gunned down, the overwhelmingly sad thought that maybe the Dream was now gone with the Dreamer. This had dramatically affected the way that black and white relationships progressed, or digressed, from that point on.

It is truly one of the saddest stories in rock music. Slowly but surely all the black musicians stopped recording at Fame, leaving their white musician friends deeply saddened that their soul brother friends no longer wanted to be around them. When this collaboration ended, so too did the magic and energy that was coming out of the Fame studios in Muscle Shoals. Soul music would keep growing and evolving, but its musical path would no longer be guided by a bunch of rural Southerners raised on everything from delta blues to rockabilly.

Soul music in general had also seemed to run its course by the end of the decade. New musical styles were emerging in both black and white music. The blues revival had mixed in with the beat-oriented counter culture in San Francisco creating a new style called psychedelia. James Brown had introduced true funk music; Sly and the Family Stone had developed it into a solid style, mixing it with psychedelia; and George Clinton took it to its ultimate expressive extreme. The 1960s was a time when there was always something new on the musical horizon, just like there was in all the other aspects of life in America in that time period. The public's thirst for new sounds generated a sense that it was okay to sound any way you wanted to in the search for those new sounds. As soon as a new sounding band or musician was clinging to the top rungs of the fame and fortune ladder, another new sound would come along and dethrone them to claim their own moment at the top.

The idea that a constant stream of new musical ideas were vital to peaking interest in music would still play into the 1970s, but gradually the major label music industry would gain a better understanding of mass promotion of formulaic popular trends. There was no solid hit-making formula in the late 1960s except to create music that was new and different. Throughout the late 1970s, and into the 1980s and 1990s, through the medium of MTV and musical styles like disco, new wave, grunge, hip hop, and techno, the major labels have consistently been increasingly successful at collaring authentic sounds, draining out the vitality, and producing cookie cutter, look alike pop stars where there once was an innovative or creative idea.

Listening:	*I Never Loved a Man*	**Aretha Franklin**
	Do Right Woman	" "
	Chain of Fools	" "

James Brown

"The hardest working man in show business," is how James Brown was known, and he deserves every bit of that sentiment. There has never been a more self made man in the history of all American music. James Brown is so important in so many ways. His style of soul music influenced nearly every rock musician to come along after him. James Brown is the very definition of a full-throttle performer. His stage show was an unrelenting pandemonium of energy and action.

Musically, James Brown introduces the drums and bass driven sound of funk music in 1965 with *Papa's Got a Brand New Bag,* expands on the idea in 1968 with *Say It Loud—I'm Black and I'm Proud,* and influences the sexuality of its development with *Get Up I Feel Like Being A Sex Machine* in 1970, signalling the decline of purely gospel-based music and the increase of purely rhythmically-driven funk music.

His primary influence musically was the raucous rhythm and blues style of Louis Jordan and His Tympany Five. Brown claimed that he was mentored in music by listening to the fast-paced Louis Jordan's recordings. Brown was also heavily involved in church music as a youth. He learned to play organ and eventually would learn literally every instrument that he used in his ensembles. Drums, horns, guitars, keyboards; you name it and James has played it. This knowledge of all the instruments, and what they can and cannot do, gave James a thorough understanding of the abilities of the ensemble.

By 1957, James Brown had gained regional success with his band, the Famous Flames, and their recording of *Please, Please, Please.* This recording began the long association between Brown and the King Record label in Cincinnati, Ohio. Brown's King recordings, from 1956 until 1970, are the most vital for him as a musical innovator. In 1959, Brown formed a new version of the Famous Flames and began performing at the Apollo Theatre in New York City. During the 1960s he became the biggest drawing artist at the Apollo and kept developing the rhythmic drive of his music until the release of *Papa's Got a Brand New Bag* in 1965. It was that song that pushed Brown over the soul edge and into a clearly defined rhythmic funk sound. Even the name of the song announces a "new bag," or new music on the scene. At that time, as the Beatles and the Beach Boys were the dominant figures on the pop charts, Brown was named the top R&B Artist of the Year. By 1966, Brown was selling out not only the Apollo Theatre, but Madison Square Garden as well. His importance in the evolution of soul music into funk was becoming more solid with every song he released.

Personally, James Brown set a precedent for black performers in America. He was the best selling rhythm and blues artist in history and used the money to buy his own private jet airplane in 1966, a first for an African American performer in any field. To remind him of where the money and fame came from, he had the names of all his hit songs painted on the side of the jet, right next to the door so that he would see them every time he boarded the plane. He was the richest black performer in America, and used the money to create many social empowerment programs. He also used his music for empowering messages to the youth who idolized him. In 1966, he released a song called *Don't Be a Dropout* to inspire black youths to get an education.

Brown's commitment to social issues only grew larger from that point. He used his wealth to create college scholarship programs and a highly publicized "stay in school" campaign aimed at black youth. He also started a chain of restaurants that celebrated

The Godfather of Soul: James Brown. © Neal Preston/CORBIS

African American heritage by serving traditional southern soul food. He bought radio stations and record labels to promote black culture. But his commitment went far beyond just using his image as a figurehead on these issues. He didn't isolate himself away from the public the way most superstar performers do. Brown would go into the black neighborhood to be part of the people. He visited the prisons to give the inmates a sense of hope. He even traveled with the USO entertaining U.S. troops in Vietnam. When Martin Luther King was assassinated and the threat of racial riots hung like a dark cloud ready to burst at any moment, Brown went to the people to calm their anxiety. He was the most influential black man in America at that time, especially to other black males. If he would have said riot, there would have been an awful lot more blood in the streets, but Brown counseled restraint to his fans at his concerts. In this way, James Brown was really a part of and completely dedicated to the people from where he came, and the social issues that concerned them.

His definitive social statement and impact came in 1968 with the release of *Say It Loud—I'm Black and I'm Proud*. Brown always preached for peace and understanding, but in the black community the song became the rally cry of the black power movement on both the peacable side and the confrontational side. The significance of the song is again contained in the title. It's not passive like the *All You Need is Love* and *We Shall*

Overcome rally cries. It has a direct, in-your-face attitude. Not only are you supposed to say "I'm black and I'm proud," but you're commanded to say it loudly. This coincides perfectly with the rise of the Black Panthers, who were fighting the state of California for their right to bear arms. The Panthers were issuing the same message as *Say It Loud* did to America, that the black people of America had reached a point where they were not going to sit back and passively absorb the racist regime of America any longer. That song certainly must have made more than a few people entrenched in old world thinking sit up and take notice.

The shift to a complete funk style of music came in 1970 in Cincinnati when Brown fired his whole band over a pay dispute. As replacements he hired a local group called the Pacesetters, whose bass player, Bootsy Collins would later go on to star in Funkadelic. The group already knew all of Brown's material before they ever worked with him, and the magic of the godfather of soul was revitalized. The result was a music even more harmonically simplistic, extremely rhythmic, and downright tribal sounding than anything he had done so far. It was after a gig that James was riding in the tour bus with his new band, when suddenly they started playing around with some rhythmic vocals. James got excited at the fresh sound and ordered the bus to the recording studio that night. When they were done, *Get Up, I Feel Like Being a Sex Machine*, or more commonly just known *Sex Machine*, was on tape. The song has one chord throughout and relies on the rhythm section's staccato jabs and slashes and Bootsy's sliding bass lines to propel the music against Brown's searing voice.

James Brown had created the raw materials of funk. But it would be up to a guy named Sly to form it into a movement, and a happily-crazed man named George to build it into a spaceship of the imagination.

Sly and The Family Stone

Sly and the Family Stone, formed in San Francisco in 1967, were the first band to bring together all the different styles of rock music from the 1960s. Their music was a combination rhythm and blues, soul, funk, hard rock, and psychedelia, with an added flavor of pure tribal drum chanting, all rolled into one package of versatility, unbridled energy, and unpredictability. Sly and the Family Stone emerged as a funk band out of the psychedelic environment of San Francisco.

Sly and the Family Stone was the first band where the roles of each performer were interchangeable. Vocalists might play percussion instruments. The bass player might play keyboard. And everyone on stage would dance. The Family Stone was a fully integrated band, with each member on a mission to express themselves, yet the cacophony would mold together into a rhythmically precise single unit. The Family had both white and black, male and female musicians, and though Sly was the leading force in the band, on stage it was the whole picture that caught the attention, not just one person. In this way, Sly and the Family had broken down many of the boundaries of how a band should function. It seemed more egalitarian, like a tribe or extended family.

There was also a shift of focus from vocals, as in the music of Motown, James Brown, the Stax and Fame recordings, and other soul music, to a more rhythmic and instrumentally-driven musical style. This idea coincides with the other music coming out of San Francisco at the same period. One of the hallmarks of the whole psychedelic movement in music is the shift from vocal-based music to instrumental music based on the ideas of improvisation and instrumental virtuosity. That's a rather big way of saying jamming.

Mainstream America was, and still is, a society that placed the highest esteem on those who displayed an image of polite sophistication. Sly and the Family Stone were anything but that. The biggest boundary that the Family Stone broke through was the feeling that black performers should steer far away from any portrayal of tribalism, or true

Sly Stone (b. Sylvester Stewart, 1944).
© Hulton-Deutsch Collection/CORBIS

African music. The Family Stone refreshingly embraced their tribal roots in both their music and stage show, which played perfectly into the hippies' earthly vision and their embracing of neo-paganism. The hippies could see in Sly the essence of what they were trying to capture. Sly even went as far as to use such obvious tribal vocal references like "boom chaka-lakah-lakah."

Black musicians, with the sole exception of Screamin' Jay Hawkins, would never have gone that far for fear of playing into the stereotype of African Americans as people from the jungles of Africa. It just wasn't done, but Sly had the ignorance of youth on his side. He didn't care what the rest of the America had done, and his vision of society and community was embraced and strongly emulated by every funk band to follow. Sly Stone had created the funk standard by which all the others would be judged. He took the idea of "statement of identity" to its logical conclusion, and in doing so brought funk into mainstream attention.

The culmination of his influence came at the Woodstock Festival in 1969. Regardless of the way Sly lived his personal life, and he certainly had his troubles, here was a magical moment in the story of American music as it relates to cultural shifts. Like a fervent preacher, Sly Stone captured the imaginations of the neo-pagan, neo-tribal hippie movement when he broke down the song *I Want To Take You Higher* into a pulsing sermon. Half a million people sat in a field in the dark screaming "higher" along with the chorus, throwing their arms into the air to give the peace sign after Sly told them the message they had come to hear.

Although the hippies didn't know exactly what they had come to hear, something had spontaneously brought together over a million people (though only half a million made it to the performance field) who were seeking some direction in their earth-based quest for understanding their own humanness. Sly gave it to them when he got everyone in the main field to make witness to communal solidarity. Consequently, the Family Stone's performance at Woodstock is greatly regarded as the best of the whole festival.

In the moment where Sly delivers his sermon, the band lays back, quietly continuing their soft pulsing rhythm of the song and allowing sonic space for Sly to speak. Slowly he built the tension and fervor with these words.

> What we would like to do is sing a song together. Now you see, what usually happens is you get a group of people that might sing, and for some reasons that are not unknown anymore, they won't do it. Most of us need approval. Most of us need to get approval from our neighbors before we can actually let it all hang down . . . ya dig. Now what is happening here is we're gonna' try to do a sing-along. Now a lot of people don't like to do it because they feel like it might be old fashioned. But you must dig that it is not a fashion in the first place. It is a feeling, and if it was good in the past, it's still good. We would like to sing a song called Higher, and if we could everyone to join in, we'ld appreciate it. What we'ld like you to do is say "higher" and throw the peace sign up, it'll do you no harm. Still again some people feel that they shouldn't because there are situations where you need approval to get in on something that could do you some good. (Sly: I want to take you . . . —audience yells: higher) If you throw the peace sign up and get everybody to do it . . . there's a whole lot of people here and a lot of people might not want to do it because they can somehow get around it. They feel that there are enough people to make up for it, and on and on.

Sly and the Family Stone then built the music to a crescendo. The ever increasing volume and the repeated call and response of Sly chanting "I want to take you . . ." and the audience yelling out "higher" had significant impact. The idea was clear that he was not referring to drugs as the "higher," but that the term higher meant to take the human race up a step higher through cooperation and joint effort. For the hippies, who were not talking about Communism, but rather experimenting with living their life communally, Sly's message cut right to the heart of how that is done.

He built up the frantic call and response of "I want to take you higher" as everyone in the field stood up to participate and share in the moment. Then he stopped singing the call, and just let the audience repeat the responsory "higher" as he left the stage and disappeared into the offstage darkness like some messenger sent by the ancient ones to tell the hippies how to achieve their goals. If the movement is gone today, it wasn't because no one told the people how to proceed—cooperation and community. The messages were everywhere in the music, and especially in the image that Sly and the Family Stone presented, a truly integrated, multi-racial collaboration of effort toward a common musical goal. Just take out the word "music" and you have the key to how the human race must proceed if it is to survive its own technological advancements.

Free Your Mind: The Essence of Sundiata

In order to understand where a guy like George Clinton and his message of "Free your mind and your ass will follow" comes from, there is an old African story that sheds light on the issue. It is the story of Sundiata. As the story goes, Sundiata was an African king in a time long ago when people were more in tune to their magical selves. Sundiata and his tribal warriors were going to battle the next day with a neighboring king and his warriors. It is not the battle that we are concerned with, but what takes place the night before the battle. Sundiata literally flies to his opponent king during the night. It's not meant to be a metaphor. He literally takes on the form of an owl and flies right into the encampment of his rival king to tell him that he was going to be utterly defeated in the next day's battle. Then Sundiata flies back to his own encampment. One of his generals came to him and asked him how it was that he could fly. Sundiata responds with the classic simplicity of a shaman that "In order to fly, you must first lose your s**t."

By that statement he was referring to all the baggage that we acquire that weighs us down. Flying, in this case, was not meant as a metaphor, but that we could actually fly if we could break completely free of all the burdens in our life. This meaning your worries and concerns about anything and everything. It also is a reference to being open-minded enough to acknowledge the possibility of anything.

George Clinton took this ideal, built upon the funk movement that Sly and the Family Stone had developed, then took it all into a wholly new place of the imagination. He developed a whole mythology around the spirit of Sundiata's message, that we can fly if we can free our minds completely. Then Clinton took it a step farther, right out into space and the universe. In this view, it wasn't that just the Earth was ours, but that the whole universe was ours to be a part of.

Funkadelic—The Mothership Has Landed

Led by the ever colorful George Clinton, Funkadelic formed in 1967, spinning out of a softer and more accessible soul band. Clinton built his vision of music and mythos completely out of what Sly had done with the Family Stone. Funkadelic merged the ideas and imagery of psychedelia, glam rock, with the driving power of funk, soul, jazz fusion, and hard rock, then Clinton surrounded the music with the mythos of his alter ego, Dr. Funkenstein and his army of funksters. The mythos of Dr. Funkenstein transported the whole image of this hard-rocking band into a space-faring army of followers whose job it was to rid the universe of all those who "faked the funk."

Funkadelic began in the early 1960s as the soft soul, doo wop group Parliament. By 1967, Clinton had recruited more hard-rocking musicians into his funk army, most particularly guitarist Eddie Hazel, and renamed the group Funkadelic. Though Parliament continued to remain a separate entity, the two bands were essentially the same band that functioned under two different names, and as a conflation called Parliment-Funkadelic, or P-Funk. The P-Funk sound solidified in 1970 with the addition of music conservatory-trained keyboardist Bernie Worrell for their second album, *Free Your Mind And Your Ass*

© Lynn Goldsmith/CORBIS

Will Follow. Bootsy Collins, former bassist with James Brown's band, was added to the lineup after Clinton saw him performing in Detroit in 1972, and the P-Funk army hit its full stride.

In 1972, Funkadelic released their third album, *Maggot Brain*, containing the studio version of the title cut. Maggot Brain is similar to a program piece. **Program music** is a reference to a classical style that provides a story, image, or title that suggests the imagery of the music. In classical music, the program is usually either printed in the program as something for the listeners to read before the performance, or is simply contained in the work's title. Programs give the listener something to think about while the music unfolds. At the beginning of *Maggot Brain*, Clinton delivers his program, "Mother Earth is pregnant for the third time, for you all have knocked her up. I have tasted the maggots in the mind of the universe, and I was not offended by it, for I knew that I had to rise above it all or drown in my own s**t." This is then followed by eleven minutes of instrumental guitar solo jam on four simple chords that allows the listener to contemplate Clinton's words. Eddie Hazel's guitar solo on that song is one of the best to be found in all of rock music. Because of the searing and masterful sound that emanates from his guitar on *Maggot Brain*, the song is still getting ritual airplay on Saturday nights at midnight on classic rock radio stations all over America. It is the Pachelbel Canon of the

20th-century. Though it is certainly anything but a driving funk song, it does carry the Funkadelic concept of oneness with the universe, and its simplicity, virtuosity, and beauty insures that it will be getting radio airplay as long as there are radio stations.

Funkadelic destroyed all who stood in their funk path. Their concerts were a seemingly chaotic mass of humanity on stage, sometimes having as many as forty performers on stage together. They had colorful leather "clone" costume outfits made to outdo any other funk band. The main attraction at a Funkadelic show was the Mothership landing. Clinton had a life-size UFO-like spaceship built, complete with strobe lights, lasers, and spewing smoke. After the band slowly built up the first song's groove, the Mothership would descend from above the stage in all its flashing glory, land, and out emerged Dr. Funkenstein from a cloud of smoke to administer the medicine of funk. Members of Funkadelic had their own spin-off groups as well. There was the Brides of Funkenstein and Bootsy's Rubber Band, whose quest it was to continue the battle against non-funk on as many fronts as possible.

Funkadelic enjoyed some high points in the 1970s, climbing into the top rungs of the R&B charts on numerous occasions, but due to label conflicts they abandoned both the names Parliment and Funkadelic. In 1982, the band that was Funkadelic began touring as the P-Funk All Stars, the name they are still known by. They continued to tour extensively under that name throughout the 1980s and 1990s, and continue to put on a show that is not soon forgotten. No other funk band could keep in stride with Clinton's unrelenting experimentation with music, imagery, and ensemble. After Sly Stone, Clinton redefined funk and became the new standard by which all other funk bands would be measured. In the end, though many bands like Earth, Wind and Fire and Kool and the Gang tried, not one of the competitor bands could keep up with Clinton's expansive stage show of extended family tribal imagery. His music was far from accessible to the mainstream music market, yet Funkadelic will be forever known as the true masters of funk music.

Gil Scott-Heron

One of the most important seminal artists in the creation of rap and hip hop music, Gil Scott-Heron, took his awareness of social issues and his love of poetry and rhythm, and molded it into a musical form that today shows no sign of fading. Its message has shifted considerably since its arrival in music in 1970 from the purely black pride association of the Civil Rights Movement from which it came. The rhythmic word use that Scott-Heron helped pioneer is still the mold into which all rappers pour themselves.

Born in Chicago in 1949, and spending his high school years in the Bronx after some time with his grandmother in Tennessee, Gil Scott-Heron developed his love of writing and poetry by reflecting the world around him. This is very different from what George Clinton did. Scott-Heron's formation of lyric content comes from the school of thought that proclaims that music reflects reality, while Clinton's formation comes from the school of thought that says that we create our own reality. While Scott-Heron's *The Revolution Will Not Be Televised*, released in 1970 and the first clearly definable rap song, acted as a

© Neal Preston/CORBIS

social mirror of earthly reality and a call to action, Funkadelic's music and image acted as a fantastic looking glass into future possibility as cosmic citizens. The former dwells on the reality we did create, while the latter dares to dream of the reality we could create. As Yin balances Yang, as life needs death to create new life, as black needs white, both reality and possibility have a place in music, and both are indeed necessary for us to evolve as humans and as a society.

The primary musical difference between the rap that Scott-Heron developed and the rap music that it evolved into is that Scott-Heron's music was music, the same as Funkadelic. Their music was intricate and complex with rhythmic variants played by musicians, on musical instruments that you have to learn how to play. Rap music from the late 1970s on has relied more and more on the technology of drum machines, samplers (digital recordings of sound bits with instant playback ability), and, of course, turntables to collage interwoven spoken vocal lines with found sound bits over a downbeat oriented and repetitive drums and bass. On the other hand, the primary similarity between the rap of then and the rap of now is that both rely on poetic rhythm and precise delivery of the lyrics to propel the music.

Early rap, like Scott-Heron's, developed more out of the jazz and poetry Beat scene of New York City, but after DJ Kool Herc brought turntable mixing of reggae music of Jamaica to dance parties in New York City in the late 1970s, and his protege, Grand Master Flash developed the multiple turntable scratch technique into a new form of backdrop for the poetry, rap music took off in a wholly different direction.

Gradually, the availability of audio technology provided a means by which young black poets could express themselves to a larger audience than a street corner or coffee shop provided. It is interesting that both Scott-Heron and DJ Cool Herc had direct family links to Jamaican culture, which has a long tradition of rhythmic, spoken-word singing over music.

The significance of Gil Scott-Heron in a social context is his timing. *The Revolution Will Not Be Televised* was released in the same year that four students at Kent State University were killed by Ohio National Guardsmen during protests against the war in Vietnam. The radical factions of the Civil Rights Movement had polarized away from their hippie collaborators in vision.

While the hippies went down the path of dropping out of society to just live life the way they thought it should be lived, the radical left pushed more towards direct confrontation with the U.S. industrial military complex. The hippies had already realized that it was a fight that could not be won if it was fought on those terms. But white hippies are able to grow their hair long and drop off into the forests of Oregon and Vermont and mingle into other backwoods' communities. African Americans had no choice. They couldn't meld into the American landscape if they wanted to. They had no choice but to confront institutional racial inequalities. The Dreamer, Martin Luther King, Jr., had been assassinated, and it seemed for many that the only solution left was confrontation in the streets of the cities. *The Revolution Will Not Be Televised* delivers the message clearly that if change was to be made, all the people have to get up on their feet and march in the streets to make their voices heard.

Gil Scott-Heron sang songs about many of the problems facing the world, from drug abuse, the nuclear war and nuclear power malfunctions, to foreign imperial domination of indigenous people, yet *The Revolution Will Not Be Televised* hits the nail on the head for problem solving any social issue. Though the song deals directly with the mind numbing effects of corporate media (which plays a tremendously larger role today than it did in 1970) and the ignorance that the rest of America had of the oppressive plight of the inner city, the overall message is the that it's up to the people as a whole to stand up and let their voices be heard.

That is, in fact, what the whole soul movement was all about, a people standing up to let their voices be heard. They sang loud, and they sang proud. In all the forms of authentic soul music discussed here, we hear the collective voice of a people. We only need to listen to understand. That is, after all, the mark of any folk music, and if authentic rock and roll is anything, it is the music of the folk.

Listening:	*Papa's Got a Brand New Bag*	**James Brown**
	Say It Loud—I'm Black and I'm Proud	" "
	Get Up, I Feel Like Being a Sex Machine	" "
	I Want to Take You Higher	**Sly and the Family Stone**
	Maggot Brain	**Funkadelic**
	Lunchmeataphobia *(Think, It Ain't Illegal Yet)*	" "
	One Nation Under a Groove	" "
	The Revolution Will Not Be Televised	**Gil Scott-Heron**

Roots of Rap:
The History of Reggae Music

Rasta forms the base of reggae music, the vehicle that artists such as Bob Marley used to spread Rasta throughout all over the world. This indigenous music grew from ska, which had elements of American R&B and Caribbean styles. It also drew from folk music, Pocomania church music, Jonkanoo fife and drum bands, fertility rituals, adaptations of quadrilles, plantation work songs, and a form called mento. Nyahbingi is the purest form of music played at Rasta meetings or grounations. It uses three hand drums of different sizes, the bass, the funde, and the repeater. (An archetypal example of nyahbingi is the three LP set from Count Ossie and the Mystic Revelation of Rastafari.) "Roots" reggae explores the themes of the suffering of ghetto dwellers, slavery in Babylon, Haile Selassie as a living diety, and the hoped-for return to Africa.

Reggae music is a combination of traditional African rhythms, American rhythm and blues, and indigenous Jamaican folk conventions. The synthetic style is strictly Jamaican and includes offbeat syncopations, up-stroke guitar strums, chanted vocal patterns, and lyrics associated with the religious tradition of *Rastafari*. Though many commercial ventures have been made into Babylon via reggae, the strict monetary sentiment is antithetical to many of the religious elements but not the political aspects of Rastafari.

Reggae music style is strongly based on American soul music but with inverted rhythms and massively prominent bass lines. The themes of reggae lyrics include Rastafari, political protest, the 'rudie' (hooligan hero), and most dominantly a profession to living in love and peace with each other as a human species. Bob Marley (1945–81) and his group, the Wailers, were largely responsible for the widespread popularity of reggae. The film The Harden They Come (1973) brought the style to the United States. Reggae influenced a generation of white musicians—notably Paul Simon and Eric Clapton—and reggae modes can often be detected in today's rock and rap music. After the death of Bob Marley, the style lost much of its international energy, with the exception of a few bands such as Black Uhuru and Steel Pulse, and single Linton Kwesi Johnson, a Jamaican poet living in England.

In the 1960s the term reggae was used in reference to a "ragged" form of dance rhythm popular in Jamaica. The music and its rhythms were comprised of elements of American rhythm and blues, soul, and rock being heard on local radio stations and in dance halls, Afro-Caribbean rhythms (calypso, merengue, rhumba); and folk music style called mento, which was rich in African heritage. Early forms of reggae (ska, rocksteady) reflected stronger influences from African-American music, although the guitar scratched chords on the offbeats, and the drums played complex cross-rhythms. Contemporary reggae draws from Rastafarian ritual drumming, chanting, and mysticism, thus slowing down the tempo and giving emphasis to the music's social, political, and humanistic messages.

Reggae is a music unique to Jamaica, but it ironically has its roots in New Orleans R&B. Reggae's direct forefather is ska, an uptempo, rhythmic variation based on the New Orleans R&B that Jamaican musicians heard as broadcasted from the United States on their transistor radios. Relying on skittering guitar and syncopated rhythms, ska was their interpretation of R&B, and it was quite popular in the early 1960s. However, during one very hot summer, it was too hot to either play or dance to ska, so the beat was slowed down and reggae was born. Since then, reggae has proven to be as versatile as the blues, as it lends itself to a number of interpretations, from the melodic rock steady of Alton Ellis and the rock and folk-influenced songwriting of Bob Marley to the trippy, near-psychedelic soundscapes of dub artists like Lee 'Scratch' Perry. It has crossed into the mainstream through the bright, bouncy 'Reggae Sunsplash' festivals and pop-oriented bands like UB40, but more adventurous reggae artists, such as Marley and Perry, have influenced countless reggae, folk, rock, and dance artists. Their contributions resonate throughout popular music.

The merging of rap and reggae into a style called dub or toasting, as well as the appearance of younger performers such as Ziggy Marley (Bob's son), revitalized reggae in the late 1980s and 1990s. In fact, reggae music is a survivor. Offshoot genres that play into the mainstream American music market come, play themselves out, become tools for corporate America marketers, die, and go away, but the roots are always there for the next generation to discover. The language of reggae music continues to evolve as well. Reggae music is showing absolutely no signs of stagnation, if you know what to listen for. And new authentic, grassroots styles are emerging like spring flowers all over the Caribbean islands, from Bermuda to West Indies to Trinidad, with each artist exploring their own unique roots and possibilities in innovative and evolving ways.

Many of the new breeds of players in the current Caribbean musical environment are incorporating vastly fun and danceable styles from their own cultures. Of primary important is calypso music. This is a form of folk music developed in Trinidad, West Indies, and originally sung at carnivals. Frequently improvised, the words of calypso songs usually concern topical or satirical themes, and they are characterized technically by arbitrary shifts in the accentuation of everyday English words. In Trinidad, calypso music is generally sung to a guitar and maraca accompaniment that establishes a complex counter rhythm with the voice of the singer in a style probably based on the percussive rhythms of native African music. Since about 1945, steel drums (oil drums, modified and tuned) have also been used, often played in bands. These new musicians merging reggae and calypso traditions are bringing much needed fun and youth back into music.

While only a few Jamaican recordings have crossed over to audiences beyond the Jamaican community, it's hard to think of any genre of popular music that has had a greater influence in the past two decades. Reggae hits have been covered by mainstream rock stars from Eric Clapton and the Stones to the Clash and the Fugees, but more important has been Jamaica's music effect on the worldwide dance scene. Major features of Jamaican dancehall culture—the megawatt sound systems, the exclusive *"one-off"* echo recordings, the foregrounding of drum and bass, and the practice of rapping over rhythm tracks—have been appropriated by rave and dance culture. Other reggae innovations, like the dub remix, have been assimilated into wider popular music.

Though pure reggae music has always been a tough sell in the United States, it has enjoyed many instances of adoption by underground musicians in the United States. The

Police certainly can lay claim to some of that mainstream acceptance of reggae music, but it goes much deeper than that. Hearing the Police do a reggae-influenced song was mainstream America's only probable exposure. They were just the tip—albeit a very popular one—of an iceberg. A Top 40 band copping (pun intended) in on a style and culture that was well understood already by other musicians, most notably, and most surprisingly, the punk rockers.

In the mid to late 1970s, punk and reggae were coexisting as underground genres, and there are many instances of the two feeding off each other. It wasn't an even exchange for the most part. Mostly it was the punks going to after hours reggae shows in New York City. And strangely enough, the musical exchange always seemed to be amazingly minimal considering the exposure each had to the other's music. After a night of banging your head down at CBGBs, the punks frequently held after hours court at reggae clubs, more so to relax and unwind to another underground music and that scene than anything else. Punks couldn't, or wouldn't trust most people, but they felt an affinity with the Rastafarians and their music. If there is one element that the New York punks and reggae musicians shared and could connect with each other on, it was politics. But musically, reggae seemed the perfect down-time music for the overly energetically charged punks, who truly could not tolerate anything corporate or mainstream.

Today, reggae music and the authentic grassroots offshoots of it coming from the rest of the Caribbean islands are as vital as ever and spreading throughout the world dance scene at an infectious rate.

Worksheet Assignment: Chapter 7
From Soul to Funk

1. Soul music reflected a renewed sense of pride for what Americans?

   _____

2. The most dominant rally cry for the black rights movement came in a song called, "Say It Loud—I'm Black and I'm Proud" written and performed by

   _____

3. What region of the United States became the growing fields of authentic soul music?

   _____

4. Name the studio, city, and state where authentic soul music gained its strongest foothold.

   Studio _____

   City _____

   State _____

5. Name the house band from that studio.

   _____

6. What was so unique about this band?

   _____

7. What authentic soul performer were they the back-up band for at the Monterey Pop Festival?

   _____

8. What female vocalist on Atlantic records brought the sound of authentic, gospel-based soul music into the popular limelight?

   _____

9. Who can lay legitimate claim to the creation of funk music?

_____

10. Who developed funk music into an imaginative new direction by merging it with hard rock music?

_____

11. Who developed funk music into a movement based on science fiction and dance, bringing as many as thirty or forty performers onto the stage to deliver his message?

Real Name _____

Stage Name _____

Band Name _____

12. Highlight the state of Alabama, and draw a line from Alabama to Memphis, Tenn., to Chicago, Ill.

13. Circle the general region of the Caribbean Islands.

14. Draw a line between the Caribbean Islands and New York City.

8 Folk Rock
The Voice of the Poet

Woody Guthrie

Woody Guthrie was the most important American folk music artist of the first half of the 20th-century, taking the guitar and turning it into a weapon against injustice. Coming out of Oklahoma, Guthrie had firsthand knowledge of the dustbowl diaspora chronicled in John Steinbeck's novel, *The Grapes of Wrath*. In fact, Guthrie wrote his own version of the story in a song called *Tom Joad*. By the time he gained recognition in the 1940s, Guthrie had written hundreds of songs, many of which remain folk standards to this day. When he was interviewed by Alan Lomax for the Library of Congress in March 1940, Guthrie punctuated his reminiscences by singing *So Long, It's Been Good to Know You*, *Dust Bowl Blues*, *Do-Re-Mi*, *Pretty Boy Floyd*, *I Ain't Got No Home*, and other songs. He later wrote *Pastures of Plenty*, *The Grand Coulee Dam*, and his masterpiece, *This Land Is Your Land*. He was also an author (*Bound for Glory*) and a newspaper columnist.

Guthrie made some recordings for RCA in 1940, but much of his work was issued on the small Folkways label. Meanwhile, in the late 1940s and early 1950s, versions of his songs became hits for such artists as The Weavers. By then, Guthrie himself was in physical decline, suffering from Huntington's chorea, a hereditary neurological disorder. But during his long illness, Guthrie's influence spread to the next generation, fostering the folk boom of the late 1950s and early 1960s. Not only is Bob Dylan unimaginable without him, but large segments of popular music are permanently affected by his concerns as a songwriter and his approach to the form. Guthrie also composed a body of children's music toward the end of his performing career in the early 1950s, when he was raising a family with his wife Marjorie. The songs, many sung from a child's point of view, have been covered and performed extensively since.

Woody Guthrie.
© <CRDPHOTO>/CORBIS

Folk music is the music of the common folk, and rock and roll is really just electrified folk music. Rock music is truly the music of the poor and working classes of the United States. But authentic, grassroots folk rock music is even more so aligned to this idea than any other genre. Folk rock is the banner on which the message of social change is written. Not only is folk rock that voice of social change, but sometimes it bypasses that idea and delivers a message for your life. A guidepost, or warning to you, the listener, to guard and protect certain aspects of yourself, your life, your beliefs and ideals.

American folk music has a very deep tradition. Rooted strongly in musical styles of Ireland, Scotland, and England, yet performing the same function as the classic griot styles, namely chronicling history, folklore, and beliefs. But folk music of the 1960s took on a new urgency. The Civil Rights Movement found its voice in the many poet-musicians of the era. The songs gave the participants strength and fortitude to endure through trying times. During the 1960s, people gathered to sing "We Shall Overcome" countless times as they marched in the streets to peacefully confront the institutional injustices of America.

The obvious starting point is to take a step back beyond the 1960s and look at the rich tradition of folk music in America. The first example that pops into most people's minds is Pete Seeger and his song *This Land Is Your Land*, a song many people learned in grade school. What is the message in a song like this?

Obviously Seeger was rallying people to see for themselves the beauty of America, and against the almost immediate elitism of the new American rich, who had, and still have, high mobility. The idea is that you are here now, and that this land was made for you to experience. The American working class had more a sense that they are stuck, unable to travel, unable to buy the train tickets that allow them to travel the land. But when Seeger's song became popular, it rallied the poor of America to an idea. America was here exactly for those people. The working class Joe; the poor family still looking for freedom in the land of the free, might just find their pot of gold if they kept exploring this land of opportunity—to not just accept the structures of the eastern states, somewhat still entrenched in European idealogy. There was more to America than just the poor Bronx neighborhood they grew up in. All someone really had to do to find the freedoms promised in America was to go into the land. Your specific opportunities to freedom might not be in the shops of New England states, or the farms of Virginia, or the steel mills in Cleveland. Anything is possible if you have the gumption to pack your bags and "Go west, young man." Just listen to the song. It tells you what to do if you're not happy with things in your neck of the woods. "This land is *your* land," the song says, from and to every corner of it.

This specific song bears witness to the folk ideal of Americans, and is, in fact, the ideal which this country is founded upon. Pioneers, explorers, and settlers were needed to fill the land. That *is* our tradition, very much lost today on a people now thoroughly entrenched in couch-potatoism, generic shopping malls, and gentrified radio and television. The song tells you, if you want your dreams to come true, get on your feet, travel the land, and find your own path. It also tells you with the same words that the world will not

Joan Baez sang in support of the Free Speech Movement at U.C. at Berkeley.
© Ted Streshinsky/CORBIS

come knocking at your door. That you must challenge *yourself* to go explore the land-scape of opportunity in America.

Musically, folk rock is one of those forms where simplicity is employed. With many exceptions, usually folk songs fit into that classic I-IV-V progression, or some variation of, with the minor iii and vi added into the progression on occasion. This is a generaliza-tion, and there are many folk songs that deviate strongly, but for the most part the true beauty of folk music *is* that simplicity (the exact same can be said of rock music in gen-eral). Keeping the musical form and harmonic progression simple allows the message of the lyrics to shine through, and it allows anyone with the ability to learn a few chords to write music. Virtuosity can develop if the musician sticks with it, but the important thing is to pick up an instrument in the first place, and give voice to words, ideas, emotions, and concerns in song form. The other side of the coin is lyric writing. As a musician, you must ask yourself, what is it that I have to say?

Folk music is exactly what the term indicates; the music of *folk*—the common people of the land who work hard to survive—in the farm fields, the factories, the mines, and the shipyards. Folk music gives voice to their concerns, triumphs, hardships, politics, spirituality, and awareness just as the blues gave voice to early 20th-century black America. In the 1960s, all sorts of song lyrics can be found in folk music, though historical focus today falls more on the *protest song* in an effort to fully understand the depth of social and cultural change of that era.

To listen to folk music of the late 1960s, you simply must place the song within context. All the aspects of social change of the late 1960s must be viewed in order to understand where the musicians were coming from. If you place these songs in today's context, they don't really strike home as they used to. We *don't* have an unpopular war today sucking in large numbers of our young people. We *do* have today black studies and women's studies programs offered at our universities. We even have diversity training at corporations and schools. In the 1960s, those ideas just weren't popular, until they were taken into the public forum by protesters (mostly college students) and musicians. One song can become a rally cry. One song can become an anthem for a cause. One song can change people's minds. One song can open people's minds. One song can also rally people to fight and die. *That* is the power of the folk song. There are so many stories of a person's path in life being dramatically altered upon hearing a song.

Let's take a look at a few very different folk songs to see just how a strong message, in poetic form and set to music, can influence our emotions, feelings, and opinion. Words, whether they are set in song form, printed in a book, or delivered in a speech by a talented communicator, have the power to move people at both emotional and intellectual levels.

One classic style of folk song, especially for protest songs, is to simply write new words for well-known traditional tunes. One very cutting example was a song written on the U.C. Berkeley campus during the FSM (Free Speech Movement) in the mid-1960s. The sarcastic and pointed lyrics are aimed right at the forces they opposed. Sung to the tune of *"Jingle Bells."*

chorus:　　　 Coffee shops, pom pom girls, UC all the way.
　　　　　　 Oh what fun it is to have your mind reduced to clay.
　　　　　　 Civil rights, politics . . . just get in the way.
　　　　　　 Questioning authority when you should obey.

verse:　　　 Sleeping on the lawn—in an unfolded sleeping bag.
　　　　　　 Doesn't get things done. Freedom is a drag.
　　　　　　 Chuck your principles, Don't stand up and fight.
　　　　　　 You won't get democracy if you yell all night.

One of the best things about this form is that people would ad their own verses, those verses would spread around, become popular, and the song itself becomes alive . . . ever changing to accommodate a new twists in the civil rights plot.

Another very sarcastic and pointed song of the era, and a song that really did become an anthem for the young Americans faced with being sent off to an unpopular war, was

Country Joe McDonald's *Feel Like I'm Fixing To Die Rag*. Every young person seemed to know this song in the late 1960s, and when he performed it at Woodstock, he had a half-million people standing and singing along.

🎼   **Listen:**   *Feel Like I'm Fixing To Die Rag*   **Country Joe and the Fish**

Those songs are incredibly pointed. But other songs were also picked up as civil rights anthems in that era that made use of metaphors to make their point. At the same time period, the Black Panthers also used songs to rally their cause. Based more on the gospel style, but still just as moving to hear a large group of people singing together, "The revolution has come. Time to pick up the gun," or "You gotta' march when the spirit say march."

Bob Dylan, (Robert Zimmerman b. May 24, 1941), probably the biggest name then and now in the folk scene, was a huge fan of Woodie Guthrie and moved from Minnesota to New York City in 1961, where Guthrie was living. He met his hero and began cutting a name for himself in the New York coffeehouses and folk music scene in Greenwich Village. The folk music scene there had evolved from the Beat poets who called Greenwich Village home before relocating to San Francisco in the mid-1960s.

Bob Dylan

Bob Dylan's influence on popular music is incalculable. As a songwriter, he pioneered several different schools of pop songwriting, from confessional singer/songwriter to winding, hallucinatory, stream-of-conscious narratives. As a vocalist, he broke down the notions that in order to perform, a singer had to have a conventionally good voice, thereby redefining the role of vocalist in popular music. As a musician, he sparked several genres of pop music, including electrified folk-rock and country-rock. And that just touches on the tip of his achievements. Dylan's force was evident during his height of popularity in the 1960s—the Beatles' shift toward introspective songwriting in the mid-1960s never would have happened without him—but his influence echoed throughout several subsequent generations. Many of his songs became popular standards, and his best albums were undisputed classics of the rock and roll canon. Dylan's influence throughout folk music was equally powerful, and he marks a pivotal turning point in its 20th-century evolution, signifying when the genre moved away from traditional songs and toward personal songwriting. Even when his sales declined in the 1980s and 1990s, Dylan's presence was calculable.

For a figure of such substantial influence, Dylan came from humble beginnings. Born in Duluth, Minn., Bob Dylan was raised in Hibbing, Minn., from the age of six. As a child he learned how to play guitar and harmonica, forming a rock and roll band called the Golden Chords when he was in high school. Following his graduation in 1959, he began studying art at the University of Minnesota in Minneapolis. While at college, he began performing folk songs at coffeehouses under the name Bob Dylan, taking his last name from the poet Dylan Thomas. Already inspired by Hank Williams and Woody Guthrie, Dylan began listening to blues while at college, and the genre weaved its way into his music. Dylan spent the summer of 1960 in Denver, where he met bluesman Jesse Fuller, the inspiration behind the songwriter's signature harmonica rack and guitar. By the time he returned to Minneapolis in the fall, he had grown substantially as a performer and was determined to become a professional musician.

Dylan made his way to New York City in January of 1961, immediately making a substantial impression on the folk community of Greenwich Village. He began visiting his idol Guthrie in the hospital, where he was slowly dying from Huntington's chorea. Dylan also began performing in coffeehouses, and his rough charisma won him a significant following. In April, he opened for John Lee Hooker at Gerde's Folk City. Five months later, Dylan performed another concert at the venue, which was reviewed positively by Robert Shelton in the *New York Times*. Columbia A&R man John Hammond sought out Dylan on the strength of the review and signed the songwriter in the fall of 1961. Hammond produced Dylan's eponymous debut album (released in March 1962), a collection of folk and blues standards that boasted only two original songs. Over the course of 1962, Dylan began to write a large batch of original songs, many of which were political protest songs in the vein of his Greenwich contemporaries. These songs were showcased on his second album, *The Freewheelin' Bob Dylan*. Before its release, *Freewheelin'* went through several incarnations. Dylan had recorded a rock and roll single, *Mixed Up Confusion*, at the end of 1962, but his manager, Albert Grossman, made sure the record was deleted because he wanted to present Dylan as an acoustic folky. Similarly, several tracks with a full backing band that were recorded for *Freewheelin'* were scrapped before the album's release. Furthermore, several tracks recorded for the album—including *Talking John Birch Society Blues*—were eliminated from the album before its release.

Comprised entirely of original songs, *The Freewheelin' Bob Dylan* made a huge impact in the U.S. folk community, and many performers began covering songs from the album. Of these, the most significant were Peter, Paul and Mary, who made *Blowin' in the Wind* into a huge pop hit in the summer of 1963 and thereby made Bob Dylan into a recognizable household name. On the strength of Peter, Paul and Mary's cover and his opening gigs for popular folky Joan Baez, *Freewheelin'* became a hit in the fall of 1963, climbing to number twenty-three on the charts. By that point, Baez and Dylan had become romantically involved, and she was beginning to record his songs frequently. Dylan was writing just as fast and was performing hundreds of concerts a year.

By the time *The Times They Are A-Changin'* was released in early 1964, Dylan's songwriting had developed far beyond that of his New York peers. Heavily inspired by poets like Arthur Rimbaud and John Keats, his writing took on a more literate and evocative quality. Around the same time, he began to expand his musical boundaries, adding more blues and R&B influences to his songs. Released in the summer of 1964, *Another Side of Bob Dylan* made these changes evident. However, Dylan was moving faster than his records could indicate. By the end of 1964, he had ended his romantic relationship with Baez and had begun dating a former model named Sara Lowndes, whom he subsequently married. Simultaneously, he gave the Byrds *Mr. Tambourine Man* to record for their debut album. The Byrds gave the song a ringing, electric arrangement, but by the time the single became a hit, Dylan was already exploring his own brand of folk-rock. Inspired by the British Invasion, particularly the Animals' version of *House of the Rising Sun*, Dylan recorded a set of original songs backed by a loud rock and roll band for his next album. While *Bringing It All Back Home* (March 1965) still had a side of acoustic material, it made clear that Dylan had turned his back on folk music. For the folk audience, the true breaking point arrived a few months after the album's release, when he played the Newport Folk Festival sup-

Bob Dylan and Joan Baez. © Hulton-Deutsch Collection/CORBIS

ported by the Paul Butterfield Blues Band. The audience greeted him with vicious derision, but he had already been accepted by the growing rock and roll community. Dylan's spring tour of Britain was the basis for D.A. Pennebaker's documentary *Don't Look Back*, a film that captures the songwriter's edgy charisma and charm.

Dylan made his breakthrough to the pop audience in the summer of 1965, when *Like a Rolling Stone* became a number two hit. Driven by a circular organ riff and a steady beat, the six-minute single broke the barrier of the three-minute pop single. Dylan became the subject of innumerable articles, and his lyrics became the subject of literary analyses across the United States and U.K. Well over 100 artists covered his songs between 1964 and 1966; the Byrds and the Turtles, in particular, had big hits with his compositions. *Highway 61 Revisited*, his first full-fledged rock and roll album, became a Top Ten hit shortly after its summer 1965 release. *Positively 4th Street* and *Rainy Day Women #12 & 35* became Top Ten hits in the fall of 1965 and spring of 1966, respectively. Following the May 1966 release of the double-album *Blonde on Blonde*, he had sold over ten million records around the world.

During the fall of 1965, Dylan hired the Hawks, formerly Ronnie Hawkins' backing group, as his touring band. The Hawks, who changed their name to the Band in 1968, would become Dylan's most famous backing band, primarily because of their intuitive chemistry and "wild, thin mercury sound," but also because of their British tour in the spring of 1966. The tour was the first time Britain had heard the electric Dylan, and their reaction was disagreeable and violent. At the tour's Royal Albert Hall concert, generally acknowledged to have occurred in Manchester, an audience member called Dylan "Judas," inspiring a positively vicious version of *Like a Rolling Stone* from the Band. The performance was immortalized on countless bootleg albums (an official release finally surfaced in 1998), and it indicates the intensity of Dylan in the middle of 1966. He had assumed control of Pennebaker's second Dylan documentary, *Eat the Document*, and was under deadline to complete his book Tarantula, as well as record a new record. Following the British tour, he returned to America.

On July 29, 1966, Dylan was injured in a motorcycle accident outside of his home in Woodstock, N.Y., suffering injuries to his neck vertebrae and a concussion. Details of the accident remain elusive—he was reportedly in critical condition for a week and had amnesia—and some biographers have questioned its severity, but the event was a pivotal turning point in his career. After the accident, Dylan became a recluse, disappearing into his home in Woodstock and raising his family with his wife, Sara. After a few months, he retreated with the Band to a rented house, subsequently dubbed Big Pink, in West Saugerties to record a number of demos. For several months, Dylan and the Band recorded an enormous amount of material, ranging from old folk, country, and blues songs to newly written originals. The songs indicated that Dylan's songwriting had undergone a metamorphosis, becoming streamlined and more direct. Similarly, his music had changed, owing less to traditional rock and roll and demonstrating heavy country, blues, and traditional folk influences. None of the Big Pink recordings were intended to be released, but tapes from the sessions were circulated by Dylan's music publisher with the intent of generating cover versions. Copies of these tapes, as well as other songs, were available on illegal bootleg albums by the end of the 1960s; it was the first time that bootleg copies of unreleased recordings became widely circulated. Portions of the tapes were officially released in 1975 as the double album *The Basement Tapes*.

While Dylan was in seclusion, rock and roll had become heavier and artier in the wake of the psychedelic revolution. When Dylan returned with *John Wesley Harding* in December of 1967, its quiet, country ambience was a surprise to the general public, but it was a significant hit, peaking at number two in the United States and number one in the U.K. Furthermore, the record arguably became the first significant country-rock record to be released, setting the stage for efforts by the Byrds and the Flying Burrito Brothers later in 1969. Dylan followed his country inclinations on his next album, 1969's *Nashville Skyline*, which was recorded in Nashville with several of the country industry's top session men. While the album was a hit, spawning the Top Ten single *Lay Lady Lay*, it was criticized in some quarters for uneven material. The mixed reception was the beginning of a full-blown backlash that arrived with the double album *Self Portrait*. Released early in June of 1970, the album was a hodgepodge of covers, live tracks, re-interpretations, and new songs greeted with negative reviews from all quarters of the press. Dylan followed the album quickly with *New Morning*, which was hailed as a comeback.

Following the release of *New Morning*, Dylan began to wander restlessly. In 1969 or 1970, he moved back to Greenwich Village, published Tarantula for the first time in November of 1970, and performed at the Concert for Bangladesh. During 1972, he began his acting career by playing Alias in Sam Peckinpah's *Pat Garrett and Billy the Kid*, which was released in 1973. He also wrote the soundtrack for the film, which featured *Knockin'* *on Heaven's Door*, his biggest hit since *Lay Lady Lay*. The *Pat Garrett* soundtrack was the final record released under his Columbia contract before he moved to David Geffen's fledgling Asylum Records. As retaliation, Columbia assembled Dylan, a collection of *Self Portrait* outtakes, for release at the end of 1973. Dylan only recorded two albums— including 1974's *Planet Waves*, coincidentally his first number one album—before he moved back to Columbia. The Band supported Dylan on *Planet Waves* and its accompanying tour, which became the most successful tour in rock and roll history; it was captured on 1974's double-live album *Before the Flood*.

Dylan's 1974 tour was the beginning of a comeback culminated by 1975's *Blood on the Tracks*. Largely inspired by the disintegration of his marriage, *Blood on the Tracks* was hailed as a return to form by critics and it became his second number one album. After jamming with folkies in Greenwich Village, Dylan decided to launch a gigantic tour, loosely based on traveling medicine shows. Lining up an extensive list of supporting musicians—including Joan Baez, Joni Mitchell, Rambling Jack Elliott, Arlo Guthrie, Mick Ronson, Roger McGuinn, and poet Allen Ginsberg—Dylan dubbed the tour the Rolling Thunder Revue and set out on the road in the fall of 1975. For the next year, the Rolling Thunder Revue toured on and off, with Dylan filming many of the concerts for a future film. During the tour, *Desire* was released to considerable acclaim and success, spending five weeks on the top of the charts. Throughout the Rolling Thunder Revue, Dylan showcased *Hurricane*, a protest song he had written about boxer Rubin Carter, who had been unjustly imprisoned for murder. The live album *Hard Rain* was released at the end of the tour. Dylan released *Renaldo and Clara*, a four-hour film based on the Rolling Thunder tour, to poor reviews in early 1978.

Early in 1978, Dylan set out on another extensive tour, this time backed by a band that resembled a Las Vegas lounge band. The group was featured on the 1978 album *Street Legal* and the 1979 live album *At Budokan*. At the conclusion of the tour in late 1978, Dylan announced that he was a born-again Christian, and he launched a series of Christian albums that following summer with *Slow Train Coming*. Though the reviews were mixed, the album was a success, peaking at number three and going platinum. His supporting tour for *Slow Train Coming* featured only his new religious material, much to the bafflement of his long-term fans. Two other religious albums—*Saved* (1980) and *Shot of Love* (1981)—followed, both to poor reviews. In 1982, Dylan traveled to Israel, sparking rumors that his conversion to Christianity was short-lived. He returned to secular recording with 1983's *Infidels*, which was greeted with favorable reviews.

Dylan returned to performing in 1984, releasing the live album *Real Live* at the end of the year. *Empire Burlesque* followed in 1985, but its odd mix of dance tracks and rock and roll won few fans. However, the five-album/triple-disc retrospective box set *Biograph* appeared that same year to great acclaim. In 1986, Dylan hit the road with Tom Petty & the Heartbreakers for a successful and acclaimed tour, but his album that year, *Knocked Out Loaded*, was received poorly. The following year, he toured with the Grateful Dead as his backing band; two years later, the souvenir album *Dylan & the Dead* appeared.

In 1988, Dylan embarked on what became known as "The Never-Ending Tour"—a constant stream of shows that ran on and off into the late 1990s. That same year, he released *Down in the Groove*, an album largely comprised of covers. The Never-Ending Tour received far stronger reviews than *Down in the Groove*, but 1989's *Oh Mercy* was his most acclaimed album since 1974's *Blood on the Tracks*. However, his 1990 follow-up, *Under the Red Sky*, was received poorly, especially when compared to the enthusiastic reception for the 1991 box set *The Bootleg Series, Vols. 1–3 (Rare & Unreleased)*, a collection of previously unreleased outtakes and rarities.

For the remainder of the 1990s, Dylan divided his time between live concerts and painting. In 1992, he returned to recording with *Good As I Been to You*, an acoustic collection of traditional folk songs. It was followed in 1993 by another folk album, *World Gone Wrong*, which won the Grammy for Best Traditional Folk Album. After the release of *World Gone Wrong*, Dylan released a greatest-hits album and a live record.

Dylan released *Time Out of Mind*, his first album of original material in seven years, in the fall of 1997. *Time Out of Mind* received his strongest reviews in years and unexpectedly debuted in the Top Ten. Its success sparked a revival of interest in Dylan—he appeared on the cover of *Newsweek* and his concerts became sell-outs.

Columbia Records signed Dylan, a somewhat risky move for the label to sign an unproven folk artist to a major contract. But the risk payed off. His second album, *The Freewheelin' Bob Dylan* contained one of the songs that became an anthem for the Civil Rights Movement. *Blowin' In the Wind,* mixes some creative metaphor with straight prose to get the point across. This song strikes right to the heart of many aspects of the Civil Rights Movement. Not just free speech. Not just Vietnam. Not just the women's liberation, gay rights, and the black power movements. It speaks to them all.

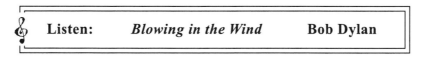

Listen: *Blowing in the Wind*   **Bob Dylan**

The amusing thing about Bob Dylan is the acoustic versus electric debate. As has been discussed in nearly every rock history textbook, their is a notion that Dylan started as a solo acoustic folk musician, then after a couple of albums, turned electric, hiring on a band and turning his back on the acoustic soloist folk tradition. Selling out for the big rock sound (and money) is the allegation leveled against him. Thus, we have half his fans liking only the folky Bob, and half liking only the folk-rockin' Bob. It's as if the authors themselves agree that a musician is not allowed to grow as a composer or evolve as a musician and poet, which is all he was doing.

His evolution musically is expected, as any fan of any long-time performer knows. It's the same with the Rolling Stones. As a Rolling Stones fan, you know they're going to do goofy stuff now and then, but then you also know they'll not let you down. That in the end they'll still jam on the blues and play *Jumpin' Jack Flash* and *I Can't Get No Satisfaction*. That's why you're a fan. But the popular opinion of many authors and the music industry alike seems to be the notion that you get famous on one sound, and your fame should always be associated with that sound, and how dare you go a different path? You're upsetting the order of things. The music industry has a vested interest in being able to pigeonhole an artist. It's understandable why the music industry plays this game, but why authors play into this game is anyone's guess. It's not very rock and roll.

However, the reality is that people in general either like Dylan's music or they hate it. If there is a split in opinion, that is where it lies. There are not a lot of middle-of-the-road Dylan fans. To some, his lyrics are upsetting and dark. To others those same words inspire to action. His lyrics are always—through every phase of his career, whether we're talking about the folky Bob, the born-again Bob, or the rockin' Bob   the main thrust of his impact on the history of American music and his influence on today's musician/singer-songwriter. Always thought-provoking, challenging, and with a master's use of metaphor, he strikes deep at the truths of the day. And HEY!!! At least he didn't make a disco album to pump up his career in the 1970s. The one thing about Bob Dylan that is not debatable is the strong impact he had on musical styles and social and culture shifts alike. By the late 1960s, after Dylan's successful musical experimentation that helped create folk rock, nearly every rock band and performer was paying tribute to Dylan in the way they sang, wrote songs, and performed them.

Let's put the gist of the protest song in perspective and context of the hippie era. The prevailing idea was that: I may be right, I may be wrong, but my voice is strong and I'm going to use it. I'm learning every day. We're learning every day. What doesn't break us, makes us stronger. Our society is sick. Either we'll change society, or be crushed under its weight. We have no intention of being crushed. We are young and strong. We will endure. We shall overcome.

That was the feeling in the late 1960s of American youth. There was a battle being fought. Not the one in Vietnam, but here. A battle for the young person's mind. On one side was the status quo, on the other was the winds of change and growth. The phrase "Either you're part of the solution or you're part of the problem," gained great popularity then. Though it wasn't a revolutionary situation, the late 1960s took on many of the aspects of a revolution. Dylan and the many other great folk singers and protest songwriters, like Joan Baez, Phil Ochs, Arlo Guthrie (Woodie's son—check out what he's up to these days at http://www.arlo.net) and many others, were inextricable from the climate of social change and the Civil Rights Movement.

Little Boxes

But music doesn't necessarily have to be obviously confrontational and dark to get its point across. Some folk songs that are most pointed and challenging are also some of the happiest sounding songs you could write. Although popularized by Pete Seeger, Malvina Reynolds, a California singer/songwriter, wrote the song *Little Boxes* in 1965 while gazing at a hillside of new homes in San Francisco. Her version of the song, recorded in 1965 but not released until early 1967, sounds so lighthearted and upbeat that it's a shock when the thought hits you, about halfway through the song that . . . "Hey! Wait a minute. You're not talking about me, are you?!"

> 🎼 **Listen:**   *Little Boxes*   **Malvina Reynolds**

The gentrification of America was a hot topic then, and even more so now with small town folks protesting in the streets against large chain stores and new malls, and *Little Boxes* certainly attacks that gentrification, but does it in as lighthearted and happy a sound as could be imagined.

Sounds of Silence

Paul Simon and Art Garfunkel, friends and occasional musical collaborators since their teens, were well known in the folk rock culture of the 1960s, mostly for their more bouncy and lighthearted songs like *Feeling Groovy* or the bigger folk rock sound in songs like *I Am A Rock*. Probably the most analyzed song from Simon and Garfunkel was *Bridge Over Troubled Water*. As an exercise, listen to *Bridge Over Troubled Water*, and answer the questions for yourself. What is the bridge? What is the water? What or who is the "silver girl" that sails on by? Why is she silver? The answers will be different and insightful for each individual. *Bridge Over Troubled Water* takes a seemingly dark lyric idea and places it in a setting that leaves the listener with a sense of hope as the final chorus swells and soars to the line, "Like a bridge over troubled water, I will lay me down."

Their late 1965 release of *Sounds of Silence*, however, was a darker song with a dark warning in it's lyrics. It's even written in a minor key. In spite of that, *Sounds of Silence* climbed to the top of the charts. And therein lies to true beauty of a song like this. The words issued a strong warning *and* received heavy airplay. (It still gets airplay today on oldies stations.) Everyone hears it. Everyone knows it. But did they listen to the words? Really listen?

It starts out with a greeting. Then each verse builds on the one before. For instance, the first verse sings about having a vision or dream. The second verse tells about the dream, and introduces a "stabbing neon light." Then the third verse sings about that light and introduces ten thousand people, maybe more. The fourth verse sings about addressing and warning the mass of people, to no avail, as the fifth and final verse is about the people ignoring the warning, and the consequences of doing so.

> 🎼 **Listen:**   *Sounds of Silence*   **Simon and Garfunkel**

What is the neon light that the masses bow and pray to? What is the light that creates the sound of silence? Maybe television?! Maybe today it's your computer. Nevertheless, the technological warning is in strong evidence. Remember . . . "the revolution will not be televised."

Art Garfunkel and Paul Simon. © Bettmann/CORBIS

This song is written with a catchy hook, masterly produced (a mixture of an earlier recorded acoustic version mixed with drums, bass and a searing guitar background solo added in later), and performed with such professionalism that it was soon number one on the charts and heard in every household. It was a hit, but did the message get through? To some it surely did, but one thing is for sure, the message is just as pertinent today— probably more so—as when it was released.

Puff the Magic Dragon

Peter Tarrow, Paul Stookey, and Mary Travers, professionally known as Peter, Paul and Mary, were among the musicians to come out of the thriving New York City-Greenwich Village folk music scene of the 1960s. Their first album release in 1962 contained such strong hits as *If I Had A Hammer* and *Lemon Tree*. The folk rock style was popular on radio in that period between 1959 (the end of the first era of rock and roll) and the British Invasion of 1964. It proved to fit in well with the watered down, big production pop rock of that era. Though the words to the music possibly contained strong messages, the sound was nonthreatening and very marketable. Their second album release in 1963 contained a song that will be a part of our culture for hundreds of years to come, *Puff (The Magic Dragon)*.

(My confidence arises from work I did for the Cleveland Opera Inc., a few years ago. My job was to drive out to Oberlin (no small bastian of musical talent there) and work with first and second graders. My task was to work with them to write an "opera." They wrote the words and I mentored them, which really meant I came into their class one or two hours per week and helped them set there words to music, and hopefully give their young brains some insight into the art of songwriting. I hope it was insightful for them, because it sure was for me. I always remember the songs we wrote and their smiling faces when we stumbled upon a hook. On one of my first sessions with them I wanted to break the ice by vamping on a sing-a-long. I thought I'd play Puff, not sure if they'd even know it. It was written over 35 years earlier. After a two bar intro they already had me pegged. They got all excited and came right in on cue, words memorized. Excuse the pun, but it was one of the most

Peter, Paul and Mary. © Bettmann/ CORBIS

magical moments I've ever had in music. Realizing what immortality Peter, Paul and Mary had achieved—that this song would probably be sung by children as long as humans walk the earth; it made me jealous that I wasn't one of them.)

Like *Sounds of Silence, Puff* is a warning song. It warns us to guard a certain part of ourself; the little kid you once were; your inner child, as the popular phrase is now used. But all new age hokum aside, our inner child really is important. We never know when we're going to need that connection to the innocence and simpleness we once were masters of. One thing is certain, days will come when we all *do* need to reconnect with our inner child. We all do, when life takes those turns that just don't make sense, and we are powerless to change it. The fact that *Puff* is indoctrinated at such a young age, then and now, insures that the message, if not the song itself, finds a place in our psyche for life.

When we look at the masterful construction of the words, the imagery, and the way the song thoroughly captures the essence of childhood, we see exactly why Puff deserves its popularity.

𝄞   **Listen:**   *Puff the Magic Dragon*   **Peter, Paul and Mary**

Look at some of the specific imagery. In the first verse there's Puff, a magic dragon (our imaginations) and Little Jackie Paper (your inner child; the you, you were as a kid). So there's paper, strings, and sealing wax (the first crayons were made of sealing wax candles). Now, what happens when a small child is left alone for a while with crayons, paper, and string (besides them eating the crayons)? Their imaginations go wild and they create. They do it naturally, and they're in their own world when they're doing it. (I've always enjoyed how the Charlie Brown television cartoons portrayed adults not with words, but with a muted trombone.)

The second verse shows the power of a child's imagination. Royalty bows and pirates hide. (Now *that's* power.) The third and fourth verse segue together, and detail the putting away of our inner child as adulthood looms. Jackie Paper comes no more to play with Puff. But the true magic here is the ending. Does Puff die or suddenly disappear? No. He dissipates—green scales fell like rain, and without Jackie, Puff simply cannot be, so he sadly slips into his cave (wherever it is in our brains where we store our inner child). And even the way Peter, Paul, and Mary sing the chorus twice at the end indicates that Puff is indeed not dead, and gives a sense of hope. The first time it is sung softly and subdued, almost sad, while the last chorus swells in exuberance and joy.

These are some of the things that a good folk song can do. From rallying a people to a cause, to warnings of danger in our paths in life, folk music styles have endured to this day because they strongly address the concerns and needs of folk. Folk rock reunited the idea of giving voice to the common person with the electric style of rock music. But after all, on many levels rock music is folk music—electrified. The union of folk with rock was a natural.

Worksheet Assignment: Chapter 8
Folk Rock: The Voice of the Poet

1. Name the father of the American folk music movement.

   _____

2. What was the saying he painted on all his guitars?

   "This machine_____"

3. Folk music gave voice to and is most primarily the voice of what class of people in America?

   _____

4. In the tumultuous 1960s, folk music became the voice of a growing social movement in America, inextricably connected to the concerns of people involved in the

   _____

5. The prime motivator of the musical shift from acoustic folk music to electrified folk rock music was Bob Dylan. What is his real name?

   _____

6. Who was directly or indirectly influenced by this Dylan's music and vocal style?

   _____

7. Who did Bob Dylan idolize and emulate?

   _____

8. The song *Little Boxes* is a jab at urban withdrawal and suburban sprawl, as well as the tendency for suburbanites to look and live very much the same. This is known as

   _____

9. Probably the most important singing duo in popularizing the folk rock sound, bringing social context topics into the popular mainstream, and challenging the listener in many ways was

_____ and _____

10. Today, the creators of "Puff the Magic Dragon," Peter, Paul and Mary are still musically active performing and recording children's music under the name

_____

11. Highlight the states of Oklahoma and Texas.

_____

12. Circle and identify New York City.

_____

9 The Late 1960s Psychedelia
Mind Revealing

The Social Issues of the Late 1960s

Political activism exploded onto the University of California at Berkeley campus in the early 1960s. The images were broadcast to the rest of America causing ripples throughout cities and small towns of the country, and suddenly young Americans were heading west to partake in the experience. It sprang out of the free speech movement, then blossomed into the anti-Vietnam War crusade. Black rights and women's liberation would also be on the agenda in time.

College age Americans had realized that people in positions of power, the establishment of the older generation, would enact any strategy to maintain those positions of power. Whether it was the campus administrators at Berkeley, the military generals engaged in foreign conquest, or the corporate and institutional hierarchy that benefitted from gross exploitation of human and natural resources and kept women and minorities out of the board rooms, the youth of America was sickened by the social and political system it was about to inherit. The very people who would soon inherit the system were marching in the streets to voice their discontent with the way things were.

In the last couple of years of the decade, the stakes were rising as more and more confrontations with authority erupted in the streets of cities throughout America. 1968 was such a terribly bad year for America, and the vision of the radical left seemed doomed in the face of such violent reprisal from the established authority of the country. California Governor Ronald Reagan had trapped the radicals inside of People's Park and had them strafed from above with tear gas. The Dreamer, Martin Luther King, Jr., and the political voice of youth, Senator Bobby Kennedy had both been brutally murdered. More and more young men were coming home from Vietnam either in body bags or horribly maimed. More and more imagery from Vietnam was sickening people as they saw footage of the seemingly senseless brutality, and as their sons came home from fighting in senseless battles to tell them what they had seen and done. More and more industrialized countries were joining the nuclear arms club.

There was a tremendously high sense in the common people of America (who actually fought the battles that the rich elite sent them into) that life on earth was terribly out of balance. Protest songs were sung and people marched singing them, but the war kept escalating, the pollution kept getting worse, the inequalities remained, and the threat of complete and total nuclear annihilation hung over their heads like dark storm clouds.

People looked around at the structures of modern society and asked themselves, "What kind of way is this to live?" Anthropologists and biologists were even beginning to add their input with stern warnings about the end results of unrestrained exploitation of people and resources, or the dismal future of a nuclear winter. Apollo 8 had shown the people of earth just how fragile and precious our little blue spaceship is, and with that imagery, a new path emerged.

Near the end of the 1960s, the radical left seemed to have reached the limitations of direct confrontation. They had their chance, and the results didn't look promising. The only strategy that seemed to make sense was to drop out of the old system instead of trying to change it. A new age of tribalism and paganism emerged that embraced the ideas of community and living in harmony with the planet and all the people on it.

The true hippie ideal view maintained that we are all one race, the human race, and that the earth is to be honored and undesecrated. They became known as hippies, and they had no intention of marching on Washington DC. The hippies realized that the only way to create long lasting change was to live their lives in the way that they thought it should be lived, and that maybe through that example others would follow. In that way, the hippies took the essence of the Civil Rights Movement to a true grassroots level. They just wanted the freedom to "go back to the Garden." The saying, "Tune in, turn on, drop out" became the mantra of this new generation's vision, completely separated in idealism from their radical political comrades. The hippies were not involved in academic discussions about communism, as the radical left was. They were living communally. They just *did* it. And they did it with every age, race, and spiritual belief all mixed in together, and all contributing to their sense of community, making it grow.

It was this new way of looking at life, culture, and society that drove much of the ideology of the psychedelic movement. Counterculture had found a home across the bay from Berkeley, in San Francisco. Many of the Beat poets had left New York's Greenwich Village and adopted San Francisco as their new home. Jack Kerouac's *On the Road* romanticized the idea of "going west." The Beats, and others like Dr. Timothy Leary, became like the elders of a new tribe that embraced the variety of world music and spirituality, forming both into something new.

Psychedelia

If we translate the term psychedelia from Latin, *psych* translates to mind and *delos* (delia) translates as visible, or "mind visible." The meaning then for the term **psychedelia** is **mind revealing**. LSD (lysergic acid diethylamide) falls into the category of a psychotropic drug, although it is synthesized, it has similar effects as other natural psychotropic plants such as psilocybin mushrooms or peyote buttons when taken internally. The use of naturally growing psychotropic drugs by tribal cultures has a long history. It is quite interesting to note that anthropological studies have shown that psychotropics are used most for shamanic purposes in regions where the shaman can not use the drum, the favorite tool of the shaman. There are two things that drums don't like; too much moisture and too little moisture.

In the ever wet regions of rainforests there are a lot of varieties of psychotropic plants that grow due to the climate, but that same ever-wet climate prevents drum use. Drum heads need some moisture, but need to be kept fairly dry else they get too soft from dampness and lose their tension. A wet drum is not a pretty sound. There is an interesting instrument in use in rainforest regions called a Birimbau: a six-foot bamboo pole strung with a steel piano wire, or other suitable steel wire. To get the instrument to sound, a hollowed out gourd with one end cut open, the other end looped with string is forced down over the pole and wire, fastened by the loop of string. It's played with is just a stick about as long as a small arrow by bouncing the stick on the suspended wire. It looks just like a bow and arrow with a big food bowl attached to one end. Pitch can be altered by bending the bamboo pole slightly in either direction. A rattle is frequently held in the same hand as the playing stick to help accompany the beat. Although it is a percussion instrument, prolonged exposure to the sound of the Birimbau creates a sense of one long, sustained pitch.

Alternately, in the extremely dry desert regions of the southwest United States and northern Mexico drum heads need to be kept moist by either applying moisture or using a fresh skin on the drum. If a drum head completely dries out, the tension will exploit the first crack that appears. Drums are used in many Southwest tribal ceremonies, where preparation for use can be maintained, but the primary sonic tools of the shaman of northern Mexico and the southwest United States are the rattle and voice. The drum is used, just not as much as in temperate regions. The extremely dry desert areas are relatively small regions; southern Arizona and New Mexico, and northern Mexico. Interestingly, this is also the only region on the planet where peyote grows naturally.

Most of North America has an average temperate climate that is perfect for drums. A shaman in the moderately humid temperate zones of North America has no other need than his drum to ply his trade, while one in the jungle rainforests of Central America or some southwest U.S. regions may rely on the assistance of psychotropic plants that achieve the same goals. Most tribal shaman use a combination of both music and psychotropics, if both are available.

The use of LSD began with its development by the U.S. military. When it was first discovered, and the ability of its effect to heighten perception realized, the idea was that the army could give it to their soldiers to create super-aware fighting machines. When that didn't work, mostly because the proper dosage was not known, resulting in turning soldiers into blithering idiots from overdose, the military thought maybe they could still use it by somehow dosing the enemy, turning them into blithering idiots in the heat of battle.

The military eventually gave up on the new drug, but the psychologists who had been working with LSD realized that it deserved further research. It was not a controlled substance in any way, and certain doctors started experimenting with it in small doses with their psychiatric patients. The doctors who worked in this area, including Dr. Timothy Leary, were enjoying phenomenal results using it with all their patients in treating everything from alcoholism to extreme mental neurosis. They started taking the drug themselves to determine its benefits to an average person. That's when they hit on the drug's true effect. In the average person, the effect was heightened awareness. LSD soon emerged in the underground counterculture in San Francisco, due in no small part to the help of its researchers, resulting in an end to all legitimate medical research when LSD was classified as a controlled narcotic substance in the mid-1960s. By the time it was made illegal, however, the cat was out of the bag, and soon everyone was finding out what the "tune in, turn on" part of the phrase meant.

When the counterculture emerged, both the radical left and the hippies started to realize that the shifting in social and cultural thought was much bigger than the war in Vietnam or the Civil Rights Movement. In their view, there were major problems with all the mechanisms of modern, industrialized civilization. They didn't want to have anything to do with a system that was slowly destroying the planet or that had the ready ability to wipe out every bit of life in an afternoon. That was the "drop out" part of the phrase. Today's new age and ecological movements spring directly from the neo-paganism, sense of spiritual enlightenment, and tribal understanding of community and nature that emerged in America in the mid-1960s.

Just like the shaman of tribal culture uses psychotropics to raise awareness, the hippies started turning on to the same idea. Psychotropic use, as well as other techniques like yoga and meditation, were seen as tools to achieve an opening of the windows of perception. Many people opened those windows, and found that once opened, they couldn't be shut. Heightening their awareness in this way made it difficult to view life and the world in the same old American way. The hippies had started down a path that was not at all a part of the American way of looking at the world. Tribalism, in fact, was seen for the most part of America's history as in direct opposition to the American way of doing things. Many tribal customs and practices were, in fact, outlawed by the U.S. government during the Indian wars of the 19th and early 20th-century. There are even instances where the drum itself was outlawed.

Synthesizers

A new musical instrument made its timid debut into the marketplace in the mid-1960s. Developed over the past few decades, and used in that time by various art music composers, synthesizers had finally been made for popular use in a keyboard format. As the name indicates, they synthesize sound out of electricity using voltage controlled oscillators, amplifiers, and filters. Synthesizers came into use in the 1960s, but it would be in the 1970s that they would find heavy use as companies like Moog, Arp, and Univox filled music stores with affordable, relatively easy-to-use instruments. The early instruments that manipulated electricity to achieve their sound are known as analog synthesizers. Today, there are no more completely analog synthesizers in production. Every electronic keyboard instrument on the market today is really a computer. Digital synthesizers creates sound by manipulating zeros and ones. If you open up an analog synthesizer, it looks like miles of wire packed inside. If you open up a digital keyboard, all you see is a small green panel with a microprocessor mounted in the middle.

Concert Halls and Theaters

On a more musical level, there are some important shifts in how rock music was presented in this time period that also help usher in a new way of doing things that are still with us today. Besides the festival scene, rock music moves from the dance halls and community centers into the concert hall. From then on, the music was something to be listened to as opposed to ritual dance music. The culmination of that comes when Pink Floyd introduces their 360 degree sound system and giant projection screen in 1969.

With the exception of the Grateful Dead, who insisted on having the seats removed in concert halls so people could dance, known as **festival seating**, rock music became an event that you would fall into, much like going to see a play or musical. Where in the 1950s and early 1960s, a person was usually drawn to the musician aspect of music, once the music transfers into concert halls and performance theaters, more and more musicians, now exposed to the magical backstages of theater houses, became increasingly drawn into the theatrical and show business aspects of music. It wouldn't be long before the rock musicians started to use all the pulleys, ropes, drop screens, lighting, and other visual effects in standard use in the worlds of theater, circus, vaudeville, and show business. The days of running away with the circus may have faded, but the rock musicians would find a way to bring a little of it back to the stage.

AM to FM Radio

Another important change came in the shift from AM (amplitude modulation) to FM (frequency modulation) radio. The advantages of FM over AM are numerous. AM radios fade out under solid obstructions like bridges or tunnels and crackle with static in storms and under power lines. The FM signal is clear and unobstructed by physical barriers. AM radio could only be broadcast in mono, while FM could be broadcast in high fidelity stereo.

Tom Donahue was the biggest convert on the west coast to the hippie ideal. He was one of the most popular disc jockeys in AM radio on the west coast, until he also turned on, quit his job, and soon resurfaced on FM radio. The progressive FM format would become the new frontier in radio. This is a lot easier said than done. FM radio had been around all along, but it was the domain of classical music and international ethnic programming. In the mid-1960s, if you wanted FM radio in your car, you had to buy a Swedish-made Saab or a Volvo. American automobiles came with a standard AM radio with one speaker mounted in the center of the dashboard. Portable transistor AM radios were the norm, though most home stereos came with an FM receiver. To market the new FM format meant that big changes had to take place. The FM band would have to become standard in cars and portable radios. But once the marketability became obvious, the changes came fast.

The whole style of radio changed with the new format and shift to FM. How a disc jockey talked on the air was as different as night and day. Where the AM voice was fast-paced, high-pitched, and conveyed a sense of urgency, the FM disc jockeys reflected the laid-back attitude of the hippies. They spoke in a slow, low-pitched, almost contemplative manner. The more stoned you could sound, the more popular you could become on the airwaves. Radio stations started converting over to the progressive format. A new kind of radio station emerged, the **AOR** (album oriented rock) station format allowed for the longer cuts and whole album sides of the new music. FM disc jockeys also had great flexibility in what they could play on the air. They were really more than just DJs, but programmers as well, working in collaboration with the music directors; unlike today where every song played on the air is preprogrammed based on corporate marketing formulas.

Improvisation

The prime concept that drove psychedelic music at first was the idea of improvisation. Later on it would become a parody of itself as bands rushed to cash in, but the driving factor in the early days was improvisation, instrumental virtuosity, and a friendly competition among each other. Bands like Grateful Dead and Quicksilver Messenger Service didn't even want to go into the studio to record. The three-minute song format was not even seen as relevant to what they were doing, which was basically a blues format as backdrop for experimentation, aptly described by members of Big Brother and the Holding Company as "the blues in technicolor." The feeling prevailed that it was OK to experiment in any way you wanted to with music. Not surprising since American society was experimenting in so many realms at the same time. Not only was there friendly competition with each other for virtuosic status, providing the motive to musically explore deeper and longer, fostered by some degree by the heightened awareness of their LSD trips, but the audience, also tripping, had no need for three minute pop songs. They wanted to hear something that developed over a long period of time, that kept synthesizing into something different than when it began, and that allowed them to work out their own experience with the music.

Transcendentalism

To get a better understanding of what the psychedelic musicians were attempting with music in the 1960s, let's take a look at what the American transcendentalists were doing with music in 1900. It's almost like the first form of music therapy, self-administered. The hippies were exploring the possibilities of music as it relates to stream of consciousness, to heighten awareness of self, and transcend that sense of self. There are some very close associations to the exact same thing that the transcendentalist composer Charles Ives was doing with music at the turn of the 20th-century. The whole idea of stream of consciousness that Ives explored was that one could use music to transcend the individual self in order to become more in tune to a greater self or awareness.

That's very close to what the hippy ideal was all about. In getting in tune to a greater self that is made up of all awareness, then together we can raise the level of human development and evolution up a notch or two; taking it away from the realms of aggression and territorialism and into realms of cooperation and egalitarianism. Another similarity between the hippy ideal and the American transcendental movement was they both regarded an understanding relationship and connection with nature—the earth, sun, and sky—as essential to understanding self.

Ives' composition, *The Unanswered Question*, was the culmination of his work in this field and is highly recommended as a listening experiment and experience. There are three parts, or roles, in the music, each superimposed over the other. The strings play a soft and slowly changing harmony in the background, voicing "the silence of the Druids" that—like the emptiness of space—knows, sees, and hears nothing. The lone trumpet asks seven times the age-old human question of existence, who are we and why are we here? The woodwinds, a flute, oboe, and clarinet, search for the answer in response, each time increasingly frantic and dissonant. But they only answer six times. The last time the trumpet asks the question, the woodwinds give up their futile attempts. The question remains unanswered as the strangely calming string harmony, "the silence of the Druids," slowly fades and dissipates into nothing.

The hippies never really achieved their ideal as a whole. Many individuals did find a path for life, and there are alternative communities spread all over the country today, but the short-term influence on American culture as a whole faded as the true hippies vanished into the forests, and those just in it for youthful experimenting drifted into normal American pie lives of a job, two cars in the garage, and 2.5 children. But any judgment seems premature, as the changes discussed here may take dozens of generations living their lives in dozens of different ways to fulfill, if at all. After all, we *are* human. Our nature is to explore.

While many of the people involved in the counterculture movent, whether musicians or not, began with lofty goals, many also pursued success in the world they rebelled against. For many it was just a matter of the reality of life. If you have bills to pay, and someone offers you a lot of money to bring your band in to record, it can't help but change the direction of the path you take and the path of your music. If, for example, you have a band that improvises for long periods on any given song, and the record label brings you into the studio to record, suddenly you have to try to make your style of music fit into an entirely different format of three to five minute songs that can be played on the radio. Even if you fail, just the attempt is going to change the way you were looking at music creation.

Just like the soul musician had the conflict between sacred and secular interests, the psychedelic musician had the conflict between staying true to their vision or selling out to "the man." Few succeeded in walking both sides of the fence, maintaining a fair amount integrity while producing marketable albums. The major labels had sent legions of A&R men (**A**rtist and **R**epertoire) to San Francisco to sign psychedelic bands after the music proved to be commercially successful. At one time, there were over 1,000 bands in the Bay area trying to make a name for themselves in the new music scene. Only a few had true lasting impact.

Haight-Ashbury

The focus of the psychedelic movement centered in the small San Francisco neighborhood of Haight-Ashbury. The hippies lived side-by-side with the superstars of their music scene. The Grateful Dead's house was open at all hours to all visitors. The Charlatans, Big Brother and the Holding Company, Janis Joplin, and Quicksilver Messenger Service all lived among the regular folks of the neighborhood, helping to instill a true sense of community. The musicians of the psychedelic movement were easily accessible. They hung out at the parks and concerts right along with everyone else. The hippies, the radicals, the musicians, and the guru-Beat elders were all visionaries striving for a deeper sense of community. In time they would go down different paths, but in the mid-1960s in the Haight-Ashbury neighborhood they celebrated their connection.

The freshness of the San Francisco music scene was that it departed from the old rock style of aggressive sexual tension and attitude. Instead of being sexual, the music became sensual. Instead of ritual, it became intellectual, both in song lyrics and in musical expression.

A few of the early San Francisco bands bridged the gap between the west coast music scene of the early 1960s and the late 1960s. In their music, usually only a couple of albums before they disappear into rock obscurity, we find the missing links between the two distinctly different periods. They merged the guitar techniques of the surf bands; double-picking, reverb, vibrato, and the various melodic modes, with folk music styles, and created the more contemplative jamming style that would mark the psychedelic sound and scene.

Formed in 1965 as a rock project when folk singer Dino Valenti combined forces with guitarist John Cipollina, **Quicksilver Messenger Service** was one of the most beloved of the San Francisco bands. They had a tight sound but could improvise for extended periods with ease. By 1967, they had developed such a strong grassroots fan base that their only real competition for prime status among the San Francisco scene was Moby Grape and the Grateful Dead. Their music embraced the blues and folk music as a background for their medium tempo guitar improvising. Their sound was a model for what other San Francisco bands would do musically, especially the Dead and Jefferson Airplane. In fact, the musical similarities are so strong that their first self-titled album sounds like it could be an early Jefferson Airplane recording.

Another of the early groups, today associated more with the garage band scene than psychedelia, was **Chocolate Watchband**. The band started in the southern Bay area of Los Altos in 1965, although due to frequent personnel changes didn't start performing until 1966. Much of their music has a strong, energetic, and edgy Rolling Stones feel to it, which is why they are considered one of the best of the garage bands, but there are a couple of cuts from their first album, *No Way Out*, recorded in 1966, but not released until 1967, that reveal the links between the old west coast sound and the new. They musically mixed together the sound of the British blues bands with surf rock sensibility and techniques; expanded the use of world music elements like African rhythms and instruments like the sitar (*Gone and Passes By*); and out came a wholly new sound. Their music has an edge that stands up today. Also of note is their creative use of backmasking the guitar solo on the song *No Way Out*.

Ironically, two of the tracks from that first album that have the biggest impact weren't by the Chocolate Watchband at all. The two instrumentals on the album were creations of the studio's engineers, Ritchie Polodor and Bill Cooper, and tacked onto the album without the band even knowing about it until the album was released. *Dark Side of the Mushroom* is a creatively-produced instrumental with a dark haunting quality as the guitar and organ play the melody in unison on top of a fuzz guitar laden musical backdrop. But the single work that stands as a missing link between west coast surf music and psychedelia is *Expo 2000*. All of the surf rock signatures are found in this hard driving instrumental, like double-picking, heavy-handed melody played in the lowest range of the guitar, with the added introduction of a new instrument, the synthesizer playing a heavy role.

The re-release on CD of *No Way Out* on Sundazed Records also contains a previously unissued instrumental that is composed by the whole Watchband. *Psychedelic Trip* captures the feel of the true San Francisco sound as it was performed live, a rhythm and blues backdrop for fuzzed out guitar solos.

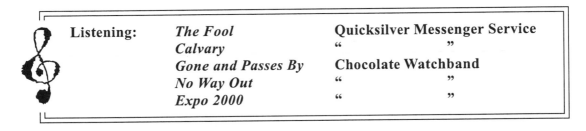

Listening:	*The Fool*	Quicksilver Messenger Service
	Calvary	" "
	Gone and Passes By	Chocolate Watchband
	No Way Out	" "
	Expo 2000	" "

The Grateful Dead

The Grateful Dead travelled their own path, maintaining full integrity to their fans without a care in the world about ever having a smash hit. They played for their fans through and through. Their multi-generational extended tribe of fans, known as Deadheads, rewarded them with undying loyalty.

The Grateful Dead was the band most tied into the Haight-Ashbury community. They achieved prophet status in the psychedelic movement simply by having the gall to speak about it in public and the fact that they were the band that played at many of the acid test parties held by Ken Kesey and his Merry Pranksters. Jerry Garcia, the voice of the Dead and figurehead of the psychedelic movement, described what they did as "Rhythm and blues with a large amount of weirdness thrown in. Once we started to do it, we couldn't seem to not do it." In reality, their music was an extension of the folk music they had started out playing when they were known as the Warlocks. They would improvise for very long periods of time on slow to medium-paced blues and country backdrops as their fans danced, and danced, and danced some more.

The Grateful Dead fed off of their fans' energy live in concert. Deadheads developed a tradition of following the band around on their tours and recording every live perfor-

The Grateful Dead. © Bettmann/CORBIS

mance on any battery operated tape recorder they could carry. It is those live recordings that are most cherished by their fans. The Grateful Dead was not really fond of studio work, preferring the live performance outlet for their creativity.

Until Jerry Garcia's death in 1995, the Grateful Dead enjoyed the status of one of the longest running, continuously working rock bands. It was then also that thirty years of building a fan base had a dramatic effect on the multi-generational Deadheads, especially the younger converts into their extended family who were now orphans. What band would they follow now? As it turns out, there are a few national bands, along with an army of regional bands throughout America that have taken the Dead's musical ideal of improvisation, and their fan base, and kept the torch lighted.

Years after psychedelia's short stint in the spotlight, and long after the big record labels moved on to other styles of music, the counterculture was left to its own devices. The Grateful Dead continued on, inspiring new converts to their family as each generation came of age, and continue to inspire musicians who desire a larger sense of community associated with their music. Today, bands like Phish are employing the same long-term strategies that allowed the Grateful Dead such a long run as prophets of the counterculture movement. In doing so, Phish and other more regional bands, like Ekoostik Hookah in the Midwest, are lighting the path for the orphaned Deadheads and keeping the counterculture movement alive at a grassroots level, which is right were it belongs.

Jefferson Airplane

The other prophets of the counterculture movement, voicing the vision of the hippies, was Jefferson Airplane. Their beginnings also evolve out of the San Francisco folk music scene. Like many of the other psychedelic bands, they took the members of a small folk group, in this case, Marty Balin and Paul Katner, electrified, added more instruments, and turned on. They were the first of the San Francisco bands to sign on with a major label when RCA came calling in 1966.

Their first album did nothing for them. Then, in 1966, they replaced their pregnant lead singer, Signe Anderson, with Grace Slick, who had recently been orphaned herself from the break-up of her band, The Great Society. Slick's voice was aggressive and earsplittingly powerful. She either prowled the stage initiating the seekers as she sang, or stood in one spot and menacingly clutched the microphone to her mouth, staring at the audience like an angry mother as she delivered her metaphor-laden songs of awareness and vision, with no small tinge of sarcasm.

Their first big hit, *Somebody to Love*, encapsulates all the aspects of the Civil Rights Movement, from free speech, to Vietnam, to the assassination of the youthful and promising leadership of John F. Kennedy, to the confusion of coming of age. When this song hit the airwaves, the hippies knew exactly what Jefferson Airplane was talking about with the forcefully sung words, "When the truth is found to be lies, and all the joy within you dies, don't you want somebody to love?" It perfectly captures both the "us versus them" sentiment the hippies had of the establishment, but also indicates the needed sense of community and solidarity in the face of conflict.

This is a common theme in the period. When Joe Cocker soulfully covered *With a Little Help From My Friends* at Woodstock, most people knew exactly what he meant by his passionate cry of "I get high with a little help from my friends," and it had nothing to do with drugs. The "high" is that elevation of the human awareness and spirit described earlier in this chapter. The rising sense that we could achieve great things together if we took better care of each other was being reflected in the music for those who already knew, and directed from the music for the newly-arrived seekers.

Jefferson Airplane is the band credited with bringing the psychedelic sound and image into national attention with the release of their second album, *Surrealistic Pillow*. The Airplane hit their stride in full throttle with that album. Almost every single song on it received heavy airplay, and with good reason. Each cut has a hook to it that won't quit. There are hard, fast, and heavy rockers (*She Has Funny Cars*, *Somebody to Love*, and *3/5 of a Mile in 10 Seconds*) alongside introspectively slow and melodious ballads (*My Best Friend*, *Today*, and *Comin' Back to Me*), and perfect combinations of the two that help define the psychedelic style (*How Do You Feel* and *Plastic Fantastic Lover*). They enjoyed manipulating formal structure, rhythmic tempo, and meter to create a vast variety in each song. But as much of a vital new sound they had achieved in the studio, creating highly marketable songs that fit into the three to five minute radio format, they were consummate professionals at weaving those three minute songs into twenty minute jams when they performed live.

One song from the *Surrealistic Pillow* album became the signature piece for them as a band, as well as for the counterculture movement, *White Rabbit*. The song begins with the growing sound of a snare drum playing a military march rhythm, painting the picture that some sort of battle is going to take place. The ominous low guitar intro over the field drum ads to the suspense. Then Grace Slick delivers her beginnings lines calmly, almost matter of fact, of the story of *Alice in Wonderland*.

Slowly, as the story in the song progresses, the band and the vocals build into a frantic sense of urgency. Direct drug references and metaphors of battle and chess (a game of war) are included in the lyrics. Then at the end of the song, Slick leads the listener into the true message of the song with "and the White Knight is talking backwards, and the

Grace Slick at Woodstock. © Roger Ressmeyer/CORBIS

Red Queen's lost her head. Remember what the Door Mouse said: 'Feed you head.'" Though the song was intended by Grace Slick as a stab at the hypocrisy of the older generation, most hippies understood that last line as a call to action in the face of a seemingly absurd and misunderstanding society.

To "feed your head" meant to be a person of knowledge and understanding through study, experience, and expanded awareness, however it was achieved. But more than that, you must remember to do it more than ever in the midst of crisis. Another interesting aspect is that the message to "feed your head" is delivered by the lowly and humble Door Mouse (which could be seen as analogy to common folk) when the White Knight and Red Queen (maybe those in positions of political power) are in a state of chaos.

Whatever conclusions are drawn from a song like *White Rabbit*, the important aspect is that it made you think. Rock music had truly become the voice of a generation, expressing their concerns and deepest thoughts both lyrically and musically. It was no longer just music to dance to, and it was now evolving beyond even the "music as art" threshold that the Beatles surpassed. It had a message, and as the youthful complaint went, "They get down on our music, but do they ever listen to the words?"

Though the group's founder, Marty Balin, had left, and two other members left to form Hot Tuna, Jefferson Airplane continued on with Grace Slick and Paul Katner at the helm into the 1970s and 1980s with frequent personnel changes, eventually renaming themselves Jefferson Starship. In 1975 they achieved their first number one album when Marty Balin returned to the Starship and they released *Red Octopus*. They continued to grow up with their generation, and were able to release new material and perform live with popular success in that period.

In their time, Jefferson Airplane completely captured the imagination of their generation, giving prophetic voice to the hippie counterculture. Their early San Francisco concerts were not just rock shows, but social events that brought hippies together in fellowship.

Their stage presence combined with the direct message of some of the songs lead to their priestly role as figureheads of the counterculture. They were creative and inventive musicians as well, but there was always a message to feed your head. Grace Slick never failed to espouse their commitment to creating thought-provoking music and has always been humorously sarcastic and direct in her quest to get people to make better use of their brains. She still never misses a chance to take her shots when doing interviews for rock documentaries.

Grace Slick is one of the survivors. Her sudden success was *not* followed by the sudden failure of judgment that destroyed other pioneers in music, maybe depriving her of the icon status heaped on the others who did self-destruct. But for a time, Grace Slick was as powerful a force in rock music as there ever was, and in being a survivor, she's proven her point all the more, to always "remember what the Door Mouse said."

Janis Joplin

The Pearl, Janis Joplin, along with Jimi Hendrix and the Who, broke into national attention as a result of their performance at the Monterey Pop Festival in 1967. Her vocal intensity is only matched by Aretha Franklin in its true grassroots grit. Janis was a powerful voice in the San Francisco music scene, and her true power and beauty was in her sense of energy and soul. Her confidence transcended her stature, and through her scruffy hippie-chick image and her powerful music, she helped redefine the notions of female attractiveness and beauty in America in the late 1960s.

Janis grew up learning blues styles around her home in Port Arthur, Tex., and later in the small clubs in Austin. In 1966, she moved to San Francisco and teamed up with local favorites Big Brother and the Holding Company. Their first album together on Mainstream Records didn't do much for them. Mainstream was a jazz label that focused on, as their name would indicate, mainstream jazz. They really didn't know what to do with a fireball blues singer like Janis and Big Brother's extremely unorthodox approach to music. But once people saw

Janis Joplin: The Pearl. © Henry Diltz/ CORBIS

them perform at Monterey, their intense energy gained them a high place in the rungs of the psychedelic ladder. In 1968, their second album, *Cheap Thrills*, now on Columbia Records, was an overwhelming success, holding the #1 Billboard Album spot for eight weeks.

Big Brother was a highly unstructured band. They were not schooled musicians at all and taught themselves to play without any care if what they were doing made sense to others. They improvised on the craziest ideas, and no musical idea was too far out for them, many times just making it up as they went along. To give an idea of their unorthodox approach, they had an idea for a song called *Bacon* that included putting a microphone up to a skillet of frying bacon, and jamming along with it until the end of the song, which was when the bacon was done. Big Brother was the perfect match for Joplin, who was quite unorthodox in her own way. She sang from the heart with intensity, power, and with a sense of full-throttle output that was unmatched in its rawness and precise attack.

Janis sang to everyone when she performed. She created a relationship on stage between herself and the whole audience, male and female. She rebelled against the perceived notions of American beauty, growing her hair, wearing folksy clothes, never with a bra. She was raspy-voiced, straight forward, and gave the image of a farm girl that sang the blues. This is all in direct opposition to the sex kitten image that most female performers utilized for success. In an age of women's liberation, she had said to American women through her vocal style and public image that it was O.K. to break from the old stereotypes and just be yourself.

Eventually, the talented Janis outgrew Big Brother's creative but musically limited structure, and in 1970 put together a new, more professional band called Full Tilt Boogie. Before the world would find out just what she could do with a professional band, she became a casualty of the era's excess. On October 4th, 1970, she died of a heroin overdose. She was one of the biggest voices of the peace and love movement while maintaining a rebellious style and stage presence, but her own inner battle with self prevailed, destroying all that might have been.

The Doors

The Doors were from media crazy Los Angeles, a significant factor in understanding the difference between the message of the flower power and free love San Francisco psychedelia and what Jim Morrison had to say. Although their sound may have been limited in scope, their talent and musicianship in defining their own style was tremendously high. Their popularity and cult status only seems to grow more and more as time goes on.

Their sound was so unique you can tell any Doors song within the first two bars of hearing it. The musical core of the band, Robbie Krieger on guitar, Ray Manzerek on organ, piano and bass, and John Densmore on drums, created lush backdrops for their bohemian poet vocalist, Jim Morrison. Their use of the dark minor key, flowing electric organ riffs, and Native American rhythms, modes, and lyric imagery set them so far apart from what anyone else was doing, yet can be linked directly to the music of southern

California just before the Doors' arrived on the scene. Many Doors songs have a musical shadow of surf rock hiding in the background. Like the Doors, surf also made use of the minor key to great effect, used open fifth harmony, and always had a rhythmic pulsing in the bass. They slowed down the frantic pace of surf, creating a more atmospheric effect over which Morrison could work.

Morrison projected a stoic image on stage and off, frequently seeming indifferent, or even disconnected, as he delivered his low monotone vocals. The aspect of the Doors that continues to draw people into their music is the thought-provoking poetry that Morrison set to music. Morrison frequently used the music medium as a vehicle to espouse rebellion against the destroyers of the Earth, a direct reflection of his own intense attraction to Native American thought. Indeed, the story of his belief in a transference of a Native American spirit into his own is well-documented.

In an age when anything seemed acceptable on some level, Morrison shocked

Jim Morrison: The Lizard King. © Henry Diltz/CORBIS

everyone, even the other freaks, with the song *The End*. Sex in the 1950s was one thing, embracing pagan religions in the 1960s was another, and even Morrison's own chant of "We want the world and we want it now," didn't compare to the dramatic nature of *The End*. In it, Morrison updates the story of Oedipus in epic fashion as the band weaves subdued, dark backdrops and powerful crescendos behind him. Morrison climbs into the dark thoughts of insanity as his psycho-killer character "takes a vase from the ancient gallery and he walks on down the hallway" before killing his father and making love to his mother. The listener is taken right into the mind of the killer as the song ends as Morrison croones slowly, "This is the end."

Morrison's own life, though he was an intensely talented poet and his band was at the top of the rock music hill, was the picture of life out of balance, and on July 3, 1971, at just 27 years old, he found his only friend.

Jimi Hendrix

The man who started heavy metal, Jimi Hendrix, will always be regarded as the most talented, innovative, and impactful guitarist in all of rock music. He is forever the ulti-

Jimi Hendrix reinvented the electric guitar. © Hulton-Deutsch Collection/CORBIS

mate king of the hill, standing on the shoulders of Chuck Berry, Little Richard, and Dick Dale. In the short time that he was given, he completely redefined how the guitar was played. He didn't just innovate on the guitar, he reinvented it.

Jimi Hendrix was born in Seattle, Wash., and soaked up all the music from up and down the west coast. During the early 1960s, Hendrix payed his musical dues on the rhythm and blues dance-hall circuit, performing with the likes of Wilson Pickett, Jackie Wilson, the Isley Brothers, and eventually Little Richard, soaking up the maniacal stage presence of the master of outrageousness. The most influential moments for him as guitarist came as he was touring with Little Richard in the early 1960s.

Two important aspects fell into place. One was when he was on tour on the west coast and he saw Dick Dale perform. Hendrix became a huge fan of Dale's machine-gun playing style and distorted volume. Both were southpaws who played the guitar backwards. Of particular note is the borrowing of the "wet" sound that Dale had developed through double picking. Hendrix came up with the similar fast fluttering effect that made him so beloved to the psychedelic crowd, but did so using a fast finger tremolo. His hands were huge by all accounts, and he developed a playing style where he could accompany his own high string solos by reaching over the other side of the guitar neck with his thumb to allow him to play different parts simultaneously. He also incorporated a collage of fast manipulation of volume and toggle switches (the toggle switches control tone color), feedback, fuzztone, and wah-wah peddles, and a display of unparalleled mastery of the whammy bar. He used all these effects in such fast juxtaposition that even other seriously talented guitarists watched in utter awe of his prowess and creativity.

The second vital aspect in his development came after Little Richard, fed up with Jimi's lateness, packed up the tour bus and left Hendrix in New York City. In 1966, Hendrix put together a blues oriented band called Jimi and the Blue Flames and started playing the Greenwich Village bar scene. This is the time period that a New York music reviewer described Hendrix's music as "the sound of heavy metal falling from the sky," officially coining the phrase. Former Animals' bassist turned talent manager, Chas Chandler, heard the buzz going on about this new guitar player and decided to check out a performance. As everyone else who saw him in those early days, Chandler was completely awestruck by Hendrix's prodigious talent. Chandler took Hendrix to England and teamed him up with guitarist turned bassist Noel Redding and drummer Mitch Mitchell to form the Experience.

The full scope of Jimi's talent and maniacal stage presence was released on American audiences at the Monterey Pop Festival. He stunned the audience with his jarring guitar style and outlandish performance techniques of playing the instrument behind his head or body or picking it with his teeth without missing a beat or note from the solos. Then he stunned them some more by ritually setting fire to his Stratocaster guitar before smashing it on stage. Songs like *Purple Haze*, *Foxy Lady*, *Hey Joe*, and *The Wind Cries Mary* became anthems for the generation and inspiration for aspiring guitarists and the soon-to-emerge hard rock, heavy metal bands.

The moment that truly endears Hendrix to the generation came on the last day of Woodstock. Hendrix was given the unenviable slot of Sunday morning. He took that slot and created a moment in time that will reverberate through music for many years to come. Hendrix woke up the Woodstock population with the most creatively deviant version of the Star Spangled Banner that has ever been performed.

The Experience released two albums, *Are You Experienced?* in 1967 and *Electric Ladyland* in 1968, that fully defines the full power of what Jimi Hendrix did with music. In 1970, Hendrix opened his own studio in New York City called Electric Ladyland, with the intent of recording and getting back on track as a musical innovator and recording artist. In August of 1970, Hendrix left for a European tour that included the Isle of Wight Festival. He died in London on September 18 of an apparent suffocation from drug overdose. Another brilliant voice in music was forever silenced, yet his influence and reputation as the primary innovator of the electric guitar grows increasingly dominant as time goes on through the few recordings he left.

The Iconoclasts

Iconoclasm is the attacking of established institutions, practices, or attitudes. An iconoclast is anyone who destroys sacred images or attacks traditional or popular ideas or institutions. Iconoclasm was not something foreign to musicians of the mid-to-late 1960s, as has been seen throughout this book, but few focused their attention completely on iconoclastic lyric content. Certain rock musicians, however, have made a career out of iconoclasm, and a few even did it with tremendous success and critical acclaim. Others existed in relative obscurity and are just beginning to be recognized for their contributions.

Frank Zappa and the Mothers of Invention

The king of iconoclasm, and the undisputed champion of free speech in music was Frank Zappa. He was also one of the most naturally talented and musically knowledgable guitar players to emerge from the 1960s. Musically, Zappa was doing things that were eons away from what anyone else was doing. The early Mothers of Invention albums are a mix of doo wop, deviant psychedelic music, and serious art music composition. Each of the songs on Mothers' albums were unique from each other, yet had an element of musical unity.

Born in Baltimore, Md. in 1940, Frank Vincent Zappa spent his early childhood in a frequently sickly condition. His parents moved the family to the west coast in the early 1950s, first to Monterey, then later to southern California. One of the most formative events for Zappa's musical development was his purchase of a copy of modern avant-garde art composer Edgard Varese's *Ionisation*, which Zappa saw reviewed in *Look* magazine that described the music as "Nothing but drums—it's dissonant and terrible; the worst music in the world." Zappa listened to *Ionisation* over and over for a couple of years, absorbing all of the strange sounds, unorthodox musical form and musical landscaping employed by Varese.

Frank Zappa: The main Mother of Invention. © Hulton-Deutsch Collection/ CORBIS

The work is a trying piece to listen to even for people involved in composition and theory, with wild juxtapositions of percussion, sirens, wind machines, and just about every single special effect available to modern composers of the 20th-century. *Ionisation* completely captured Zappa's musical imagination. In every stage of his musical career, he would always display the techniques of the theory and composition that he learned by listening to *Ionisation*. The work opened a window for him into the truly bohemian and secluded world of 20th-century experimental composition.

Varese was certainly not the only composer involved with experimentalism, as any music conservatory student can attest, but he was one of the best. The curious thing about the direction that 20th-century art composition has taken is how inaccessible and removed from the common public it is, happily secluded from the real world and existing on government welfare (grants) as it churns out music no one wants to hear. No one except Frank Zappa, who heard it and found inspiration in its inaccessible strangeness. Interestingly, his own career would also always reflect a certain inaccessibility and strangeness to the general public.

In 1965, the Mothers of Invention released their first album, *Freak Out,* which was released as a double album set on Verve Records. Double albums were not unheard of, but were certainly rare, and for a band to release a debut double album was unprecedented. Frank Zappa always maintained that he never actually took any LSD, but listening to this first album without the Varese context would convince anyone otherwise. With the Varese context, *Freak Out* makes crystal clear sense without any need to attach a reference to psychotropic influence. The music varies from song to song. Some are fuzztone dominant hard rock, some are classic 1950s doo wop parodies, some are pure 20th-century art compositions, and some are acid-soaked dirges or bopping ditties that parody the hippie culture itself. The difference in styles from song to song couldn't be larger, but upon listening, there is a sense that Zappa is at his best in the pure strangeness of the art music instrumental sections of the ending trilogy of songs: *Help, I'm a Rock*, *It Can't Happen Here*, and especially *The Return of the Son of Monster Magnet*. His experimentation with musical color and landscapes over shifting rhythms is tirelessly creative in *Monster Magnet*, as is the juxtaposing of spoken word bits from various voices.

As innovative and creative the music from *Freak Out* is, the lyrics of the songs strike the hardest blows to sensibility. The first song, *Hungry Freaks, Daddy* slams the apathy of suburban complacency. With lines like "Mr. America, walk on by your schools that do not teach. Mr. America walk on by the minds that won't be reached. Mr. America, try to hide the emptiness that's you inside. But once you find that the way you lied will not forestall the rising tide of Hungry Freaks, Daddy." The song suggests the question, what were the freaks hungry for? Remembering what the Door Mouse said in Jefferson Airplane's *White Rabbit* might be a clue.

Each song after that attacks some aspect of American culture. Zappa is at his best when he attacks his own world of the hippies. *Who Are the Brain Police?* is a musical depiction of a bad acid trip, complete with inner voices weaving in and out, over and over again, "I think I'm gonna' die . . . I think I'm gonna die . . ." The musical accompaniment also is quite convincing in its portrayal. *Wowie Zowie* and *You're Probably Wondering Why I'm Here* are R&B style sarcastic parodies of the flower-children hippies, with the added color of Kazoo solos. The hardest-hitting commentary comes on the song *Trouble Every Day*, which attacks the media's attraction to sensational imagery, like the riots and bloodshed of war.

Zappa would continue down this iconoclastic path throughout his life while continuing to evolve musically both in the rock realm and in serious art composition. One of the songs that captures the essence of Zappa's view of the absurdity of humans is one of the shortest he ever recorded, *What's the Ugliest Part of Your Body* from the *We're Only In It For the Money* album. It lasts about 20 seconds, first asking, then answering, "What's the ugliest part of your body? Some say your nose. Some say your toes. But I think it's your mind."

Zappa's career was one of the most inspiring and ever changing in all rock music. He constantly toured, from the Mothers' inception in 1965 until his death of cancer in 1993. He worked with symphony orchestras and the top names in jazz, made movies, and was always provocative on stage and off.

He testified in favor of free speech and against censorship of music against America's official soccer-mom, Tipper Gore, and the Parents Music Resource Center in nationally televised congressional hearings, and won. Gore and the PMRC wanted congress to create a censorship law making it illegal to release offensive musical material. The result was the voluntary labeling of offensive albums with a parental advisory sticker by the music industry. No law was actually passed; instead, the sticker places the burden of parenting children squarely on the shoulders of the parents. He then released an album of the hearings called, *Frank Zappa and the Mothers of Prevention* in 1990. The album is a mixture of Zappa's standard satirical songs, instrumentals, and excerpts of Zappa's testimony.

Whatever else there was about Frank Zappa, there was always one moment in his concerts that his true fans waited for, when Frank would rip into one of his signature guitar solos as only he could play. He even named an album *Shut Up and Play Your Guitar* in response to fans' constant plea for the same. Frank Zappa was one of the true heroes of his time. His fervently sarcastic social voice and his inspiring guitar solos are sadly missed.

Listening:	*Freak Out*	The Mothers of Invention
	Cruising with Ruben and the Jets	" "
	Live at the Fillmore	The Mothers of Invention with Flo & Eddie
	Roxy and Elsewhere	The Mothers of Invention
	Joe's Garage trilogy	Frank Zappa
	White Rabbit	Jefferson Airplane
	Get It While You Can	Janis Joplin
	When the Music's Over	The Doors
	The End	The Doors
	Hey Joe	Jimi Hendrix

The Velvet Underground: The Original Punks

The east coast had their own version of psychedelia, the trouble was that no one knew about it until it was over except for a few musicians and the quirky elite art crowd of New York City. There was a big difference between what was happening musically in New York's underground and on the west coast. The New York scene wasn't tied into any lofty goals of self awareness, civil rights, or the Vietnam War. It was about sexual deviancy, heroin addiction, and a dead-end sense of future. Indeed, the Velvet Underground disdained performing on the west coast due to the fact that the peace-and-love, flower-children hippies were so far removed from their own experience in the *when it rains, it pours* environment of New York City. But when the hippie ideal faded in the 1970s, it was the Velvet Underground that influenced every punk and grunge band to come along afterwards. The era of earthly love and unlimited future of the 1960s was somehow replaced in the 1970s with the era of no future social alienation as punk rock became the new model and big city bohemian imagery became the new look of "cool."

The Velvet Underground formed in 1965 when classically-trained pianist Lou Reed teamed up with a promising classically trained violist named John Cale. The two met at a sit-in jam session and decided to form a band together with Reed on vocals and Cale on bass. The other members of the group, Sterling Morrison on guitar and Maureen Tucker on drums completed the true Velvet's lineup. They got the band name from a sadomasochism paperback book they found discarded on a city street. They played any gig they could get, including film showings and art openings. They were frequently fired from jobs in the middle of their set for being too dark and disturbing. People had seen a lot of new things in music, but this was something totally different.

In 1965, pop artist Andy Warhol (who became independently wealthy from his creation of the Campbell Soup label design) saw them perform and became their mentor and manager. He put them to work playing openings at his art studio and gallery, the Factory. Warhol, who was hosting many parties at the Factory for New York's strange and eccentric art crowd, encouraged Reed to document the people and their curious attraction to fetishism,

Lou Reed. © Neal Preston/CORBIS

narcotics, and just plain weirdness. Warhol also introduced the band to Nico, who sings vocals on some of the first album.

The Velvet Underground released their first album on Verve Records in 1967. Titled *The Velvet Underground with Nico*, the album was soaked in a minimalistic, primal pounding feel, contrasted with eerie childlike songs that chronicled the New York art scene and its kaleidoscope of celebrities, gold diggers, porn queens both male and female, overly colorful art and theater tramps, sexual deviants, transsexuals, and drug addicts. It was the farthest thing from Haight-Ashbury as can be imagined.

The first song on the album belies the coming assault. *Sunday Morning* uses a toy piano bell sound in a happy little major key ballad of hopeful inspiration. Then, when your guard is down, Reed takes you for a walk into the seedy underground of New York City. *I'm Waiting for the Man* is a pure pounding, head-banging dirge that details waiting for the drug dealer to show up to make a score. The now immortal *Heroin* is an epic adventure into the escapist reasoning of heroin addiction in stunning poetic fashion.

The repetitive pulsing darkness of the accompanying music, almost out of tune and never very tight, adds to the sense of alienation and misty focus of the addict's rationalizations. There is an authentic, anxious and unsettling grit throughout all the Velvet Underground recordings, and it starts right here on this first album as powerful as it would ever become. There are a couple of other songs like *Sunday Morning*; particularly of note is *I'll Be Your Mirror*, the song that indicates exactly what Reed is doing. Sung by Nico in her slightly off-pitch, breathy way, calmly reflecting the need for misery to love company.

Venus In Furs musically captures more eastern mysticism than all the San Francisco songs combined, and it's not even trying to. The music here is a masterfully worked backdrop of **word painting** (matching the music to reflect the image of the words). The song reaches deeper than even *Heroin* does, exposing the black-walled eros dungeons of the S&M scene. Each whiplash is heard in Cale's slashing technique on the viola as an ominous background drone shadows the proceedings as the song sings about shiny boots of leather and whiplashed girl-childs in the dark, and really exposes to the core of the whole S&M scene with as the song commands, "strike, dear mistress, and cure his heart."

Obviously this is not something for major market radio, or even minor market, or even still, college radio. Yet their music did get around through the underground network of independent record stores and musicians. It just took a little more time than if there had been a big record label promotional push. Still, how could you push this? It had to spread via the grassroots underground or not at all. By the early 1970s, garage bands throughout the East and Midwest that would soon coalesce into punk bands were covering Velvet Underground songs, along with the Rolling Stones, the Who, the Kinks, and the new hard rocking glammers, New York Dolls. *The Velvet Underground with Nico* album continues to inspire and influence legions of young rockers, especially today, in their home New York City where they are forever the true originators of punk and garage grunge.

The Velvet Underground gained more attention after they broke up than they ever came close to enjoying when they were together. Lou Reed pursued a very successful solo career, hitting what many saw as his full potential on the live *Rock & Roll Animal* album released in 1974, which, some say diluted, others say empowered, the punk style he helped create by performing Velvet's songs with a professional and tight band of pure, seasoned rockers. The fact remains that *Rock & Roll Animal* was, and is still, one of the best pure rock albums in all of rock music. It is one of those rare albums that stands the test of time sounding as vital today as when it was released.

Lou Reed drifted away from iconoclasm in his efforts to have a wider appeal, though there was no small tinge of it in the popularly aired song, *Walk on the Wild Side*. Reed's iconoclasm was always pointed at specific, identifiable targets—messed-up individuals. Though their first album is a landmark in music innovation, its focus and relatively disturbing quality left the Velvet almost completely unknown during the time they were together as a band.

Pink Floyd and the Birth of Space Rock

Pink Floyd not only ruled the psychedelic scene in England, in the late 1960s, they were the best and purest, most experimental, unconventional, and creative of all the psychedelic bands. The other bands had their music, but not many of the could play it for six hours straight or create a soundtrack to the psychedelic experience the way Pink Floyd did. They weren't iconoclastic in the early days at all, but starting with the album *Dark Side of the Moon*, they would evolve into something completely different, rightly claiming the title of the biggest show in rock music. In their early days, however, no one captured the musical essence of psychedelia like Pink Floyd. A few tried, but in the end, they didn't come close.

Pink Floyd was a creation of guitarist Syd Barrett and named after American blues men Pink Anderson and Floyd Council. Under his guidance, with Roger Waters on bass, Rick Wright on organ and synthesizers, and Nick Mason on drums, Pink Floyd became the fathers and pioneers of space rock, and in spite of that were still able to pay the bills by recording pop-type psychedelic hits like *See Emily Play* and *Arnold Layne*. Syd Barrett had a tremendous talent of capturing their space tripping style in the three-minute pop formula. But in concert they refused to play any of the radio hits, preferring instead to develop their improvisational space music in front of the audience.

Their first album, *Piper At the Gates of Dawn*, was released on EMI Records in 1967. The very first thing you hear on the album is a strong indication of the direction they would go with their music. *Astronome Domine* slowly swells with a low pitched mechanical sounding voice, like a distorted train station public address system. Into that comes the pulsing rhythm of Barrett's guitar. Suddenly a frantic sounding Morse Code message starts streaming into the picture, louder and louder until Mason hammers the introductory tom-tom drum beats that lead into the song. The Morse Code and pulsing rhythm builds in urgency as the guitar slashes and jabs over it. Then, Barrett's and Waters' silky vocal harmony calm the scene a bit as they sing metaphoric imagery of space. The song lets up a little before slamming the listener into two full minutes of instrumental space-truckin' complete with a return of the train station voice before the song returns to its original form for the final verse.

In *Astronome Domine* they hit on the style from which they would make a long career. In April 1967, as Haight-Ashbury was immersed in its Summer of Love, Pink Floyd performed in the Technicolor Dream, a fourteen-hour concert held in London's Alexandra Castle. Ten thousand people showed up for the afternoon-to-sunrise event, including John Lennon and Yoko Ono.

Syd Barrett's attraction to psychedelia would be his ultimate undoing. He dropped out a little too far, and soon the band couldn't work with their own leader. He had become far too unpredictable, glopping strange gelatinous stuff on his head just before performing, not playing on stage, and going catatonic in front of live TV cameras just for kicks when he was supposed to be singing a song. David Gilmour, a guitarist friend of Syd's, was brought into the band in 1968 as a sort of fill in. He would play the actual guitar parts while Syd did whatever Syd wanted to. The band was on their way to a gig one night and looked around at each other to ask if they really wanted to keep going on like this. The answer was no, they simply didn't pick Syd up for the gig that night, or any night after that. This move is important in that it would later haunt bassist Roger Waters and end up being material for future works and guided his lyric direction.

Pink Floyd in 1966: Roger Waters, Nick Mason, Syd Barrett, and Rick Wright.
© Hulton-Deutsch Collection/CORBIS

Their second album, *A Saucerful of Secrets*, was recorded without Barrett at all. David Gilmour would now guide the band's musical direction while Waters would dominate the lyric songwriting. With Gilmour on guitar and main vocals, Pink Floyd would enter its most creative and productive period. Pink Floyd's management sided with Syd, who was after all the band's originator, songwriter, lead vocalist, and guitarist, putting their efforts into a solo career for him and leaving the band out of the picture. Syd, however, was in no shape to maintain any

David Gilmour. © Roger Ressmeyer/ CORBIS

semblance of sanity, much less a musical career, and promptly disappeared into his own inner world after a few critically acclaimed solo albums. Pink Floyd kept moving on, and would achieve heights only dreamed of by any band except the 'Stones.

Though much of the music on subsequent albums like *Ummagumma* and *Meddle* sound as if they're being improvised in real time, there is actually solid structure to every bar of their music. Various recordings of the same songs, like *Astronome Domine* and *Set the Controls for the Heart of the Sun*, have the same formal structure from recording to recording. It may *sound* improvised, and there is a lot of room for variation within the confines of the form, but each recording of the same song reveals just how controlled the music actually is. Historically, critics have torn them apart, calling their lengthy exploratory music the equivalent of "watching paint dry." But to their fans, there is no better band on the planet for exactly that reason. If you innately understood what they were doing with music, no amount of critical torpedoing could dissuade you of their genius.

In 1969, they released the double album set *Ummagumma*, one LP containing the full band, the other containing a collection of solo works. The musical mastery and spaced-out aspects of the long cuts on *Ummagumma* made it a mandatory album for every space cadet. Listening to album one is like stepping into some fantasy world cross between a Middle Eastern harem dream world and a glowing spaceship of the imagination careening through the cosmos. Album one, containing *Astronomy Domine, Careful with that Axe-Eugine, Set the Controls for the Heart of the Sun*, and *A Saucerful of Secrets*, with its tribal power, slashing guitar work, frantic climaxes that settle back into cloudy mists, and atmospheric Middle Eastern modal feel was a refreshing musical shift for those seeking something quite different. The truly amazing thing is that they were able to pull it all off live in concert with great precision and passion.

In 1970, they introduced an idea that would revolutionize the concert experience. A 360 degree sound system was installed in the concert halls for their performance, completely surrounding the audience with speakers. The sound man could pan the various sounds they were creating around the concert hall. The effect was described in a Los Angeles Free Press concert review in 1970:

The great thing about Pink Floyd is that they can make freaks sit down and listen. It was not an easy thing to do; it was obvious that a lot of the 3700 people were there to trip. When the sound of the 360 degree sound system started moving around the room, the people were forced into submission to be able to appreciate the effect. From then on, it was an honest concert with the audience in their seats listening.

The prototype work they recorded that would set the stage for the *Dark Side of the Moon* album was *Echoes*, off of the *Meddle* album released in 1971. Clocking in at just under twenty-four minutes, *Echoes* is as much a serious art composition as it is a space rock song. The unifying theme of the "echo," actually a Fender Rhodes piano fed through a Leslie amplifier, unites the work throughout the beginning, middle, and end.

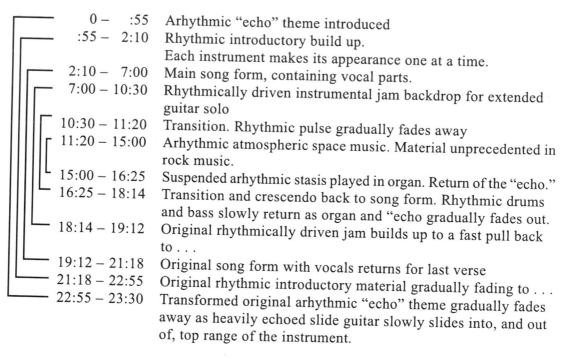

0 – :55	Arhythmic "echo" theme introduced
:55 – 2:10	Rhythmic introductory build up. Each instrument makes its appearance one at a time.
2:10 – 7:00	Main song form, containing vocal parts.
7:00 – 10:30	Rhythmically driven instrumental jam backdrop for extended guitar solo
10:30 – 11:20	Transition. Rhythmic pulse gradually fades away
11:20 – 15:00	Arhythmic atmospheric space music. Material unprecedented in rock music.
15:00 – 16:25	Suspended arhythmic stasis played in organ. Return of the "echo."
16:25 – 18:14	Transition and crescendo back to song form. Rhythmic drums and bass slowly return as organ and "echo gradually fades out.
18:14 – 19:12	Original rhythmically driven jam builds up to a fast pull back to . . .
19:12 – 21:18	Original song form with vocals returns for last verse
21:18 – 22:55	Original rhythmic introductory material gradually fading to . . .
22:55 – 23:30	Transformed original arhythmic "echo" theme gradually fades away as heavily echoed slide guitar slowly slides into, and out of, top range of the instrument.

Listen: *Echoes*   **Pink Floyd**

The piece is written in what is called **retrograde form**, meaning that the work progresses to the middle point, then from the middle of the work, the form is run backwards to the beginning, which now becomes the end. A work that ends as it begins and develops a unifying theme, not only unites the music together, but is also an expression of cyclical nature. Since rhythm is cyclical, the formal structure of the work takes on its own larger sense of rhythm. We don't sense the rhythm in the form for the same reason we don't sense the rhythm of the earth going around the sun. The time scale is larger than what we interpret as real-time rhythm. With this kind of musical understanding and ability under their belts, Pink Floyd was poised for a date with destiny. Until *Dark Side of the Moon*, Pink Floyd was well known by underground musicians and fans, but not thought of by the music industry as a band that would do much more than compose weird, marginally marketable space rock albums.

Here also, the cat was out of the bag, and space music started catching on with other musicians who would craft their own versions of it. Tangerine Dream and Hawkwind each took the space rock aspects of what Pink Floyd did and developed their own unique style of the form. The popularity of space rock has enjoyed an underground resurgence in the 1990s and into the 21st-century. Space rock festivals carry on for days on campgrounds and parks throughout the country in the summer months. The sound, the lighting, and the cosmic-oriented stage shows are all being preserved by the faithful in the same way the Deadheads are still preserving the hippie ideal. No surprise, since they're pretty much the same people.

Pink Floyd would use the musical techniques they developed up to this point, but would largely drift away from this sort of formal development of large, mainly instrumental works. Instead they would be guided more and more by the provocative metaphoric content of Waters' lyrics. *Dark Side of the Moon* was released in 1973. With its metaphors of the sun (lightness and sanity) and the moon (darkness and insanity), *Dark Side of the Moon* remains the ultimate concept album. It begins as it ends, with a heartbeat, and has thematic unity in both the music and the lyrics throughout the album. At only one point, for the song, *Money*, is there a break in the musical flow from one song to the next. The album is an iconoclastic heavyweight as well. In *Dark Side* of the Moon, stern warnings are flung about like "You run and you run to catch up with the sun, but it's sinking, and racing around to come up behind you again," and "No one told you when to run. You missed the starting gun." The big message, transformed into metaphor, comes at the end of the album, each song building into the next as the vocals cry out like a lost soul in the wilderness, when "everything under the sun is in tune, but the sun is eclipsed by the moon."

Two years later, in 1975, Pink Floyd released *Wish You Were Here*, a musical letter to their friend who they had left behind, Syd Barrett. Again, metaphor is in heavy use in the song lyrics. Everyone knew that in the song *Shine On You Crazy Diamond*, that the crazy diamond was Syd. The letter continues, almost too personal, as if you're reading somebody's diary.

> And did they get you to trade your heroes for ghosts?
> Hot ashes for trees? Hot air for a cool breeze?
> Cold comfort for change? And did you exchange
> A walk on part in the war for a lead role in a cage?

In 1977, they released the album, *Animals*, Waters' view of the people as either pigs, dogs, or sheep, and in 1979, *The Wall*, Waters' ultimate statement of self iconoclasm. *The Wall* certainly has some prime musical moments in it, but is essentially another walk with

Waters into the darkness of insanity. Throughout this period of personal iconoclasm on Waters' part, David Gilmour continued to be the star attraction at concerts with his ever-developing masterful guitar playing. On every Pink Floyd album, and at every Pink Floyd concert, there are those moments of musical inspiration and awe when Gilmour unleashes his prowess and talent on the guitar. Without his musical input, it is highly unlikely that Pink Floyd would hold the lofty spot it does in the annals of rock music.

Future Influences on Rock

Music would go down different paths in the 1970s, building upon the music that came before, as it always does given enough time. A new group, the New Yardbirds, renamed Led Zeppelin, would dominate the musical ideal of the 1970s with their blues-based power rock, inspiring an army of copycat bands playing hard rock and heavy metal. As flashy as a lot of the hard rock bands of the 1970s were, underneath all of the music was still the blues. In some ways, Jimmy Page filled the void left by Jimi Hendrix's death. That's really always how rock music has been. Whenever one superstar departs the scene, there is always a someone waiting in the wings to take their spot in the history books. And as soon as one style of music wears out its public lifetime, there's another style forming on the edges, just waiting for the chance to take center stage.

Besides Led Zeppelin's tremendously large influence on the 1970s, another new band released an album just as the 1960s came to a close that would influence hard rock music for many years to come, right up until today. In 1969, a new band called Black Sabbath released their second album, *Paranoid,* an album so pure in its heavy metal intent that it hasn't lost even one bit of edge, even compared against the deathliest of death metal bands today. True doom and destruction heavy metal was now on the agenda. Plainly speaking, Black Sabbath were the fathers of every single heavy metal band to come along since. There are no metal bands, not even one, that do not pay tribute to Ozzy Osbourne and Black Sabbath. The simple fact that someone may even be in a metal band, that itself, is a tribute to Black Sabbath. They defined what a metal band is.

Other spin-offs from the 1960s would have some lasting impact on rock music into the 1970s and beyond. Mark Bolan, a.k.a. T.Rex, single-handedly invented glam rock. David Bowie would slide onto that path and develop it into a national craze of glitter-covered space cadets in an eternal search for Ziggy Stardust and the "Star man waiting in the sky. He'd like to come and meet us, but he thinks he'd blow our minds." The New York Dolls formed in 1971, taking the energy of the Rolling Stones, dressed it up in women's clothes, and almost single handedly invented fast and furious American punk rock. A bunch of guys from the Bronx saw the New York Dolls perform and decided to out do the ever naughty she-males. The band they created was called KISS. The New York Dolls were better musicians though. In the end, however, punk, glam, and disco all came together into what became known as new wave, as the music industry once again removed the overly hard edges and milked the genres for all they were worth.

By the end of the 1960s, the psychedelic movement was waning in mass popularity, or maybe the music industry just made all the money they could from it. Regardless, it would soon drift back into the counterculture underground from where it emerged. New ideas and bands were beginning to emerge that would guide authentic hard rock of the 1970s. But before the decade was out, something unique would happen to culminate the effects of the music and movement. After Woodstock, those immersed in the counterculture would go down their own individual paths. The focus of popular attention would shift away from the hippies in the 1970s. Their image now a parody for Hollywood and Broadway shows, the counterculture faded back into the grassroots. It all still exists as much as it ever did, counterculture, the hippie ideal, neo-paganism, civil rights activism, it's just that you have to seek it out on your own. It is just as experiential as it ever was, necessitating that a person leave their house and goes out into the natural world to experience it. They don't show it on your TV.

Worksheet Assignment: Chapter 9
The Late 1960s Psychedelia

1. The term "psychedelia" translates into two words. They are

_____ _____ and _____

2. The hippies in San Francisco descended culturally from the Greenwich Village, New York City

_____

3. A new electronic musical keyboard instrument made its appearance popularly in the mid- to late-1960s, opening up for availability to musicians many new sounds, and was called a

_____

4. A massive shift in how music was delivered to a radio audience took place in the shift from

_____ to _____

5. The prime musical concept that drove psychedelic music, much like jazz, forcing musicians to explore the abilities of their instruments, was

_____

6. Stream of consciousness is an idea related to what American literary, musical, and even spiritual movement of the early 1900s?

_____

7. The hippie idealism and the people involved in it had another, more academic name for the movement, called the

_____

8. In San Francisco, the hippie culture centered around one intersection in a particularly open minded part of town. That intersection, as well as the scene itself, was called

_____ - _____

9. Draw lines connecting the following band with the leader, originator, or lead singer to the corresponding band.

The Grateful Dead   Frank Zappa

Jefferson Airplane   Big Brother & the Holding Company

Janis Joplin   Jerry Garcia

The Doors   Lou Reed

Mother of Invention   Jim Morrison

Velvet Underground   Syd Barrett

Pink Floyd   Grace Slick

10. Highlight the state of California.

11. Circle and identify San Francisco, Calif.

12. Draw a line between New York City and San Francisco, Calif.

10 From Woodstock to the Moon

Framework for Woodstock

The festival movement, or "meetings of the tribes," as they were frequently called, of the late 1960s arose from the sense of community that was shared by the hippies. That sense of community arose from the hippie's attraction to neo tribalism and neo paganism as an alternate way of life to a seemingly uncaring industrial culture. In many ways, tribalism flies in the face of corporate hyper-industrialization and the nuclear family, and paganism certainly flies in the face of the prevailing American Christian majority.

To understand why the hippies and American counterculture gravitated to neo tribalism we must first understand the nature of tribal culture versus modern industrial culture. We may then engage the possibility that the culmination of the hippie ideal—Woodstock—was possibly just a resurfacing of a way of life ingrained right into our genes through hundreds of thousands of years of evolution—a way of life we as humans have only relatively recently abandoned. The fact that music was used as a portal into neo tribalism also cannot be ignored.

A sequence of events led to Woodstock, each showing the growing potential of cooperation among the hippies. The first of the big festivals was the Monterey Pop Festival in 1967, that launched the national careers of Jimi Hendrix, Janis Joplin, and the Who, as well as introduced the hippies to authentic Indian music with the stirring performance by Ravi Shankar. Monterey had proven the potential of music to draw large crowds, outgrowing the trappings of the concert halls, and embracing the idea of presenting music to massive audiences in open outdoor settings. Other festivals in the 20,000 to 30,000 attendee range popped up around the country throughout 1968 and 1969. Though 1968 was a bad year for the radical left, the hippie movement was growing in size, bonded by their meetings of the tribes, a.k.a. music festivals.

The Apollo Factor

As well, the heightened awareness and relationship between hippies and the earth, later termed environmentalism when it became trendy, and completely validated in 1968 with the first images of Earth from deep space cannot be ignored. It's sort of like the earthrise images came streaming in from the Apollo moon missions, and some people instantly and without thought realized something deep within us as humans, that our survival as a species depended upon a nuturing relationship with our planet and each other. Remember, this was the time when humans had, for the first time in the history of humanity, been able to see themselves as inhabitants of a fragile and quiet little blue oasis suspended in the cold and unimaginably vast void of space. This paradigm shift in human awareness was not something felt by just the hippies either. Nearly ever human on planet Earth that had access to a television watched as Apollo 8 steamed back images of the earth, and later as Neil Armstrong and Buzz Aldrin represented humanity's first infant steps out of the nursery as they walked on the surface of the moon in July of 1969.

By 1969, science itself was telling the hippies what they already knew and had been practicing. There was also the feeling from the Apollo missions that we could take the best of technology into the future with us. Though the big picture of the space race was really about beating the Russians to the moon so America could sell its technology globally, when we humans took our first steps on another world, there was a overwhelming feeling that, using technology positively, we could do anything . . . go anywhere . . . achieve any goal. This is a curious dichotomy, that at the same time, and partly because of it, there was a peak in advancements in science and technology, there was also a peak in neo tribalism. In light of the old NASA saying that "we went to explore the moon and ended up discovering ourselves," the fruits of science and technology had facilitated a "return to the Garden."

In the nuclear family, we all live alone in our own little houses, with mom and dad sleeping in one room, children in another. This is very different from the way humans have lived for the vast majority of our tenure on earth. Between five and ten thousand years ago, up until the small city-states arose in Sumer, and the pyramids went up in Egypt, beginning the age of urban civilization, humans lived in small, self sufficient agricultural communities, and before the agricultural era, we lived in hunting and gathering communities. In both those communities, tribalism is the mode of social operation. Tribal cultures have existed since the beginning of humanity, between 3 and 4 million years ago. Nonstate tribal cultures were still, in fact, the major mode of human life on this planet until the expansion of the industrialized nations just 200 years ago. Even just 100 years ago, humans were tied strongly to nature by virtue of the fact that the major mode of transportation was horseback.

Another significant event of 1969 was a movie that pointed to the idea that we must be careful of what technology we do take into the future with us. *2001, A Space Odyssey* had affected a great amount of the mindset of Americans when it came out in 1969. It wasn't so much the story of a spaceships computer (HAL 9000) killing off the crew and taking control of the mission that was so infectious, though the warning about technology can not be overlooked, but the beauty of living in space that was portrayed that made people, even the Apollo astronauts, want to go there. The movie's overwhelmingly artistic and beautiful portrayal of space life, along with the very real achievements of the U.S. astronauts and the thousands of support staff working for NASA, ensured that Americans, whether mainstream or counterculture, were affected by the romantic image of humans marching forward into the final frontier. When Neil Armstrong and Buzz Aldrin walked around the surface of the Moon in July of 1969, just weeks before Woodstock, people, especially youth, were filled with the notion that we as a species could achieve anything and go any place through collaborative effort. There seemed to be no wall high enough that we couldn't throw our hat over.

Neo Tribalism: Back to the Garden

In light of the fact that our present, modern, industrialized culture in considered a recent ongoing human adaptive experiment, tribal culture is the only truly successful mode of culture that humans have ever practiced. It is similar to the biblical Garden of Eden. Everybody's needs are met, everybody meets needs, and the Earth provided the material for those needs as it was naturally. The family structure is based on the extended family of brothers, sisters, cousins, aunts and uncles, as well as other non-relatives in the tribe. In today's nuclear family, the immediate family structure is made up of just mother, father, and children. Children are left to fend off the demons of their dreams—possibly a hold over from when we were not the dominant species on the planet and had many natural predators picking on us—alone and isolated in their own rooms. Slowly, the old sense of community has been obliterated by the nuclear family of the industrial urban and suburban culture. Now, we all have our own house, usually extravagantly large in comparison to tribal housing, on a little piece of land we call our own, as opposed to shared community territory. We isolate our small children and elders away from the working adults and each other, placing the children in schools and daycare and the elders in retirement homes, as opposed to the tribal technique of utilizing a mentoring relationship between the experienced elders and the young, keeping both in vital roles.

In anthropological studies, it has been firmly acknowledged that tribal culture provides a more egalitarian and truly democratic mode of society than our present industrialized system, providing each individual a means for self-achievement that could never be explored in the stratified hyper-industrialized culture. Tribal culture is also necessarily much more in tune with a symbiotic relationship with nature—the elements, the seasons, and the earth itself—in ways that are in direct opposition to the exploitive relationship that industrialized culture has with nature. The counterculture of the hippies, realizing the apparent folly of unrestrained exploitation of nature and the absurdity of trying to change such a firmly entrenched exploitive system, gravitated back to a great amount of the tribal cultural essence. Hippies saw themselves as a tribe, linked not by family or regional, or even generational, similarity, but by the shared idealism of the tribal communal essence.

Neo Paganism

It was natural for the hippies to gravitate as well to traditional tribal spirituality, which focuses on natural elements and natural science. Tribal culture honors the earth because it provides life, food, shelter, and context. It honors the sky because the sun provides warmth and light, and the moon and stars provide more context and intrigue into our place in the universe. It honors water as the sustainer of life itself, and wind as the bringer of change. Understanding these natural elements is not a matter of romanticism. The natural world is real, and a firm understanding of it enhances the ability for a culture to survive and grow. A tribal culture may have an intense mythology surrounding the night sky, moon, and stars, but that understanding of the changing night sky also helps understand the changing seasons, a formidable ability for farmers. It's all about leaving more offspring that survive. Those that understand the seasons, farm better crops, and thus eat better, and leave more offspring. That's just simple natural selection.

The same with earth, wind, and rain. If you're hunting food and you find tracks in the mud, and have a good understanding of the erosional effects of nature, you can better tell if the tracks are old or fresh. Is the prey near? The answer lies in being able to read the clues given. Is the print worn down? Is there moss or small plants growing within the print? If so, it's an old print and the prey is far away. Or is the print fresh? Is it well defined? Are the walls of it still crumbling? If so, then the prey is near and the hunt can continue. If the hunters are successful, then the tribe eats well, and again, leaves more offspring. Or take even the age old example of moss growing on the north side of a tree. If you're lost in the forest, being able to read the signs of the natural world will point the way home. Instead of wandering in the forest until a predator finds you, in which case you will not leave many offspring, you find your way home to continue life.

The spirituality of tribal culture, known in western circles as paganism, is directly tied into the survival instincts within us. The better we understand the natural world, the more successful we become in surviving, and the more offspring we leave to continue the tribe. It should be no surprise that tribal culture should place such a high regard on the natural world as to elevate it to spiritual status. Thus the analogy to Eden, a mythical land where everything is provided for. The hippies realized that it wasn't mythical, that we could reclaim Eden if we could reconnect our traditional close relationship to the earth and the natural world.

It was this re-embracing of tribal and pagan idealism in the 1960s that gave rise to the vastly popular new age movement of today. Unfortunately, the grass-roots epiphany of tribal paganism of the 1960s has been fairly obliterated in the new age movement of today by corporate marketing profiteers. Need convincing? Check out any large bookstore's magazine section, where you will find racks of new age magazines produced for the mass market by large corporate publishers. There are a precious few authentic periodicals, but they are sadly lost in the shuffle next to the slick and stylishly produced periodical odes and tributes to Deepak Chopra, self-empowerment programs, and the rising army of sub-urban spiritual prophets for profit. Whatever authentic aspects there may be have been washed away by the same corporate strategies that smooth out the hard edges of each new style of authentic rock music to make a more marketable product for the mass market. That's not to say that earnest and sincerely authentic aspects of paganism are not to be found, just that one has to look a little deeper under the surface to find it.

In some religious doctrine, particularly western Christianity, which prevails in America, honoring the earth, sky, water, and wind is also in direct opposition to the relationship between western religion and the people. Western religion has an unseen deity, while paganism has the natural world that can be seen, felt, smelled, heard, and interacted with. Western religion claims divine dominion over the natural world, while paganism claims to be just another part of it. Thus there is a strong conflict of idealogy between the two, and there should also be no surprise that the hippies would be regarded disparagingly in their own land. But regardless of the misunderstanding in the general American public of the hippies, the deep yearning to "return to the Garden" made their numbers grow as a new generation looked around at the exploitive structures of a stratified class society, and repulsed by what they saw, sought a different path in life, socially, culturally, and spiritually. The natural choice was the system that worked for humanity successfully for millions of years before the advent of urban industrial culture—tribalism.

Tribal Idealism in Rock Music of the 1960s

The lyrics in rock music reflected many of the ideals of tribalism in the late 1960s. Songs with messages geared toward cooperation toward a common goal had replaced the songs about cars, high school, and being a teenager. The protest songwriters are the most obvious example, but also the messages in songs like *All You Need Is Love*, *Get High With a Little Help From My Friends*, *Somebody To Love*, and *I Want To Take You Higher*, to name just a few of the many, carried messages of a raising of awareness, spirit, and communal connection.

What did it all mean, and where will it lead the hippies? The answer came in August of 1969 when half a million people gathered spontaneously in a farm field in upstate New York to supposedly listen to music. Another estimated million tried, but couldn't get to the field due to road blockage. It was the largest ever gathering of people in America, and it was obvious that something much larger was taking place than just a rock music festival. Woodstock was the ultimate gathering of the tribes, and the closest the hippies had come to achieving and perfecting the hippie ideal. The hippies had proven to the world that a half a million people could come together for three days of peace and music without violence, guns, police, riots, or any of the trappings of urban conflict. The idea was that, if we could do it for three days, maybe we could do it for a week. If we could do it for a week, why not a month? Why not a year? Why not forever?

The songs were relaying the positive message of how to achieve that. Take the previously mentioned songs as examples, three of which were performed at Woodstock. *All You Need Is Love* (performed by the Beatles in front the largest television audience ever) basically says that we can achieve our goals of living peacefully with each other and the planet if we just have love for them. *Get High With a Little Help from My Friends* and *Somebody To Love* both express a need for community. *I Want To Take You Higher* expresses the need for the community to grasp itself as a community, and then raise its awareness to a higher level of cooperation.

It all came together at the Woodstock music and arts festival in Bethel, New York, on August 14, 15, and 16 of 1969. The official motto was 3 Days of Peace and Music, or as Max Yasgur, farmer and landowner that allowed the festival to happen on his land, told the massive audience "nothing but peace and music, and God bless you for it." Half a million people descended onto the festival, transforming a farm field into one of the largest cities in the world overnight. It was declared a national disaster area, food and clothes were flown in, people took care of and fed each other, and it worked. No guns. No hassles. No burning tires. No violence. No willful destruction of property. Just half a million young people living together in peace for three days and showing the world that it could be done.

Woodstock also showed the hippies how many of them there really were. They had travelled from all parts of the country, from little towns to big cities to be a part of the movement. It was so much more than the music and the bands. It was truly an army of seekers trying to find a way out of the perceived mess that had become known as the American way of life. Seekers seeking out new ways of looking at life.

List of performers at Woodstock

Joan Baez	Arlo Guthrie	Tim Hardin
Incredible String Band	Ravi Shankar	Richie Havens
Sly and the Family Stone	Bert Sommer	Sweetwater
Quill	Canned Heat	Creedence Clearwater Revival
Jefferson Airplane	The Who	Grateful Dead
Keef Hartley	Blood, Sweat and Tears	Crosby, Stills & Nash (& Young)
Santana	Jeff Beck Group	The Band
Ten Years After	Johnny Winter	Jimi Hendrix
Janis Joplin	Joe Cocker	Mountain
Melanie	Sha-Na-Na	Sebastian
Country Joe and the Fish	Paul Butterfield Blues Band	

Probably the most appropriate song performed at Woodstock was when Richie Havens returned to the stage for the sixth time. The producers were trying to figure out how to get the other performers to the site as the roads were all blocked. They kept sending Richie out to play until the helicopters could shuttle in more performers. In an act of creative desperation, Richie Havens just started playing a fast rhythmic strumming on his guitar, searching for something to sing. He looked out at the half a million people in front of him and just started to sing the word "freedom," until a song popped into his head. He then worked his improvisation into a song he used to play in the coffee houses, *Motherless Child*. The lyrics hit home with the hippies—who were greatly misunderstood, feared, despised, and outright hated by a large part of the American public—with its repeated lyric line of "Sometimes I feel like a motherless child . . . a long way from home."

Havens' "motherless child . . . a long way from home" sentiment perfectly captures the essence of what happened at Woodstock. The hippies had begun a coordinated effort to explore the possibilities of change in social and cultural structures at a grass-roots level. Because a vision of the movement as a whole had never really been worked out, to do so would take many people, one person at a time, collectively engaged in lifelong personal commitment to exploring various possibilities

The dilemma for the movement was not uncertainty in what the movement as a whole needed to accomplish, but what each individual needed to do help define the vision and goals of change. What path was right for the individual? That question drove the majority of the festival goers at Woodstock. These seekers within the movement, the majority of the hippies, went to Woodstock not because they knew something they believed to be true, but because they were seeking answers to the many different questions raised by the shift toward social and cultural awareness, and a path for themselves to follow as individuals. For many, the path defined itself when they discovered and partook in the intense sense of community and cooperation at Woodstock, realizing an authentic, if temporary, state of tribal utopia.

When their numbers grew at Woodstock into the hundreds of thousands, it was clear to the hippies that their movement was much larger in both number and scope than even they had estimated. There's no doubt that there was lots of music, but there was also seminars on yoga and meditation, speeches by eastern spiritual leaders, and in a colossal effort of cooperation, every person was fed by the free kitchens, treated by volunteer medical staff, and generally watched over by every other member of the tribe. Resources were limited, but shared equally.

A moment of pure egalitarianism flowered when it poured down rain long enough to completely drench every single person there. Suddenly it didn't matter where you were from, how much money you had, what you believed socially or spiritually, how good a sleeping bag or tent you had, even what kind of shoes you wore. Everything and everybody got wet, effectively equalizing the entire Woodstock population. Then, in the true spirit of optimism, the rain itself became an event. People on stage grabbed microphones to start a "no rain" chant picked up by the audience. One of the best recordings of music from the festival was performed by the audience in what is titled the Rain Chant. Sounding exactly like an African drum chant, the audience rallied behind a few bongo drummers in a vocal chorus of tribal singing as a way of making it through the downpour.

If they weren't in tune to a tribal sense of community when they first got there, they certainly were now. In the end, the hippies proved that we could live together in peace and harmony if we *really wanted* to. They demonstrated for the world to see that we really are all one race—the Human Race.

Worksheet Assignment: Chapter 10
From Woodstock to the Moon

1. The Woodstock festival was called "Three Days of

   _____ and _____

2. Name the man whose farm was used for the Woodstock festival.

   _____

3. The hippie movement culminated at Woodstock, with young people discovering for the first time a new (or rather, old) way of living life called

   neo _____

4. The renewed spiritual system centered on honoring the Earth and living in peace with the planet and each other that this was all based on is known as

   neo _____

5. Approximately how many people attended Woodstock?

   _____

6. Was Woodstock a financial success?

   _____

7. Was Woodstock a social and cultural success?

   _____

8. A sense among Americans that "anything is possible" was most strongly instilled in the events of the day, most predominantly by an event that brought a million people to the beaches of Florida just three weeks before Woodstock? What event was it?

   _____

9. Before that even, the entire world received a wake-up call when television images from the Apollo 8 mission (Christmas Eve, 1968) to orbit the Moon came streaming back, and the people of Earth were able, for the first time in human history, to

   _____

10. In what event did the participants and attendees of Woodstock partake in the lake that allowed them to free the inhibitions that they had been raised to adhere to?

_____

11. Though the attendees at Woodstock came from all corners of America, life, social status, and cultural background, what event equalized everyone at Woodstock?

_____

12. Highlight the state of New York on the map below.

11 The 1970s— Out with the Old—In with the New

Hard Rock

Blues Rock—Led Zeppelin: Dominators of the 1970s

Led Zeppelin was the definitive blues based hard rock band. It wasn't just their crushingly loud interpretation of the blues—it was how they incorporated mythology, mysticism, and a variety of other genres (most notably world music and British folk)—into their sound. Led Zeppelin had mystique. They rarely gave interviews, since the music press detested the band. Consequently, the only connection the audience had with the band was through the records and the concerts. More than any other band, Led Zeppelin established the concept of album-oriented rock, refusing to release popular songs from their albums as singles. In doing so, they established the dominant format for heavy metal, as well as the genre's actual sound.

Led Zeppelin formed out of the ashes of the Yardbirds. Jimmy Page had joined the band in its final days, playing a pivotal role on their final album, 1967's *Little Games*, which also featured string arrangements from John Paul Jones. During 1967, the Yardbirds were fairly inactive. While the Yardbirds decided their future, Page returned to session work in 1967. In the spring of 1968, he played on Jones' arrangement of Donovan's *Hurdy Gurdy Man*. During the sessions, Jones requested to be part of any future project Page would develop. Page would have to assemble a band sooner than he had planned. In the summer of 1968, the Yardbirds' Keith Relf and James McCarty left the band, leaving Page and bassist Chris Dreja with the rights to the name, as well as the obligation of fulfilling an upcoming fall tour. Page set out to find a replacement vocalist and drummer. Page contacted Robert Plant, who was singing with a band called Hobbstweedle.

After hearing him sing, Page asked Plant to join the band in August of 1968. John Paul Jones joined the group as its bassist. Plant recommended that Page hire John Bonham, the drummer for Plant's old band, the Band of Joy. By September, Bonham agreed to join the band. Performing under the name the New Yardbirds, the band fulfilled the Yardbirds' previously booked engagements in late September 1968. The following month, they recorded their debut album in just under 30 hours. Also in October, the group switched their name to Led Zeppelin. The band secured a contract with Atlantic Records in the United States before the end of the year.

That in itself is a stroke of music business genius. Atlantic Records had built a reputation as a predominantly black music record label, giving rise to such artists as Aretha Franklin. Atlantic Records expanded their reach in the music industry tremendously with Led Zeppelin in the fold. Certainly it was a bit of a business gamble, for who could know that Led Zeppelin would become the prime dominating force in rock music throughout the 1970s? This is in the same light as Sun Records selling Elvis Presley to RCA for forty thousand dollars just to see RCA see a return on their investment in the neighborhood of ten million records sold in just that first year that Elvis was with RCA. Atlantic records signing Led Zeppelin was probably one of the most daring and rewarding music business ventures of any record label in the whole history of rock music.

Early in 1969, Led Zeppelin set out on their first American tour, which helped set the stage for the January release of their eponymous debut album. Two months after its release, Led Zeppelin had climbed into the U.S. Top Ten. Throughout 1969, the band toured relentlessly, playing dates in America and England. While they were on the road, they recorded their second album, *Led Zeppelin II*, which was released in October of 1969. Like its predecessor, *Led Zeppelin II* was an immediate hit, topping the American charts two months after its release and spending seven weeks at number one.

The album helped establish Led Zeppelin as an international concert attraction, and for the next year, the group continued to tour relentlessly. Led Zeppelin's sound began to deepen with *Led Zeppelin III*. Released in October of 1970, the album featured an overt British folk influence. The group's infatuation with folk and mythology would reach a fruition on the group's untitled fourth album, which was released in November of 1971. *Led Zeppelin IV* was the band's most musically diverse effort to date, featuring everything from the crunching rock of *Black Dog* to the folk of *The Battle of Evermore*, as well as *Stairway to Heaven*, which found the bridge between the two genres.

Stairway to Heaven was an immediate radio hit, eventually becoming the most played song in the history of album-oriented radio; the song was never released as a single. Despite the fact that the album never reached number one in America, *Led Zeppelin IV* was their biggest album ever, selling well over 16 million copies over the next two and a half decades. Again, another stroke of genius in the music business. They knew they had a hit song with *Stairway*, and they knew that a single release of the song would take away from the album sales. So by not releasing the song as a single, album sales on *Led Zeppelin IV* remained brisk and lucrative, even so still today.

Led Zeppelin did tour to support both *Led Zeppelin III* and *Led Zeppelin IV*, but they played fewer shows than they did on their previous tours. Instead, they concentrated on only playing larger venues. After completing their 1972 tour, the band retreated from the spotlight and recorded their fifth album. Released in the spring of 1973, *Houses of the Holy* continued the band's musical experimentation, featuring touches of funk and reggae among their trademark heavy metal rock and folk.

The success of *Houses of the Holy* set the stage for a record-breaking American tour. Throughout their 1973 tour, Led Zeppelin broke box-office records—most of which were previously held by the Beatles—across America. The group's concert at Madison Square

Garden in July was filmed for use in the feature film *The Song Remains the Same*, which was released three years later.

After their 1973 tour, Led Zeppelin spent a quiet year during 1974, releasing no new material and performing no concerts. They did, however, establish their own record label, Swan Song, which released all of Led Zeppelin's subsequent albums. *Physical Graffiti*, a double album released in February of 1975, was the band's first release on Swan Song. The album was an immediate success, topping the charts in both America and England. Led Zeppelin launched a large American tour in 1975, but it came to a halt when Robert Plant and his wife suffered a serious car crash while vacationing in Greece. The tour was cancelled, and Plant spent the rest of the year recuperating from the accident.

Led Zeppelin returned to action in the spring of 1976 with *Presence*. Although the album debuted at number one in both America and England, the reviews for the album were lukewarm, as was the reception to the live concert film *The Song Remains the Same*, which appeared in the fall of 1976. The band finally returned to tour America in the spring of 1977. A couple of months into the tour, Plant's six-year-old son Karac died of a stomach infection. Led Zeppelin immediately cancelled the tour and offered no word whether or not it would be rescheduled, causing not only widespread speculation about the band's future, but wild speculations about cult activity and their attraction to mysticism.

Led Zeppelin caught in the act of dominating the 1970s. © Neal Preston/CORBIS

For a while, it did appear that Led Zeppelin was finished. Robert Plant spent the latter half of 1977 and the better part of 1978 in seclusion. But by then, the large venue rock scene was in full bloom, so rock fans barely noticed the absence, assuming that the band would certainly be back on stage sooner or later. Strangely enough though, other changes were brewing in music that would soon wipe the large, theatrical heavy metal sound and shows into the backdrop of the whole rock music landscape. Punk rock, a lashing out at the overly flamboyant arena rock environment, was gaining a strong foothold, and inner city break dancing hip hoppers and rappers were making their presence felt. As well, disco was merging with punk energy in the late 1970s, creating the first of the new wave bands like Blondie. The landscape of rock music was expanding faster than most people, even record industry executives, could keep track of. Bands that were on top of the world just a year or two earlier, were finding the musical shifts happening at a pace that few could keep up with. It seemed that every year there was a new style, new breed of rock musician, new venues and smaller halls, and shifts in all these elements as new people rushed to the scene. The late 1970s was probably one of the most uncertain and fast changing times in American music, and Led Zeppelin, as staunch and stable a rock band that ever was, was also feeling the shifts in society, culture, and fickle musical tastes.

The group didn't begin work on a new album until late in the summer of 1978, when they began recording at ABBA's Polar studios in Sweden. A year later, the band played a short European tour, performing in Switzerland, Germany, Holland, Belgium, and Austria. In August of 1979, Led Zeppelin played two large concerts at Knebworth; the shows would be their last English performances.

In Through the Out Door, the band's much-delayed eighth studio album, was finally released in September of 1979. But by then, the musical landscape was so utterly changed from just a couple of years earlier, Led Zeppelin was already seen as classic rock, a new category describing the arena and festival big show rock of the late 1960s and 1970s.

Led Zeppelin was, however, Led Zeppelin. The album entered the charts at number one in both America and England. In May of 1980, Led Zeppelin embarked on their final European tour. In September, Led Zeppelin began rehearsing at Jimmy Page's house in preparation for an American tour. On September 25, John Bonham was found dead in his bed—following an all-day drinking binge. In December of 1980, Led Zeppelin announced they were disbanding, since they could not continue without Bonham.

In 1994, Jimmy Page and Robert Plant reunited to record a segment for *MTV Unplugged*, which was released as *Unledded* in the fall of 1994. Although the album went platinum, the sales were disappointing considering the anticipation of a Zeppelin reunion. The following year, Page and Plant embarked on a successful international tour, which eventually led to an all new studio recording in 1998. The duo still perform and record, but have shunned the "Led Zeppelin" image and bombast. They have both evolved quite a bit musically right on up to today and continue to do so—Page working with numerous younger bands, and Plant exploring various aspects of world music.

Heavy Metal

Black Sabbath

Black Sabbath has been so influential in the development of heavy metal rock music as to be a defining force in the style.

Once Led Zeppelin kicked open the door to heavy metal, in came some of the most defining artists in the development of the genre as a driving force in popular music. No band defined the whole style, attitude, theatrics and musical vocabulary as Black Sabbath. Their influence is felt today in heavy metal, death metal, speed metal, and any other kind of metal more than any band to come out of the genre. They took the foundations that Hendrix and Led Zeppelin laid down, transformed it with theatrics with a "dark side" theme, and simply changed the entire landscape of the genre. All the bombastically dark heavy metal, as well as the varied offshoots we see today such as goth (oh those poor children . . . won't someone give them something to eat and tell them that living isn't so bad?), industrial, or any musical style and scene that plays up the whole tortured, dark hearted but tough, "we're gonna' eat your children" theatrics in their music can thank one band for opening that dark dungeon door.

The group took the blues-rock sound of late 1960s acts like Cream, Jimi Hendrix, Led Zeppelin, and the one-hit wonder Iron Butterfly to its logical conclusion, slowing the tempo, emphasizing the bass, and, most importantly for our musical discussion, shining the spotlight most dominantly on searing guitar solos and howled vocals full of lyrics expressing mental anguish and dark fantasies. If their predecessors clearly came out of an electrified blues tradition, Black Sabbath took that tradition, dressed it in theatrics based on a theme and guided the course of this genre right up to today.

The group was formed by four teenage friends from Aston, near Birmingham, England: Anthony "Tony" Iommi, guitar; William "Bill" Ward, drums; John "Ozzy" Osbourne, vocals; and Terence "Geezer" Butler, bass. They originally called their band Polka Tulk, later renaming themselves Earth, and they played extensively in Europe. In early 1969, they decided to change their name again when they found that they were being mistaken for another group called Earth. Butler had written a song that took its title from a novel by occult writer Dennis Wheatley,

Ozzy at his tricks. © S.I.N./CORBIS

Black Sabbath, and the group adopted it as their name as well. As they attracted attention for their live performances, record labels showed interest, and they were signed to Phillips Records in 1969. In January 1970, the Phillips subsidiary Fontana released their debut single, *Evil Woman (Don't Play Your Games With Me)*, a cover of a song that had just become a United States hit for Crow; it did not chart. The following month, a different Phillips subsidiary, Vertigo, released Black Sabbath's self-titled debut album, which reached the U.K. Top Ten. Though it was a less immediate success in the United States—where the band's recordings were licensed to Warner Bros. Records and appeared in May 1970—the LP broke into the American charts in August, reaching the Top 40, remaining in the charts over a year, and selling a million copies.

As exemplified by the diversity found in all the musical styles and sounds available by the time rock music finds itself at Woodstock, the 1960s proved without a doubt that many different aspects of popular music could be integrated into an eclectic style with broad appeal. The Beatles were as likely to perform an acoustic ballad as a hard rocker or R&B-influenced tune. The array of music styles and sounds at the Monterey Pop Festival or Woodstock was, beyond any doubt, a vastly rich gumbo of all the musical roots that went into rock music to that point. The audience had shown that it would accept any creative adaptation and interpretation.

Though the musical press at the time didn't put a whole lot of support behind an act like Black Sabbath, the band had discovered a new audience eager for its uncompromising approach. Black Sabbath quickly followed its debut album with a second album, *Paranoid*, in September 1970. This album is not only responsible for luring droves of teens to music stores to buy guitars and fuzz boxes, but drew in a young fan base seeking something new, fresh sounding, and certainly an irritant to parents, which is what a teenager wants to do anyway. Remember, this is the peak time of the generation gap, and a popular saying was "If your parents hate it, then it must be good." Black Sabbath, and particularly the *Paranoid* album, certainly gave parents something to hate, or at the very least worry about.

Master of Reality, their third album, followed in August 1971, reaching the Top Ten on both sides of the Atlantic and selling over a million copies. For *Sabbath Bloody Sabbath* (November 1973), the band brought in prog rocker and Yes keyboard player Rick Wakeman, signaling a slight change in musical direction; it was Black Sabbath's fifth straight Top Ten hit and million-seller. In July 1975, with their sixth album, *Sabotage*, they were welcomed back at home, but in the United States the musical climate had changed.

By the mid-1970s, the album oriented, big theatrical show bands were finding themselves the target of a new generation of musicians, tired of the extravagant environment of arena rock, but just as aggressive musically, if not more so—the punks. The mainstream pop market was going in a direction of less heavy, aggressive music, while the underground music world was driving into harder and darker, in-your-face political directions. Black Sabbath and the legions of new heavy metal bands who emulated them were caught in the middle of all this. Some adapted to the pop market, merging it with glam and giving rise to an army of pretty boy hair metal bands. Some went in the other direction, taking heavy metal into ever darker, slower, more aggressive death metal. Some took heavy metal in directions that had nothing to do with either selling out to the pop mainstream or singing low odes to darkness dirges—the speed metal bands. The notable aspect of what Black Sabbath started, and heavy metal as a genre, is that while heavy metal may have had its ups and downs, it's still there, and it's still branching off in differ-ent directions. It adapts and incorporates new styles—mostly from underground musical genres, such as punk and industrial or anything with an edge to it. It's real. **And it** evolves. So whether you are fan of heavy metal or not, there's no denying that there's an attraction to it when each new generation hits that rebellious youth phase of teenagedom.

Punk Rock

Iggy Pop—Birth of a True Punk

Iggy Pop was the first. Sure, there were other predecessors that had the punk sound, but Iggy Pop was the guy who put the anger and politics and attitude to it all that so many bands to follow would incorporate. Iggy was definitely an in-your-face sort of musician and songwriter. He defined what being "punk" was for just about every punk rocker to follow. Again, we have an individual whose influence can be easily seen and heard through-out the history of rock music. Since he presented his version of rock music to the world, his aggressive influence on style and attitude have guided each generation that follows.

There's a reason why many consider Iggy Pop the godfather of punk—every single punk band of the past and present has either knowingly or unknowingly borrowed a thing or two from Pop and his late 1960s/early 1970s band, the Stooges. Born on April 21, 1947, in Muskegon, Mich., James Newell Osterberg was intrigued by rock and roll. Osterberg began playing drums and formed his first band, the Iguanas, in the early 1960s. Via the Rolling Stones, Osterberg discovered the blues, forming a similarly styled outfit, called the Prime Movers, upon graduating from high school in 1965. When a brief stint at the University of Michigan didn't work out, Osterberg moved to Chicago, playing drums alongside bluesmen.

But his true love was still rock and roll, and shortly after returning to Ann Arbor, Osterberg decided to form a rock band, but this time, he would leave the drums behind and be the frontman (inspired by the Velvet Underground's Lou Reed and the Doors' Jim Morrison). He tried to find the right musicians who shared his same musical vision: to create a band whose music would be primordial, sexually charged, political, and aggres-sive. In 1967, he hooked up with an old acquaintance from his high school days, guitarist Ron Asheton, who also brought along his drummer brother Scott, and bassist Dave Alexander, forming the Psychedelic Stooges. Although it would take a while for their sound to gel—they experimented with such non-traditional instruments as empty oil drums, vacuums, and other objects before returning to their respective instruments—the group fit in perfectly with such other high-energy Detroit bands as the MC5, becoming a local attraction.

Iggy on a mission to search and destroy.
© Boutard, David/CORBIS KIPA

It was around this time that the group shortened their name to the Stooges, and Osterberg changed his stage name to Iggy Pop. With the name change, Pop became a man possessed on-stage—going into the crowd nightly to confront members of the audience and working himself into such a frenzy that he would be bleeding by the end of the night from various nicks and scratches. (Eventually, Iggy would take that aspect of his act to dangerous levels throughout the early 1970s, before recreating his image in the later 1970s to a more fit, healthy, even muscular Iggy and a music not quite so confrontational.)

Elektra Records signed the quartet in 1968, issuing their self-titled debut a year later, and a follow-up in 1970, *Funhouse*. Although both records sold poorly upon release, both have become rock classics and can be pointed to as the official beginning of what would become known as punk rock. The group was dropped from their record company in 1971 due to the public's disinterest and the group's growing addictions to hard drugs (and additionally in Pop's case, continuous death-defying acts like stage diving onto a bed of broken shards of glass), leading to the group's breakup the same year.

But Stooges fan and sky-rocketing rock star David Bowie tracked down Pop and convinced the newly clean and sober singer to restart his career. Pop enlisted guitarist James Williamson (who was briefly a second guitarist for the Stooges before their breakup), and after the pair signed to Bowie's Mainman management company and relocated to England, eventually reunited with the Asheton brothers (with Ron moving from the six-string to the bass).

Signed by major label Columbia Records and hoping to follow in Bowie's footsteps toward a major commercial breakthrough, the Stooges penned another punk classic—the brutally explosive *Raw Power*. Pop's plan for the Stooges' third release overall would be to create a record that would be so over the top sonically that it would actually hurt you when it poured out of the speakers. Although it may not have been that extreme, it came pretty close (with Bowie signed on as the producer), but yet again, the album sank without a trace in the mainstream. But the underground music scene, driven primarily by college radio, was in no way forgetting Iggy.

It was right about this time—the mid-1970s—that mainstream commercial rock radio was becoming so self-absorbed and disconnected from new trends that a new generation of rock fans were seeking something fresh, raw, and real. Commercial radio was something your older brother listened to, but college radio was hitting its most vital period. You could hear real, non-corporate rock there, and hear it commercial free all the time. Sure, you might have to put up with a Slovenian Hour or German Hour or some public service radio show every now and then, but for the most part, college radio programmers were the only vital and evolving force in rock music in the late 1970s and into the 1980s. That is, until CMJ came along (College Music Journal) as a means by which corporate record companies could tap into and exert control on the college radio music market. Just like after Woodstock, when the corporate music business world saw the numbers of people attending rock concerts and said to its collective self, "wow, look at that . . . market," the corporate music industry saw a market developing in underground college radio and the bands and audiences that fed it and rushed in to control it as best they could while attempting to maintain an image of "indie" there.

While FM album-oriented, commercial rock radio, along with their "zoo crews" and "work in the factory—party on the weekends" attitudes and format, were putting their older hippie siblings to sleep and giving them a soundtrack for their entrance into suburban life, this next generation—post Baby Boomer but pre-GenX, sometimes referred to as the "blank" generation because of that, had gravitated to the left end of the radio dial where all the college stations are. This was the realm of Iggy and the Stooges and countless other bands who could not find a place in the mainstream pop rock market no matter what the music industry marketers in New York City tried.

By 1974, Pop and most of the Stooges' star was fading fast before it even shined in the mainstream, the band called it quits for a second and final time. After a brief spell becoming very disassociated with the rock scene and more associated with hospitals and actual homelessness, Pop would soon rise again from his own ashes. During a hospital stay, an old friend came to visit him. David Bowie, whose career was still in high gear, offered to take Pop on the road with him during his tour in support of *Station to Station*. The pair got along so well that they both moved to Berlin in late 1976, during which time Bowie helped Pop secure a solo record deal with Virgin. Bowie was interested in European electronic rock (Kraftwerk, Can, etc.) and admitted later that he used Pop as a musical guinea pig on such releases as *The Idiot* and *Lust for Life* (both issued in 1977 and produced/co-written by Bowie). Both albums sold better than his previous efforts with the Stooges, but at the price of losing much of the edge that Iggy was known for in the underground music scene. Bowie also toured in support of these albums as Pop's keyboardist. Pop would vacillate between polished work with Bowie and raw punk music out on his own, but he would always maintain that essence of what it is to be punk. His influence was most strongly felt in the late 1980s and early 1990s with the emergence of neo punk and grunge bands such as Nirvana, Mudhoney, and Soundgarden.

Around the same time, a wide variety of bands covered Pop and/or Stooges tracks—Slayer, Duran Duran, Guns N' Roses, R.E.M., and even Tom Jones, while Pop issued another fine solo set, 1993's *American Caesar*. Pop enjoyed another hit when the nearly twenty-year-old title-track from *Lust for Life* was used prominently on the hit movie soundtrack *Trainspotting*, providing the punk legend with a fresh generation of fans. Iggy Pop almost single-handedly created an entire genre of music and remains one of rock's top live performers and all-time influential artists.

Glam Rock

New York Dolls

While Iggy Pop was mutilating himself and declaring to the world that he was here to "Search and Destroy," the New York Dolls created their own version of punk rock before there was a term for it. Building on the Rolling Stones' dirty rock and roll, Mick Jagger's androgyny, girl group pop, the glam rock of David Bowie and T. Rex, and the Stooges' anarchic noise, the New York Dolls created a new form of hard rock that presaged both punk rock and heavy metal. Their drug-fueled, theatrical performances and crossdressing attitude influenced a generation of musicians in New York and London, who all went on to form punk bands. The most notable fan of the Dolls that went on to create their own version of what the Dolls were trying to do was Gene Simmons, who took what he saw of the New York Dolls performances and created Kiss. And although they self-destructed quickly, the band's two albums remain two of the most popular cult records in rock and roll history.

All of the members of the New York Dolls played in New York bands before they formed in late 1971. Guitarists Johnny Thunders and Rick Rivets, bassist Arthur Kane, and drummer Billy Murcia were joined by vocalist David Johansen. Early in 1972, Rivets was replaced by Syl Sylvian, and the group began playing regularly in lower Manhattan, particularly at the Mercer Arts Center. Within a few months, they had earned a dedicated cult following, but record companies were afraid of signing the band because of their cross-dressing and blatant vulgarity.

The New York Dolls in full regalia.
© Bettman/CORBIS

Late in 1972, the New York Dolls embarked on their first tour of England. During the tour, drummer Murcia died after mixing drugs and alcohol. He was replaced by Jerry Nolan. After Nolan joined the band, the Dolls finally secured a record contract with Mercury Records. Todd Rundgren—whose sophisticated pop seemed at odds with the band's crash-and-burn rock and roll—produced the band's eponymous debut, which appeared in the summer of 1973. The record received overwhelmingly positive reviews, but it didn't stir the interest of the general public; the album peaked at number 116 on the U.S. charts. The band's follow-up, *Too Much Too Soon*, was produced by the legendary girl group producer George "Shadow" Morton. Although the sound of the record was relatively streamlined, the album was another commercial failure, only reaching number 167 upon its early summer 1974 release.

Following the disappointing sales of their two albums, Mercury Records dropped the New York Dolls. No other record labels were interested in the band, so they decided to hire a new manager, the British Malcolm McLaren, who would soon become famous for managing the Sex Pistols. With the Dolls, McLaren began developing his skill for turning shock into invaluable publicity. Although he made it work for the Pistols just a year later, all of his strategies backfired for the Dolls. McLaren made the band dress completely in red leather and perform in front of the USSR's flag; all of which meant to symbolize the Dolls' alleged communist allegiance. The new approach only made record labels more reluctant to sign the band and members soon began leaving the group.

By the middle of 1975, Thunders and Nolan left the Dolls. The remaining members, Johansen and Sylvain, fired McLaren and assembled a new lineup of the band. For the next two years, the duo led a variety of different incarnations of the band to no success. In 1977, Johansen and Sylvain decided to break up the band permanently. Over the next two decades, various outtakes collections, live albums, and compilations were released by a variety of labels and the New York Dolls' two original studio albums never went out of print.

Upon the Dolls' break up, David Johansen began a solo career that would eventually metamorphose into his lounge-singing alter-ego Buster Poindexter in the mid-1980s. Syl Sylvain played with Johansen for two years before he left to pursue his own solo career. Johnny Thunders formed the Heartbreakers with Jerry Nolan after they left the group in 1975. Over the next decade, the Heartbreakers would perform sporadically and Thunders would record the occasional solo album. On April 23, 1991, Thunders—who was one of the more notorious drug abusers in rock and roll history—died of a heroin overdose. Nolan performed at a tribute concert for Thunders later in 1991; a few months later, he died of a stroke at the age of forty.

T-Rex

Initially a British folk-rock combo called Tyrannosaurus Rex, T. Rex was the primary force in glam rock, thanks to the creative direction of guitarist/vocalist Marc Bolan (born Marc Feld). Bolan created a deliberately trashy form of rock and roll that was proud of its own disposability. T. Rex's music borrowed the underlying sexuality of early rock and roll, adding dirty, simple grooves and fat distorted guitars, as well as an overarching folky/hippie spirituality that always came through the clearest on ballads. While most of his peers concentrated on making cohesive albums, Bolan kept the idea of a three-minute pop single alive in the early 1970s. In Britain, he became a superstar, sparking a period of "T. Rextacy" among the pop audience with a series of Top Ten hits, including four number one singles. Over in America, the group only had one major hit—the Top Ten *Bang a Gong (Get It On)*—before disappearing from the charts in 1973. T. Rex's popularity in the U.K. didn't begin to waver until 1975, yet they retained a devoted following until Marc Bolan's death in 1977. Over the next two decades, Bolan emerged as a cult figure and the music of T. Rex has proven quite influential on hard rock, punk, new wave, and alternative rock.

Following a career as a teenage model, Marc Bolan began performing music professionally in 1965, releasing his first single, *The Wizard*, on Decca Records. Bolan joined the psychedelic folk-rock combo John's Children in 1967, appearing on three unsuccessful singles before the group disbanded later that year. Following the breakup, he formed the folk duo Tyrannosaurus Rex with percussionist Steve Peregrine Took. The duo landed a record deal with a subsidiary of EMI in February 1968, recording their debut album with producer Tony Visconti. *Debora*, the group's first single, peaked at number thirty-four in May of that year, and their debut album, *My People Were Fair and Had Sky in Their Hair . . . But Now They're Content to Wear Stars on Their Brow*, reached number fifteen shortly afterward. The duo released their second album, *Prophets, Seers & Sages, the Angels of the Ages*, in November of 1968.

By this time, Tyrannosaurus Rex was building a sizable underground following, which helped Bolan's book of poetry, *The Warlock of Love*, enter the British best-seller charts. In the summer of 1969, the duo released their third album, *Unicorn*, as well as the single *King of the Rumbling Spires*, the first Tyrannosaurus Rex song to feature an electric guitar. Following an unsuccessful American tour that fall, Took left the band and was replaced by Mickey Finn. The new duo's first single did not chart, yet their first album, 1970's *A Beard of Stars*, reached number twenty-one.

The turning point in Bolan's career came in October of 1970, when he shortened the group's name to T. Rex and released *Ride a White Swan*, a fuzz-drenched single driven by a rolling backbeat. *Ride a White Swan* became a major hit in the U.K., climbing all the way to number two. The band's next album, T. Rex, peaked at number thirteen and stayed on the charts for six months. Encouraged by the results, Bolan expanded T. Rex to a full band, adding bassist Steve Currie and drummer Bill Legend (born Bill Fifield). The new lineup recorded *Hot Love*, which spent six weeks at number one in early 1971. That summer, T. Rex released *Get It On* (retitled *Bang a Gong (Get It On)* in the United States), which became their second straight U.K. number one; the single would go on to be their biggest international hit, reaching number ten in the United States in 1972. *Electric Warrior*, the first album recorded by the full band, was released in the fall of 1971; it was number one for six weeks in Britain and cracked America's Top Forty.

By now, "T. Rextacy" was in full swing in England, as the band had captured the imaginations of both teenagers and the media with its sequined, heavily made-up appearance; the image of Marc Bolan in a top hat, feather boa, and platform shoes, performing *Get It On* on the BBC became as famous as his music. At the beginning of 1972, T. Rex signed with EMI, setting up a distribution deal for Bolan's own T.Rex Wax Co. record label. *Telegram Sam*, the group's first EMI single, became their third number one single.

Marc Bolan of T. Rex.
© Denis O'Regan/CORBIS

Metal Guru also hit number one, spending four weeks at the top of the chart. *The Slider*, released in the summer of 1972, shot to number one upon its release, allegedly selling 100,000 copies in four days; the album was also T. Rex's most successful American release, reaching number seventeen. Appearing in the spring of 1973, *Tanx* was another Top Five hit for T. Rex; the singles *20th Century Boy* and *The Groover* soon followed it to the upper ranks of the charts. However, those singles would prove to be the band's last two Top Ten hits. In the summer of 1973, rhythm guitarist Jack Green joined the band, as did three backup vocalists, including the American soul singer Gloria Jones; Jones would soon become Bolan's girlfriend. At the beginning of 1974, drummer Bill Legend left the group and was replaced by Davy Lutton, as Jones became the group's keyboardist.

In early 1974, the single *Teenage Dream* was the first record to be released under the name Marc Bolan and T. Rex. The following album, *Zinc Alloy and the Hidden Riders of Tomorrow*, was the last Bolan recorded with Tony Visconti. Throughout the year, T. Rex's popularity rapidly declined—by the time *Zip Gun Boogie* was released in November, it could only reach number forty-one. Finn and Green left the group at the end of the year, while keyboardist Dino Dins joined. The decline of T. Rex's popularity was confirmed when 1975's *Bolan's Zip Gun* failed to chart. Bolan took the rest of the year off, returning in the spring of 1976 with *Futuristic Dragon*, which peaked at number fifty. Released in the summer of 1976, *I Love to Boogie*, a disco-flavored three-chord thumper, became Bolan's last Top Twenty hit.

Bolan released *Dandy in the Underworld* in the spring of 1977; it was a modest hit, peaking at number twenty-six. While *The Soul of My Suit* reached number forty-two on the charts, T. Rex's next two singles failed to chart. Sensing it was time for a change of direction, Bolan began expanding his horizons in August. In addition to contributing a weekly column for Record Mirror, he hosted his own variety television show, *Marc*. Featuring guest appearances by artists like David Bowie and Generation X, *Marc* helped restore Bolan's hip image. Signing with RCA Records, the guitarist formed a new band with bassist Herbie Flowers and drummer Tony Newman, yet he never was able to record with the group. While driving home from a London club with Bolan, Gloria Jones lost control of her car, smashing into a tree. Marc Bolan, riding in the passenger's seat of the car, was killed instantly.

While T. Rex's music was intended to be disposable, it has proven surprisingly influential over the years. Hard rock and heavy metal bands borrowed the group's image, as well as the pounding insistence of their guitars. Punk bands may have discarded the high heels, feather boas, and top hats, yet they adhered to the simple three-chord structures and pop aesthetics that made the band popular.

David Bowie—The Man Who Fell to Earth

The cliché about David Bowie says he's a musical chameleon, adapting himself according to fashion and trends. While such a criticism is too glib, there's no denying that Bowie demonstrated remarkable skill for perceiving musical trends at his peak in the 1970s. After spending several years in the late 1960s as a mod and as an all-around music-hall entertainer, Bowie reinvented himself as a hippie singer/songwriter. Prior to his breakthrough in 1972, he recorded a proto-metal record and a pop/rock album, eventually redefining glam rock with his ambiguously sexy Ziggy Stardust persona. Ziggy made Bowie an international star, yet he wasn't content to continue to churn out glitter rock. By the mid-1970s, he developed an effete, sophisticated version of Philly soul that he dubbed "plastic soul," which eventually morphed into the eerie avant-pop of 1976's *Station to Station*. Shortly afterward, he relocated to Berlin, where he recorded three experimental electronic albums with Brian Eno. At the dawn of the 1980s, Bowie was still at the height of his powers, yet following his blockbuster dance-pop album *Let's Dance* in 1983, he slowly sank into mediocrity before salvaging his career in the early 1990s. Even when he was out of fashion in the 1980s and 1990s, it was clear that Bowie was one of the most influential musicians in rock, for better and for worse. Each one of his phases in the 1970s sparked a number of subgenres, including punk, new wave, goth rock, the new romantics, and electronica. Few rockers ever had such lasting impact.

David Jones began performing music when he was thirteen years old, learning the saxophone while he was at Bromley Technical High School; another pivotal event happened at the school, when his left pupil became permanently dilated in a schoolyard fight. Following his graduation at sixteen, he worked as a commercial artist while playing saxophone in a number of mod bands, including the King Bees, the Manish Boys (which also featured Jimmy Page as a session man), and Davey Jones & the Lower Third. All three of those bands released singles, which were generally ignored, yet he continued performing, changing his name to David Bowie in 1966 after the Monkees' Davy Jones became an international star. Over the course of 1966, he released three mod singles on Pye Records, which were all ignored. The following year, he signed with Deram, releasing the music hall, Anthony Newley-styled *David Bowie* that year. Upon completing the record, he spent several weeks in a Scottish Buddhist monastery. Once he left the monastery, he studied with Lindsay Kemp's mime troupe, forming his own mime company, the Feathers, in 1969. The Feathers were short-lived, and he formed the experimental art group Beckenham Arts Lab in 1969.

Bowie needed to finance the Arts Lab, so he signed with Mercury Records that year and released *Man of Words, Man of Music*, a trippy singer/songwriter album featuring *Space Oddity*. The song was released as a single and became a major hit in the U.K., convincing Bowie to concentrate on music. Hooking up with his old friend Marc Bolan, he began miming at some of Bolan's T. Rex concerts, eventually touring with Bolan, bassist/producer Tony Visconti, guitarist Mick Ronson, and drummer Cambridge as Hype. The band quickly fell apart, yet Bowie and Ronson remained close, working on the material that formed Bowie's next album, *The Man Who Sold the World*, as well as recruiting Michael "Woody" Woodmansey as their drummer. Produced by Tony Visconti, who also played bass, *The Man Who Sold the World* was a heavy guitar rock album that failed to gain much attention. Bowie followed the album in late 1971 with the pop/rock *Hunky Dory*, an album that featured Ronson and keyboardist Rick Wakeman.

Following the release of *Hunky Dory*, Bowie began to develop his most famous incarnation, Ziggy Stardust: an androgynous, bisexual rock star from another planet. Before he unveiled Ziggy, Bowie claimed in a January 1972 interview with the Melody Maker that he was gay, helping to stir interest in his forthcoming album. Taking cues from Bolan's stylish glam rock, Bowie dyed his hair orange and began wearing women's clothing. He began calling himself Ziggy Stardust, and his backing band—Ronson, Woodmansey, and bassist Trevor Bolder—were the Spiders from Mars. *The Rise & Fall of Ziggy Stardust and the Spiders from Mars* was released with much fanfare in England in late 1972. The album and its lavish, theatrical concerts became a sensation throughout England, and it helped him become the only glam rocker to carve out a niche in America. *Ziggy Stardust* became a word-of-mouth hit in the United States, and the re-released *Space Oddity*— which was now also the title of the re-released *Man of Words, Man of Music*—reached the American Top Twenty. Bowie quickly followed *Ziggy* with *Aladdin Sane* later in 1973. Not only did he record a new album that year, but he also produced Lou Reed's *Transformer*, the Stooges' *Raw Power*, and Mott the Hoople's comeback *All the Young Dudes*, for which he also wrote the title track.

Given the amount of work Bowie packed into 1972 and 1973, it wasn't surprising that his relentless schedule began to catch up with him. After recording the all-covers *Pin-Ups* with the Spiders from Mars, he unexpectedly announced the band's breakup, as well as his retirement from live performances, during the group's final show that year. He retreated from the spotlight to work on a musical adaptation of George Orwell's *1984*, but once he was denied the rights to the novel, he transformed the work into *Diamond Dogs*. The album was released to generally poor reviews in 1974, yet it generated the hit single *Rebel Rebel*, and he supported the album with an elaborate and expensive American tour. As the tour progressed, Bowie became fascinated with soul music, eventually

The starman Bowie. © Neal Preston/CORBIS

redesigning the entire show to reflect his new "plastic soul." Hiring guitarist Carlos Alomar as the band's leader, Bowie refashioned his group into a Philly soul band and recostumed himself in sophisticated, stylish fashions. The change took fans by surprise, as did the double-album *David Live*, which featured material recorded on the 1974 tour.

Young Americans, released in 1975, was the culmination of Bowie's soul obsession, and it became his first major crossover hit, peaking in the American Top Ten and generating his first U.S. number one hit in *Fame*, a song he co-wrote with John Lennon and Alomar. Bowie relocated to Los Angeles, where he earned his first movie role in Nicolas Roeg's *The Man Who Fell to Earth* (1976). While in L.A., he recorded *Station to Station*, which took the plastic soul of *Young Americans* into darker, avant-garde-tinged directions, yet was also a huge hit, generating the Top Ten single *Golden Years*. The album inaugurated Bowie's persona of the elegant *Thin White Duke*, and it reflected Bowie's growing cocaine-fueled paranoia. Soon, he decided Los Angeles was too boring and returned to England; shortly after arriving back in London, he gave the awaiting crowd a Nazi salute, a signal of his growing, drug-addled detachment from reality. The incident caused enormous controversy, and Bowie left the country to settle in Berlin, where he lived and worked with Brian Eno.

Once in Berlin, Bowie sobered up and began painting, as well as studying art. He also developed a fascination with German electronic music, which Eno helped him fulfill on their first album together, *Low*. Released early in 1977, *Low* was a startling mixture of electronics, pop, and avant-garde technique. While it was greeted with mixed reviews at the time, it proved to be one of the most influential albums of the late 1970s, as did its follow-up, *Heroes*, which followed that year. Not only did Bowie record two solo albums in 1977, but he also helmed Iggy Pop's comeback records *The Idiot* and *Lust for Life*, and toured anonymously as Pop's keyboardist. He resumed his acting career in 1977, appearing in *Just A Gigolo* with Marlene Dietrich and Kim Novak, as well as narrating Eugene Ormandy's version of *Peter and the Wolf*. Bowie returned to the stage in 1978, launching an international tour that was captured on the double-album *Stage*. During 1979, Bowie and Eno recorded *Lodger* in New York, Switzerland, and Berlin, releasing the album at the end of the year. *Lodger* was supported with several innovative videos, as was 1980's *Scary Monsters*, and these videos—*DJ*, *Fashion*, *Ashes to Ashes*—became staples on early MTV.

Scary Monsters was Bowie's last album for RCA, and it wrapped up his most innovative, productive period. Later in 1980, he performed the title role in stage production of The Elephant Man, including several shows on Broadway. Over the next two years, he took an extended break from recording, appearing in *Christine F* (1982) and the vampire movie *The Hunger* (1982), returning to the studio only for his 1981 collaboration with Queen, *Under Pressure*, and the theme for Paul Schrader's remake of *Cat People*. In 1983, he signed an expensive contract with EMI Records and released *Let's Dance*. Bowie had recruited Chic guitarist Nile Rodgers to produce the album, giving the record a sleek, funky foundation, and hired the unknown Stevie Ray Vaughan as lead guitarist. *Let's Dance* became his most successful record, thanks to stylish, innovative videos for *Let's Dance* and *China Girl*, which turned both songs into Top Ten hits. Bowie supported the record with the sold-out arena tour Serious Moonlight.

Greeted with massive success for the first time, Bowie wasn't quite sure how to react, and he eventually decided to replicate *Let's Dance* with 1984's *Tonight*. While the album sold well, producing the Top Ten hit *Blue Jean*, it received poor reviews and ultimately was a commercial disappointment. He stalled in 1985, recording a duet of Martha & the Vandellas' *Dancing in the Street* with Mick Jagger for Live Aid. He also spent more time jet-setting, appearing at celebrity events across the globe, and appeared in several movies—*Into the Night* (1985), *Absolute Beginners* (1986), *Labyrinth* (1986)—that turned out to be bombs. Bowie returned to recording in 1987 with the widely panned *Never Let Me Down*, supporting the album with the Glass Spider tour, which also received poor reviews. In 1989, he remastered his RCA catalog with Rykodisc for CD release, kicking off the series with the three-disc box *Sound + Vision*. Bowie supported the discs with an accompanying tour of the same name, claiming that he was retiring all of his older characters from performance following the tour. *Sound + Vision* was successful, and *Ziggy Stardust* re-charted amidst the hoopla.

Sound + Vision may have been a success, but Bowie's next project was perhaps his most unsuccessful. Picking up on the abrasive, dissonant rock of Sonic Youth and the Pixies, Bowie formed his own guitar rock combo, Tin Machine, with guitarist Reeves Gabrels, bassist Hunt Sales, and his drummer brother Tony, who had previously worked on Iggy Pop's *Lust for Life* with Bowie. Tin Machine released an eponymous album to poor reviews that summer and supported it with a club tour, which was only moderately successful. Despite the poor reviews, Tin Machine released a second album, the appropriately titled *Tin Machine II*, in 1991, and it was completely ignored.

Bowie returned to a solo career in 1993 with the sophisticated, soulful *Black Tie White Noise*, recording the album with Nile Rodgers and his now-permanent collaborator, Reeves Gabrels. The album was released on Savage, a subsidiary of RCA and received positive reviews, but his new label went bankrupt shortly after its release, and the album disappeared. *Black Tie White Noise* was the first indication that Bowie was trying hard to resuscitate his career, as was the largely instrumental 1994 soundtrack *The Buddha of Suburbia*. In 1995, he reunited with Brian Eno for the wildly hyped, industrial rock-tinged *Outside*. Several critics hailed the album as a comeback, and Bowie supported it with a co-headlining tour with Nine Inch Nails in order to snag a younger, alternative audience, but his gambit failed; audiences left before Bowie's performance and *Outside* disappeared. He quickly returned to the studio in 1996, recording *Earthling*, an album heavily influenced by techno and drum'n'bass. Upon its early 1997 release, *Earthling* received generally positive reviews, yet the album failed to gain an audience, and many techno purists criticized Bowie for allegedly exploiting their subculture.

Alice Cooper

Originally, there was a band called Alice Cooper led by a singer named Vincent Damon Furnier. Under his direction, Alice Cooper pioneered a grandly theatrical and violent brand of heavy metal that was designed to shock. Drawing equally from horror movies, vaudeville, heavy metal, and garage rock, the group created a stage show that featured electric chairs, guillotines, fake blood, and huge boa constrictors, all coordinated by the heavily made-up Furnier. By that time, Furnier had adopted the name for his androgynous on-stage personality. While the visuals were extremely important to the group's impact, the band's music was nearly as distinctive. Driven by raw, simple riffs and melodies that derived from 1960s guitar pop as well as show tunes, it was rock and roll at its most basic and catchy, even when the band ventured into psychedelia and art rock. After the original group broke up and Furnier began a solo career as Alice Cooper, his actual music lost most of its theatrical flourishes, becoming straightforward heavy metal, yet his stage show retained all of the trademark props that made him the king of shock rock.

Furnier formed his first group, the Earwigs, as an Arizona teenager in the early 1960s. Changing the band's name to the Spiders in 1965, the group was eventually called the Nazz (not to be confused with Todd Rundgren's band of the same name). The Spiders and the Nazz both released local singles that were moderately popular. In 1968, after discovering there was another band called with the same name, the group changed its name to Alice Cooper. According to band legend, the name came to Furnier during a ouija board session, where he was told he was the reincarnation of a 17th-century witch of the same name. Comprised of vocalist Furnier—who would soon begin calling himself Alice Cooper—guitarist Mike Bruce, guitarist Glen Buxton, bassist Dennis Dunaway, and drummer Neal Smith, the group moved to California in 1968. In California, the group met Shep Gordon, who became their manager, and Frank Zappa, who signed Alice Cooper to his Straight Records imprint.

Alice Cooper released their first album, *Pretties for You*, in 1969. *Easy Action* followed early in 1970, yet it failed to chart. The group's reputation in Los Angeles was slowly shrinking, so the band moved to Furnier's hometown of Detroit. For the next year, the group refined their bizarre stage show. Late in 1970, the group's contract was transferred to Straight's distributor Warner Bros., and they began recording their third album with producer Bob Ezrin.

With Ezrin's assistance, Alice Cooper developed their classic heavy metal crunch on 1971's *Love It to Death*, which featured the number twenty-one hit single *Eighteen*; the album peaked at number thirty-five and went gold. The success enabled the group to develop a more impressive, elaborate live show, which made them highly popular concert attractions across the United States and eventually the U.K. *Killer*, released late in 1971, was another gold album. Released in the summer of 1972, *School's Out* was Alice Cooper's breakthrough record, peaking at number two and selling over a million copies. The title song became a Top Ten hit in the United States and a number one single in the U.K. *Billion Dollar Babies*, released the following year, was the group's biggest hit, reaching number one in both America and Britain; the album's first single, *No More Mr. Nice Guy*, became a

Alice Cooper casting his spells. © Neal Preston/CORBIS

Top Ten hit in Britain, peaking at number twenty-five in the United States. *Muscle of Love* appeared late in 1973, yet it failed to capitalize on the success of *Billion Dollar Babies*. After *Muscle of Love*, Furnier and the rest of Alice Cooper parted ways to pursue other projects. Having officially changed his name to Alice Cooper, Furnier embarked on a similarly theatrical solo career; the rest of the band released one unsuccessful album under the name *Billion Dollar Babies*, while Mike Bruce and Neal Smith both recorded solo albums that were never issued. In the fall of 1974, a compilation of Alice Cooper's five Warner albums, entitled *Alice Cooper's Greatest Hits*, became a Top Ten hit.

For his first solo album, Cooper hired Lou Reed's backing band from *Rock 'N' Roll Animal*—guitarists Dick Wagner and Steve Hunter, bassist Prakash John, keyboardist Joseph Chrowski, and drummer Penti Glan—as his supporting group. *Welcome to My Nightmare*, Alice Cooper's first solo album, was released in the spring of 1975. The record wasn't a great departure from his previous work, and it became a Top Ten hit in America, launching the hit acoustic ballad *Only Women Blee*d; its success put an end to any idea of reconvening Alice Cooper the band. Its follow-up, 1976's *Alice Cooper Goes to Hell*, was another hit, going gold in the United States. After *Alice Cooper Goes to Hell*, Cooper's career began to slip, partially due to changing trends and partially due to his alcoholism. Cooper entered rehabilitation in 1978, writing an album about his treatment called *From the Inside* (1978) with Bernie Taupin, Elton John's lyricist. During the early 1980s, Cooper continued to release albums and tour, yet he was no longer as popular as he was during his early-1970s heyday.

Cooper made a successful comeback in the late 1980s, sparked by his appearances in horror films and a series of pop-metal bands that paid musical homage to his classic early records and concerts. *Constrictor*, released in 1986, began his comeback, but it was 1989's *Trash* that returned Cooper to the spotlight. Produced by the proven hitmaker Desmond Child, *Trash* featured guest appearances by Jon Bon Jovi, Richie Sambora, and most of Aerosmith; the record became a Top Ten hit in Britain and peaked at number twenty in the United States, going platinum. *Poison*, a mid-tempo rocker featured on the album, became Cooper's first Top Ten single since 1977. After the release of *Trash*, he continued to star in the occasional film, tour, and record, although he wasn't able to retain the audience recaptured with *Trash*. Still, 1991's *Hey Stoopid* and 1994's *The Last Temptation* were generally solid, professional efforts that helped Cooper settle into a comfortable cult status without damaging the critical goodwill surrounding his 1970s output. After a live album, 1997's *Fistful of Alice*, Cooper returned on the smaller Spitfire label in 2000 with *Brutal Planet*.

Rebel Rock

Allman Brothers

The story of the Allman Brothers Band is one of triumph, tragedy, redemption, dissolution, and a new redemption. Over almost thirty years, they've gone from being America's single most influential band to a has-been group trading on past glories, to reach the 1990s as one of the most respected rock acts of their era.

For the first half of the 1970s, the Allman Brothers Band was the most influential rock group in America, redefining rock music and its boundaries. The band's mix of blues, country, jazz, and even classical influences, and their powerful, extended onstage jamming altered the standards of concert performance—other groups were known for their onstage jamming, but when the Allman Brothers stretched a song out for thirty or forty minutes, at their best they were exciting, never self-indulgent. They gave it all a distinctly Southern voice and, in the process, opened the way for a wave of 1970s rock acts from south of the Mason-Dixon Line, including the Marshall Tucker Band, Lynyrd Skynyrd, and Blackfoot, whose music, at least initially, celebrated their roots. And for a time, almost single-handedly, they also made Capricorn Records into a major independent label.

The group was founded in 1969 by Duane Allman on guitar; Gregg Allman on vocals and organ; Forrest Richard ("Dickey") Betts on guitar; Berry Oakley on bass; and Butch Trucks and Jaimoe Johanny Johanson on drums. Duane and Gregg Allman loved soul and R&B, although they listened to their share of rock and roll, especially as it sounded coming out of England in the mid-1960s. Their first group was a local Daytona Beach garage band called the Escorts, who sounded a lot like the early Beatles and Rolling Stones; they later became the Allman Joys and plunged into Cream-style British blues, and then the Hour Glass, a more soul-oriented outfit. The group landed a contract with Liberty Records with help from the Nitty Gritty Dirt Band, but the company wasted the opportunity on a pair of overproduced albums that failed to capture the Hour Glass's sound. The group split up after Liberty rejected a proposed third album steeped in blues and R&B.

Duane Allman began working as a session guitarist at Fame Studios in Muscle Shoals, Ala., and it was there, appearing on records by Wilson Pickett, Aretha Franklin, John Hammond, and King Curtis, among others, that he made his reputation. In 1969, at the coaxing of ex-Otis Redding manager Phil Walden, Allman gave up session work and began putting together a new band—Jaimoe (Johnny Lee Johnson) Johanson came aboard, and then Allman's longtime friend Butch Trucks, and another Allman friend, Berry Oakley, joined, along with Dickey Betts, with whom Oakley was playing in a group called Second Coming. A marathon jam session ensued, at the end of which Allman had his band, except for a singer—that came later when his brother Gregg agreed to join. They were duly signed to Walden's new Capricorn label.

The band didn't record their first album until after they'd worked their sound out on the road, playing heavily around Florida and Georgia. The self-titled debut album was a solid blues-rock album and one of the better showcases for guitar pyrotechnics in a year with more than its share, amid albums by the Cream, Blind Faith, the Jeff Beck Group, and Led Zeppelin. It didn't sell 50,000 copies on its initial release, but *The Allman Brothers Band* impressed everyone who heard it and nearly everyone who reviewed it. Coming out at the end of the 1960s, it could have passed as a follow-up to the kind of blues-rock coming out of England from acts like Cream, except that it had a sharper edge—the Allmans were American and Southern, and their understanding of blues (not to mention elements of jazz, mostly courtesy of Jaimoe) was as natural as breathing. The album also introduced one of the band's most popular concert numbers, *Whipping Post*.

Their debut album attracted good reviews and a cult following with its mix of assured dual lead guitars by Duane Allman and Dickey Betts, soulful singing by Gregg Allman, and a rhythm section that was nearly as busy as the lead instruments, between Oakley's rock-hard bass and the dual drumming of Trucks and Johanson. Their second album, 1970's *Idlewild South*, recorded at Capricorn's studios in Macon, Ga., was produced by Tom Dowd, who had previously recorded Cream. This was a magical combination—Dowd was completely attuned to the group's sound and goals, and *Idlewild South* broadened that sound, adding a softer acoustic texture to their music and introducing Dickey Betts as a composer (including the original studio version of "In Memory of Elizabeth Reed," an instrumental tribute to Miles Davis that would become a highlight of their shows, in many differ-

Greg Allman. © Bettman/CORBIS

ent forms, for the next thirty years). It also had a Gregg Allman number, *Midnight Rider*, which became one of the band's more widely covered originals and the composer's signature tune.

By this time, the band's concerts were becoming legendary for the extraordinarily complex yet coherent interplay between the two guitarists and Gregg Allman's keyboards, sometimes in jams of forty minutes or more to a single song without wasting a note. And unlike the art rock bands of the era, they weren't interested in impressing anyone with how they played scales, how many different tunings they knew, or which classical riffs they could quote. Rather, the Allmans incorporated the techniques and structures of jazz and classical music into their playing. In March of 1971, the band played a series of shows at the Fillmore East that were recorded for posterity and subsequently transformed into their third album, *At Fillmore East*. This double album, issued in July of 1971, became an instant classic, rivaling the previous blues-rock touchstone cut at the Fillmore, Cream's *Wheels of Fire*. Duane Allman and his band were suddenly the new heroes to millions of mostly older teenage fans. Although it never cracked the Top Ten, *At Fillmore East* was certified as a gold record on October 15, 1971.

Fourteen days later, Duane Allman was killed in a motorcycle accident. The band had been midway through work on their next album, *Eat a Peach*, which they completed as a five-piece, with Dickey Betts playing all of the lead and slide guitar parts. Their second double album in a row became another instant classic, and their first album to reach the Top Ten, peaking at number five.

Despite having completed *Eat a Peach*, the group was intact in name only. Rather than try and replace Duane Allman as a guitarist, they contrived to add a second solo instrument in the form of a piano, played by Chuck Leavell. The group had already begun work on a long-delayed follow-up to *Eat a Peach*, when Oakley was killed in a motorcycle accident only a few blocks from Allman's accident site.

Lamar Williams (b. Jan. 15, 1949–d. Jan. 25, 1983) was recruited on bass, and the new lineup continued the group's concert activities, as well as eventually finishing their next album, *Brothers and Sisters*, which was released on August 1, 1973. During the extended gap in releases following *Eat a Peach*, Atco reissued *The Allman Brothers Band* and *Idlewild South* together as the double album *Beginnings*, which charted higher than either individual release.

Brothers and Sisters marked the beginning of a new era. The album had a more easygoing and freewheeling sound, less bluesy and more country-ish. This was partly a result of Capricorn's losing the services of Tom Dowd, who had produced their three previous albums. Additionally, Dickey Betts' full emergence as a songwriter and singer as well as the group's only guitarist, playing all of the lead and slide parts, altered the balance of the group's sound, pushing forth his distinct interest in country-rock. Betts also became the reluctant *de facto* leader of the band during this period, not from a desire for control as much as because he was the only one with the comparative stability and creative input to take on the responsibility.

The record occupied the number one spot for six weeks, spurred by the number two single *Ramblin' Man*, and became their most well-known album. It was an odd reversal of the usual order of success for a rock band—usually, it was the release of the album that drew the crowds to concerts, but in this case, the months of touring the band had done paved the way for the album. The fact that it kept getting pushed back only heightened the fans' interest.

Ironically, *Brothers and Sisters* was a less challenging record than the group's earlier releases, with a relatively laidback sound, relaxed compared to the groundbreaking work on the group's previous four albums. But all of this hardly mattered; based on the reputation they'd established with their first four albums, and the crowd-pleasing nature of *Ramblin' Man* and the Dickey Betts-composed instrumental *Jessica*, the group was playing larger halls and bigger crowds than ever.

An entire range of Southern-based rock acts had started to make serious inroads into the charts in the wake of the Allman Brothers. Labels such as MCA and even Island Records began looking for this same audience, signing acts like Lynyrd Skynyrd and Blackfoot, respectively, among others. For the first time since the mid-1950s, the heyday of the rockabilly era, a major part of the country was listening to rock and roll with a distinctly Southern twang.

The band began showing cracks in 1974, as Gregg Allman and Dickey Betts both began solo careers, recording albums separately from the group. Allman married Cher (twice), an event that set him up in a Hollywood-based lifestyle that created a schism with the rest of the band. They might have survived all of this, but for the increasing strain of the members' other personal habits—drugs and alcohol had always been a significant part of the lives of each of the members, except perhaps for Jaimoe, but as the strain and exhaustion of touring continued, coupled with the need to produce new music, these indulgences began to get out of control, and Betts' leadership of the group created a further strain for him.

The band's difficulties were showcased by their next album, the highly uneven *Win, Lose Or Draw*, which lacked the intensity and sharpness of their prior work. The whole band wasn't present for some of the album, and Gregg Allman's involvement with Cher, coupled with his serious drug problems, prevented him from participating with the rest of the group—his vocals were added separately, on the other side of the country.

The band finally came apart in 1976 when Allman found himself in the midst of a federal drug case against a supplier and agreed to testify against a friend and band employee. Leavall, Johanson, and Williams split to form Sea Level, which became a moderately successful band, cutting four albums for Capricorn over the next four years, while Betts pursued a solo career. All of them vowed never to work with Gregg Allman again.

Amid this split, Capricorn Records, reaching ever deeper into its vaults for anything that could generate income, issued two collections, a double-album live collection called *Wipe the Windows, Check the Oil, Dollar Gas*, showcasing the *Brothers and Sisters*-era band at various concerts, and a double-album best-of package, *And the Road Goes On Forever*. *Wipe the Windows* was a modest seller, appearing as it did when the group's sales had already fallen off, and it was compared unfavorably with the legendary work on *At Fillmore East*. The studio compilation passed with barely a ripple, however, because most fans already had the stuff on the original albums.

They were all back together by 1978, however, and over the next four years the group issued a somewhat uneven series of albums. *Enlightened Rogues* (1979) somewhat redeemed their reputations—produced by Tom Dowd, who had always managed to get the very best work out of the group, it had more energy than any record they'd issued in at least six years. It also restored the two-guitar lineup, courtesy of Dan Toler (from Dickey Betts' solo band), who was brought in when Chuck Leavell (along with Lamar Williams) refused to return to the Allmans. By that time, however, the Allmans were fighting against time and musical trends. Disco, punk, and power-pop had pretty much stolen a march on the arena acts epitomized by the Allmans; whatever interest they attracted was a matter of nostalgia for their earlier releases. The group was in danger of becoming arena rock's third big oldies act (after the Moody Blues and Paul McCartney's Wings).

Additionally, their business affairs were in a shambles, owing to the bankruptcy of Capricorn Records in late 1979. When the fallout from the Capricorn collapse settled, PolyGram Records, the company's biggest creditor, took over the label's library, and the Allman Brothers were cut loose from their contract.

Their signing to Arista enabled the group to resume recording. What they released, however, was safe, unambitious, routinely commercial pop-rock, closer in spirit to the Doobie Brothers than their own classic work, and a shadow of that work, without any of the invention and daring upon which they'd built their reputations. The group's fortunes hit a further downturn when Jaimoe was fired, breaking up one of the best rhythm sections in rock. For most of the 1980s, the group was on hiatus, while the individual members sorted out their personal and professional situations. During those years, only Dickey Betts seemed to be in a position to do much with his music, and most of that wasn't selling.

In 1989, the band was reactivated again, partly owing to the PolyGram's decision to issue the four-CD box set retrospective *Dreams*. That set, coupled with the reissue of their entire Capricorn catalog on compact disc in the years leading up to the box's release, reminded millions of older listeners of the band's greatness, and introduced the group to millions of people too young to have been around for Watkins Glen, much less the Fillmore shows.

They reunited and also restored the band's original double-lead-guitar configuration, adding Warren Haynes on lead guitar alongside Dickey Betts, with Allen Woody playing bass; Chuck Leavell was gone, however, having agreed to join the Rolling Stones on tour as their resident keyboard player, and Lamar Williams had succumbed to cancer in 1983.

The new lineup reinvigorated the band, which signed with Epic Records and surprised everyone with their first release, *Seven Turns*. Issued in 1990, it got some of the best reviews and healthiest sales they'd had in more than a decade. Their subsequent studio albums failed to attract as much enthusiasm, and their two live albums, *An Evening With the Allman Brothers Band* and *2nd Set*, released in 1992 and 1995, respectively, were steady but not massive sellers. Much of this isn't the fault of the material so much as a natural result of the passage of time, which has left the Allmans competing with two decades' worth of successors and rivals.

The group has stayed together since 1989, overcoming continuing health and drug problems, which have occasionally battered their efforts at new music. They remain a top concert attraction more than twenty-five years after their last historically important album, easily drawing more than 20,000 fans at a time to outdoor venues, or booking 2,000-seat theaters for three weeks at a time. Their back catalog, especially the first five albums, remain consistent sellers on compact disc and recently returned to the reconstituted Capricorn label (still a home for Southern rockers, including the latter-day Lynyrd Skynyrd, as well as reissues of Elmore James and other classic bluesmen), under a 1997 licensing agreement that has resulted in their third round of digital remastering.

Apart from their Arista releases, the Allman Brothers Band has remained remarkably consistent, altering their music only gradually over thirty years. They sound more country than they did in their early days, and they're a bit more varied in the vocal department, but the band still soars at their concerts and on most of their records for the last ten years.

Lynyrd Skynyrd

Lynyrd Skynyrd was the definitive Southern rock band, fusing the overdriven power of blues-rock with a rebellious, Southern image and a hard rock swagger. Skynyrd never relied on the jazzy improvisations of the Allman Brothers. Instead, they were a hard-living, hard-driving rock and roll band—they may have jammed endlessly on stage, but their music remained firmly entrenched in blues, rock, and country. For many, Lynyrd Skynyrd's redneck image tended to obscure the songwriting skills of its leader, Ronnie VanZant. Throughout the band's early records, VanZant demonstrated a knack for lyrical detail and a down-to-earth honesty that had more in common with country than rock and roll. During the height of Skynyrd's popularity in the mid-1970s, however, VanZant's talents were overshadowed by the group's gritty, greasy blues-rock. Sadly, it wasn't until he was killed in a tragic plane crash in 1977 along with two other band members that many listeners began to realize his talents. Skynyrd split up after the plane crash, but they reunited a decade later, becoming a popular concert act during the early 1990s.

While in high school in Jacksonville, Fla., Ronnie VanZant (vocals), Allen Collins (guitar), and Gary Rossington (guitar) formed My Backyard. Within a few months, the group added bassist Leon Wilkeson and keyboardist Billy Powell, and changed their name to Lynyrd Skynyrd, a mocking tribute to their gym teacher Leonard Skinner, who was notorious for punishing students with long hair. With drummer Bob Burns, Lynyrd Skynyrd began playing throughout the South. For the first few years, the group had little success, but producer Al Kooper signed the band to MCA after seeing them play at an Atlanta club called Funocchio's in 1972. Kooper produced the group's 1973 debut, *Pronounced Leh-Nerd Skin-Nerd*, which was recorded after former Strawberry Alarm Clock guitarist Ed

Ronnie VanZant leading the band in concert. © Roger Ressmeyer/CORBIS

King joined the band. The group became notorious for their triple guitar attack, which was showcased on *Free Bird*, a tribute to the recently deceased Duane Allman. *Free Bird* earned Lynyrd Skynyrd their first national exposure and it became one of the staples of album-rock radio, still receiving airplay nearly twenty-five years after its release.

Free Bird and an opening slot on the Who's 1973 *Quadrophenia* tour gave Lynyrd Skynyrd a devoted following, which helped its second album, 1974's *Second Helping*, become its breakthrough hit. Featuring the hit single *Sweet Home Alabama*—a response to Neil Young's *Southern Man*—*Second Helping* reached number twelve and went multi-platinum. At the end of the year, Artimus Pyle replaced drummer Burns and King left the band shortly afterward. The new sextet released *Nuthin' Fancy* in 1975, and it became the band's first Top Ten hit. The record was followed by the Tom Dowd-produced *Gimme Back My Bullets* in 1976, which failed to match the success of its two predecessors. However, the band retained its following through its constant touring, which was documented on the double-live album *One More from the Road*. Released in late 1976, the album featured the band's new guitarist Steve Gaines and a trio of female backup singers, and it became Skynyrd's second Top Ten album.

Lynyrd Skynyrd released its sixth album, *Street Survivors*, on October 17, 1977. Three days later, a privately chartered plane carrying the band between shows in Greenville, S.C., and Baton Rouge, La., crashed outside of Gillsburg, Miss. Ronnie VanZant, Steve Gaines, and his sister Cassie, one of the group's backing vocalists, died in the crash; the remaining members were injured. (The cause of the crash was either fuel shortage or a fault with the plane's mechanics.) The cover for *Street Survivors* had pictured the band surrounded in flames; after the crash, the cover was changed. In the wake of the tragedy, the album became one of the band's biggest hits. Lynyrd Skynyrd broke up after the crash, releasing a collection of early demos called *Skynyrd's First And . . . Last* in 1978; it had been scheduled for release before the crash. The double album compilation *Gold and Platinum* was released in 1980.

Later in 1980, Rossington and Collins formed a new band, which featured four surviving members. Two years later, Pyle formed the Artimus Pyle Band. Collins suffered a car crash in 1986, which killed his girlfriend and left him paralyzed; four years later, he died of respiratory failure. In 1987, Rossington, Powell, King, and Wilkeson reunited Lynyrd Skynyrd, adding vocalist Johnny VanZant and guitarist Randall Hall. The band embarked on a reunion tour, which was captured on the 1988 double-live album, *Southern by the Grace of God/Lynyrd Skynyrd Tribute Tour—1987*. The re-formed Skynyrd began recording in 1991, and for the remainder of the decade, the band toured frequently, putting out albums occasionally. The reunited Skynyrd frequently switched drummers, but it had little effect on their sound.

During the 1990s, Lynyrd Skynyrd were made honorary colonels in the Alabama State Militia, due to their classic-rock staple *Sweet Home Alabama*. During the mid-1990s, VanZant, Rossington, Wilkeson, and Powell regrouped by adding two Southern rock veterans to Skynyrd's guitar stable: former Blackfoot frontman Rickey Medlocke and ex-Outlaw Hughie Thomasson. With ex-Damn Yankee Michael Cartellone bringing stability to the drum chair, the reconstituted band signed to CMC International for the 1997 album *Twenty*. This lineup went on to release *Lyve from Steeltown* in 1998, followed a year later by *Edge of Forever*. The seasonal effort *Christmas Time Again* was released in fall 2000.

The bigger picture, however, in the whole discussion of Southern, or Rebel rock, and, in fact, the whole topic of American grassroots music in general, is the grassroots nature of it. The way the guitars are played, reflecting the delta blues slide styles, the many tips of the musical hat to earlier pioneers in music, and the often down home lyric content reflects images straight out of our earlier discussions of American delta, blues, gospel, and hillbilly music. The threads that trace right back to those ideas, and the people they came from are easily defined. A prime example is within the Lynyrd Skynyrd song *Sweet Home Alabama*. We've already discussed the importance of Muscle Shoals, Alabama, and the Fame Recording Studio being the hotbed of activity by names such as Booker T and the MGs, Otis Redding, Wilson Pickett, and Aretha Franklin—artists that represent the very core of soul music. In *Sweet Home Alabama*, the roots of Skynyrd's music is exposed when Ronnie sings, *"Now Muscle Shoals they got the swamp licks, and they been known to pick a song or two. Lord, they get me off so much. Pick me up when I'm feeling blue . . . now how about you?"*

The current of understanding the American heritage runs like a river through time, held together by and flowing with the diversity of all the stories and all the music of the many characters who make it up. There are so many branches to the river, but they all trace back to a central river. And all musicians who become a part of that find their way by understanding what it means to dig their fingers into the mud of the delta and tributaries of that river.

Or view the whole discussion very much like a tree. A musical tree called American music. And each individual, like the many that we've discussed, and many more we haven't—who they learned from, comes along and grafts a little piece of themselves onto that tree, and a new flower grows. To not study, appreciate, and understand intimately the diversity of culture of American roots music, from the lone bluesman wandering the Mississippi delta, to the hippies at Woodstock, is to deny us all our heritage. The experiment called America can never be more fully appreciated than by viewing it through its authentic grassroots music.

"Music is not an option."

Sam Phillips (1923-2003)

Worksheet Assignment: Chapter 11
The 1970s—Out with the Old—In with the New

1. Led Zeppelin was the creation of former Yardbirds guitarist

   _____

2. Peal away the layers of sparkled costumes and extravagant stage shows and the musical foundation of Led Zeppelin is firmly rooted in what genre of roots music?

   _____

3. The song written by Led Zeppelin that is described as THE defining song of the 1970s was

   _____

4. Heavy metal music found its hero in the music and attitudes of Ozzy Osbourne, who led what pioneering band of the genre?

   _____

5. Who was the Detroit rocker, known for his dangerous stage antics and buzzsaw voice, opens the door to hard, aggressive, and most importantly, politically driven punk rock?

   _____

6. What New York band was the seminal glam rock band, dressing in women's clothes and makeup, and putting on a risque and fun hard rock show that influenced Gene Simmons to create Kiss?

   _____

7. The epic adventures of Ziggy Stardust and the Spiders from Mars, the story about a space traveler with a message for Earth, was the creation of

   _____

8. This artist took glam rock into a fun dark side, mixing it with epic adventure, horror movie imagery, and sinister lyrics meant to shock.

   _____

9. In regard to rebel rock, the Allman Brothers certainly can lay claim to being the essential Southern rock band, but in the 1970s, a band came along, led by Ronnie VanZant, that captured the essence of the Southern rock experience better than any other then or since. They were

_____

10. Highlight Alabama on the following map.

11. Draw a circle around the vicinity of Muscle Shoals, Ala.

12. Circle and identify Detroit, Mich.

13 Circle and identify New York City.

14. Draw a route line between Detroit and New York City that goes through Cleveland, Ohio.